WITHDRAWN
FROM
UNIVERSITIES
AT
MEDWAY
LIBRARY

Abject Terrors

OUT OF PRINT ITEM

READING LIST MATERIAL

PLEASE DO NOT WITHDRAW

D1438026

TP120002936
KFINE

PETER LANG
New York • Washington, D.C./Baltimore • Bern
Frankfurt am Main • Berlin • Brussels • Vienna • Oxford

Tony Magistrale

Abject Terrors

Surveying the Modern and Postmodern Horror Film

PETER LANG
New York • Washington, D.C./Baltimore • Bern
Frankfurt am Main • Berlin • Brussels • Vienna • Oxford

Library of Congress Cataloging-in-Publication Data

Magistrale, Tony.
Abject terrors: surveying the modern
and postmodern horror film / Tony Magistrale.
p. cm.
Includes bibliographical references and index.
1. Horror films—History and criticism. I. Title.
PN1995.9.H6M248   791.43'6164—dc22   2005007036
ISBN 0-8204-7056-2

Bibliographic information published by **Die Deutsche Bibliothek**.
Die Deutsche Bibliothek lists this publication in the "Deutsche
Nationalbibliografie"; detailed bibliographic data is available
on the Internet at http://dnb.ddb.de/.

UNIVERSITIES AT MEDWAY
1 1 DEC 2012
DRILL HALL LIBRARY

Cover design by Lisa Barfield

Cover art: Francisco Goya (1746–1828), *The Sleep of Reason Produces Monsters*,
from the collection, *The Caprices*.

The paper in this book meets the guidelines for permanence and durability
of the Committee on Production Guidelines for Book Longevity
of the Council of Library Resources.

© 2005 Peter Lang Publishing, Inc., New York
275 Seventh Avenue, 28th Floor, New York, NY 10001
www.peterlangusa.com

All rights reserved.
Reprint or reproduction, even partially, in all forms such as microfilm,
xerography, microfiche, microcard, and offset strictly prohibited.

Printed in the United States of America

Once again, to Jennifer, Christopher, and Daniel Magistrale,
Ken Wagner, Colleen Dolan, Polly Binns, Kay and Norman Tederous,
Patty and Peter Kvam, and Larry and Betsy Bennett,
the little horrors in my life for whom I am most grateful

Contents

Acknowledgments

Several individuals and institutions helped to make this book possible. First, and perhaps most important, the undergraduate students at the University of Vermont enrolled in my "Horror Film" classes over the years; their unflagging interest in the subject and their verbal and written contributions helped to shape my own thinking about the genre. One student in particular, Daniel Norford, has, over time, persuaded me that *The Texas Chainsaw Massacre* is as good a film as he has staked it to be. My colleagues in the English Department, Sarah Nilsen and Hilary Neroni, read multiple versions of individual chapters and shared their wisdom and film expertise on more occasions than I deserved. Team-teaching with Professor Neroni has taught me a great deal about film scholarship and the horror film in particular. During a sabbatical year provided by the University of Vermont, I composed most of this volume, and would undoubtedly still be writing it if not for this leave. At Peter Lang, Heidi Burns was not only my unflappable editor, advisor, and linguistic magician all through the project, but also the individual who first proposed that I write this book. I would also like to thank Lisa Dillon who worked on the production process of this manuscript. A portion of chapter 7 discussing *The Shining* and *Eyes Wide Shut* was originally published in the magazine *Traffic East*; the author wishes to acknowledge and thank the magazine's editor, Mark Dellas, for permission to republish it here.

Introduction

It is likely that the very first motion picture was a horror film. Out of the dark shadows cast by a flickering candle, exaggerated and magnified by mirrors and accompanied by the artificial induction of smoke, Georges Méliés's *The Devil's Manor* (1896) was as much a magic trick as it was an effort to produce the first vampire film, where a bat flies into an ancient castle and transforms itself into the Devil. It is actually not that far a leap from Méliés's rudimentary experiments in blending science and spiritualism to the aesthetics of German expressionism that informed the cinema of the 1920s. The environmental settings for the earliest motion pictures feature the essentials of the vampire film: highly stylized sets and exaggerated use of makeup on the faces of actors provide *Nosferatu* and *The Cabinet of Dr. Caligari* with a highly psychological mise-en-scène. Lost in an angular, unnatural landscape, these early films emphasize the distortion of space and create an unsafe milieu that most resembles that of a nightmare.

What began as homage to nineteenth-century literary monsters on grainy, shadowy, black and white celluloid has, in less than a century, become one of the dominant genres within the film industry. Almost always as profitable as it is popular, the horror film reminds us of its cultural importance every couple of weeks with a new release in multiplexes across America. Although still sometimes viewed by film snobs as cinema's illegitimate child, the horror film—through its most disturbingly inventive forms as well as in its most mindless sequels—has become a mainstream art form. Much to the chagrin of neo conservatives and the liberal elite alike, the genre's pervasiveness is perhaps the most apt illustration that postmodern America is as much a culture of the Gothic as it is a culture split into oppositional blue and red state "moral value" systems. Although too reductive in his description of the Gothic as a "bitter version of experience overall" (xi), Mark Edmundson tabulates accurately that "American culture at large has become suffused with Gothic assumptions, with Gothic characters and plots" (xii). Further, it is not only American culture that has been so influenced; the horror film is, quite frankly, the most obvious and ubiquitous evidence of the Gothic's worldwide cultural permutation.

Horror art has always admired itself so excessively that it cannot resist revising and duplicating its most successful conventions and themes; thus, over time the genre has mutated into multiple subcategories. While horror often mates in inimitable ways with other genres—science fiction, detective noir, dystopian fantasy, screwball comedy, even cartoon animation—the horror aesthetic is a jealous mistress. So, regardless of whatever hybrid offshoots the horror film assumes, its story lines keep circling back to core confrontations with abject terror, otherness, and issues of gender identity, dislocation, and fragmentation. Like a striptease, a good horror film reveals its secrets a little at a time, with emphasis on build-up and anticipation.

Whether featuring a classic monster from the presound era, a space creature from another galaxy, a serial killer who has lost the ability to control his basest urges, the psychological collapse of an individual mind unraveling, or a parody of any of these horror tropes, the horror film has always been as relentless as one of its monsters in forcing us to question, to a greater or lesser extent, our most enlightened beliefs: that there is a God in Heaven keeping watch over us, that progress will inevitably lead to perfection, that in our families we will find sanctuaries against a cruel world, and that human beings share more in common with the angels than with the beasts. Motion picture history began with excursions into horror, and when—in the distant future, for whatever reasons—cinema as we now know it is absorbed into some new media technology or simply disappears altogether, it is more than likely that a horror film will be one of the last movies made. Although it is true that the genre adheres to certain core sensibilities, these elements are like a virus, possessing the ability to adapt to changing times and circumstances, to new technologies and means for redefining its terrors.

The average Hollywood theatrical release, including production, distribution, and publicity, currently averages around $100 million per film. Notably, many of the best films in the horror genre have been made for a fraction of this cost. *The Blair Witch Project*, *The Texas Chainsaw Massacre*, *The Evil Dead*, *Night of the Living Dead*, and *Halloween* were all produced with small budgets and featured actors who were virtually unknown at the time of the films' releases. Generally, horror works best when it is not a big budget project. The genre is by its very nature subversive entertainment—going to see a horror film often goes against the advice of parents, civic leaders, teachers, and church—and most Hollywood production companies are reluctant to invest huge sums of money on a product that may alienate its middle-class, suburban, essentially teenage audience. Thus, over the years independent film companies have made some of the most successful horror pictures.

In *Danse Macabre*, Stephen King suggests that horror "films which have been the most successful almost always seem to play upon and express fears which exist across a wide spectrum of people. Such fears are often political, economic, and psychological rather than supernatural" (5). The art of terror, whether literary or celluloid, has always addressed our most pressing fears as a society and as individuals. Like any other art form, horror cannot and should not be viewed as separate from its social and historical context; it is nothing less than a barometer for measuring an era's cultural anxieties.

As elaborated in chapter 2, nascent cinematic projects found horror images impossible to resist. Early directors and cinematographers were quick to learn that the camera possesses the power to frame a single image—e.g., the vampire rising majestically from his coffin, the hellish bowels of a factory—and etch it into an image that could send shivers down the spines of those watching in the dark. *The Cabinet of Dr. Caligari, Nosferatu,* and *Metropolis* still fascinate a contemporary viewer with their excursions into the realms of the surreal and the psychologically aberrant. At the same time, however, these films of the early 1920s were painfully realistic in recalling the unprecedented violence and trauma that occurred during World War I, where the combatants who somehow managed to survive often returned to civilized life as living specters, the walking dead who were more shadow than substance.

In the 1930s and 1940s, the epoch demarcating Hollywood's classic monster movies, one of the key historical developments that pushed the horror film into a place of importance in the motion picture industry was the American studio film system itself. The various lots owned by Hollywood studios, most notably Universal City, made the production of horror a recurring genre as sets of spooky houses, graveyards, cathedrals (Universal recreated to scale the front façade of Notre Dame in Paris), woods filled with smoky fog, and diabolical laboratories were recycled in film after film. The films made during this period took their inspiration from the rich tradition of nineteenth-century British Gothicism: *Frankenstein, Dracula, The Hunchback of Notre Dame,* and *The Strange Case of Dr. Jekyll and Mr. Hyde.* That the emergence of literally dozens of movies based on these literary texts corresponds historically to the rise of totalitarian dictators across Europe and in Japan is no mere coincidence. Each of these monsters comes shambling out of the shadows of Europe, threatens the members of his community and is destroyed only by collective group action. Some have argued that the Great Depression gave birth to Hollywood's age of monsters because people needed "an instinctive therapeutic escape" (Skal, *Monster Show* 115) into a fantastical realm to forget the immediate problems of unemployment and poverty. These films, however, can also be interpreted as metaphors for the very real crises of the era that spawned them: Hitler and Mussolini as vampire like threats to the stability of the civilized world.

Horror monsters can and should be interpreted as historical signifiers of their particular time, and this present volume seeks to do so wherever possible. The horror film speaks to us more about the dangers of a historical moment and less about its triumphs or its hopes. Thus, the oversized and mutated creatures of the 1950s techno-horror genre embody that age's fear of atomic radiation and the anxieties attendant to space exploration. The merging of science fiction and horror, discussed in chapter 5, gave birth to a generation of giant bugs and blobs that are the by-products of irresponsible scientific intrusions. Although the 1950s ushered in the modern age of consumerism and prosperity in America, horror cinema worried more about the escalating Cold War, nuclear proliferation, and ventures into deep space—its monsters suggest the consequences of unenlightened scientific and military incursions into fragile alien environments.

When we consider the horror films released in the 1960s and 1970s—most notably *Psycho*, *Rosemary's Baby*, *Carrie*, *The Exorcist*, *The Texas Chainsaw Massacre*, and *Halloween*—the narrative emphasis moves sharply away from space creatures and atomic terror, and turns inward, toward the home and interpersonal family dynamics. Alfred Hitchcock's films, addressed in chapter 4, as well as the range of movies considered in chapter 6, examine the horror film as psychic thriller, revealing the interior workings of diseased minds and journeys into psychological abnormality. In the post-*Psycho* world of horror art, the monster is not a foreign or extraterrestrial phenomenon but integral to the psychic life of the American family. The end of the 1960s established a new standard of violence—in part a response to Vietnam, urban race wars in American cities, and European art films—that found both an audience and a medium in this era's horror films. In addition, these chapters undertake a specific reading of the horror film in the context of gender and the rise of feminism. Indeed, the proliferation of feminist criticism that has methodically emerged in critical scholarship on the horror film, detailed in chapter 1, occurred as a natural response to movies that posed intriguing relationships between monstrosity and gender crises. In horror films following and including *Psycho*, for example, the monster's ability to foment disruptions to normalcy is frequently associated with gender ambiguity and upheaval.

Gender distress and a focus on the deteriorating family remain central concerns throughout this book's analysis of Stanley Kubrick's canon in chapter 7 as well as other narratives of postmodern horror that emerge during the 1980s and 1990s. In *The Silence of the Lambs*, *Se7en*, *The Shining*, and the horror films that chapter 8 aligns with the slasher genre, the monster emerges as a serial killer preying on random victims; he is now no longer a supernatural vampire or space alien, but one of us. Moreover, steady improvements in special effect technology forged a more intimate and visceral bond between film audience and the monster's acts of violence. As a result, the body's assault and display becomes a core element in evoking postmodern terror.

In this volume's tracing of the modern and postmodern horror film, a historical pattern slowly reveals itself. From the early cinema of supernatural monster hybrids, part human and part beast, to the slasher genre, where the monster is a very human projection of our fear of one another, what inspires terror as well as the shape terror takes has grown steadily more realistic and closer to us in proximity. In her essay "Freud's Worst Nightmare: Dining with Hannibal Lecter," Barbara Creed suggests that the history of modernity as paralleled by the horror film "has been that of exposing the audience to images which are more shocking than those of the previous decade; this, in turn, has created in audiences a desire, perhaps insatiable, to be shocked even more deeply and disturbingly than on the previous occasion" (196). The "shock quotient" to which Creed refers is synonymous with the monster and the abject moving ever closer in reference and identification to the audience itself. The image of a funnel emerges as a possible metaphor for horror's cinematic evolution: Abject terror begins as something "out there," as a supernatural creature exiled from Transylvania or mutating under the surface of the earth that, over time, gradually narrows and relocates itself into the face of a quiet young man managing the motel down the road or the dreamscape of a teenage girl sleeping in the suburbs.

The evolution of the horror film as a genre that has historically developed an ever closer intimacy with the audience is illustrated in microcosm in chapter 2. Vampire films follow the evolution and parallel the pattern that the larger genre of the horror film assumes from its inception to the present day. Celluloid vampires likewise appear to develop steadily a closer affinity to the human throughout the course of their history. Although highly sexualized as a method for helping them to satisfy their hunger, the original cinematic vampires in *Nosferatu* and *Dracula* nonetheless epitomize the role of the outsider, an alien species that violates and intrudes upon both race and culture. By the time we get to postmodern vampire movies such as *The Hunger*, *Blade*, or *Interview with the Vampire*, the vampire has assimilated comfortably among us, and in lifestyle and attitude he appears as a figure just as likely to inspire envy in his victims as fear.

The title for this book takes a part of its inspiration from Julia Kristeva's *The Powers of Horror*, wherein she defines the abject as a wide-ranging construction of otherness that threatens and disrupts the processes of life. For Kristeva, the abject is located in sexual perversity, gender ambiguity, torture, incest, bodily wastes, murder, death, and the feminine body. The various definitions of monstrosity that appear throughout the chapters in this book—from the supernatural to the psychotic—share at least some association with Kristeva's inclusive definition of the abject. The monsters either embody the abject in themselves—in the otherness of their bodies and actions—or project it onto others. Horror films, according to Cook and Bernink, are "a kind of modern defilement rite in which all that threatens the rule of order and meaning, all that is the Other, is separated out and subordinated to the paternal law" (201). Abject terrors, then, at least as this volume appropriates the term, are the core disruptions to the social order and paternal norm set in motion by the monster and invoke the response of terror, confusion, disgust, or perverse association in other characters on the screen as well as in the audience watching the film. Thus, a film such as *The Texas Chainsaw Massacre* locates the abject on several levels simultaneously: in the gender confusion of Leatherface, in the extreme level of terror that Sally is forced to undergo, in the perversion of a normal family dynamic, in the visceral slaughter of innocent teenagers, and in the practice of human cannibalism.

Despite the fact that horror has often been treated as a second-tier contribution in the hierarchy of artistic representation, the issues it asks us to ponder have always been similar to those found in classical tragedy: What do we do when faced with circumstances we can neither understand nor are in a position to control? How do we move forward when confronted with a world in ruins? The best horror cinema evokes terror from the audience through our identification with characters who have lost their bearings—geographical, psychological, and spiritual—who appear at the end of a paved road and now must venture into unmarked wilderness without a map, who have suffered long and hard and must somehow learn to live with the prospect of still more suffering to come.

Horror art has never attracted the faint of heart. It most often reveals to us truths that we do not care to know, conditions about gender and social and historical circumstances that are somber and threatening, but also disruptive and transformative. Many choose to avert their eyes under the claim that such revelations pose too great a risk, are too unnerving for a cultivated consciousness to absorb. Reminiscent again of classical tragedy, it is to the essence of the human condition that effective horror cinema transports us—stripped of our artifices and delusions and faced with a nearness to the abyss so close that we can almost feel the air from below rush up alongside our bodies. Horror films have always driven paying customers out of theaters, sometimes literally, running from the shambling monster as well as the agile Norman Bates. Even so, most of us are drawn, paradoxically, to look at what we would wish not to see: the bloodied bodies inside the mangled car by the side of the road, the mysterious shape that slinks around a dark corner. What will define abject terror in the future? It depends on what we allow ourselves to see, and, just as often, what we close our eyes to avoid.

More than any other film genre, going to see a horror movie is, ironically, a communal experience. Unlike the romantic melodrama or even the action picture, watching horror invites a communal response. In this way the horror genre probably resembles most comedy and the realm of parody (that is the subject of chapter 9), as the anatomy of terror often encourages a tongue in the cheek to accompany the flash of teeth. Part of the pleasure of going to a horror film is connecting with an active, participatory audience: Who screams and at what points? Who laughs, who mocks the plotline, and who dares to speak out directly to the monster or to its potential victims? Somehow, terror becomes less terrible when it is shared with a large, interactive theater audience. In fact, I can think of no other film genre where its audience "dialogues" more with the events and images unfolding on the screen.

I first started paying attention to horror movies when I was a teenager dating Karla Decker in the 1970s. Karla was a leggy cheerleader who was usually distant and physically unapproachable; our dates typically never progressed much further than the requisite goodnight kiss at her parents' front door. In the darkened theater of a gripping horror film, however, Karla became uncharacteristically animated: She required me to hold her clammy, manicured hand, put my arm around her trembling shoulders, and supply a brave chest to shield her exquisitely beautiful face from the terrifying action occurring on the screen in front of us. Strangely enough, we were the most intimate with one another in the shared experience of watching horror in a packed movie theater. More than any other cinematic genre, the horror film inspires and even encourages the individual members of its audience to talk with one another—to reassure and find comfort in each other, to lessen the intensity of the carnage on the screen by trying to poke fun at the monster, to recognize our common vulnerability as human beings.

I end this introduction with several apologies. I'm afraid there will be little here of interest to aficionados of zombies or the werewolf. With the most notable exceptions of *Night of the Living Dead* and *Day of the Dead*, it is my belief that the zombie movie is better off dead. *28 Days Later* shows great promise for the first half of the picture, but then loses focus and potency when it descends into some kind of military exploitation film. For this writer, the cinematic world of the werewolf is similarly limited. *The Howling* is an intriguing adaptation of the formula, but precious few other films in this subgenre hold my interest for very long. Additionally, this study leans heavily on American films because Hollywood remains the best place to find motion pictures about dreams as well as nightmares. The American horror film appears increasingly preoccupied with the evolving tradition of Japanese horror art, but remakes of the pedestrian haunted house movie *The Grudge* and the more interesting *The Ring* indicate that something is still lost in translation. The Italian work of Dario Argento certainly has its defenders, but I prefer the suspenseful *The Bird with the Crystal Plumage* to the critically acclaimed *Susperia* hands down. The latter picture is a visual feast, but absolutely incoherent; I wish I liked his films more. In the end, what is presented in this volume is an analysis of individual motion pictures—the greatest hits of the genre, if you will—that, when considered in chapter groupings and as a whole, form a coherent overview of the changing landscape of the horror film during the past century. This is a representative sampling that excludes more than it should. My hope is that what is lost in general scope will be compensated by close attention to important individual films.

Terror Theories

A Representative Survey

Once dismissed as a genre of serious interest only to adolescents and developmentally arrested adult males, the horror film has recently gained enormous intellectual currency largely due to work by academic critics. Perhaps because of its tremendous popularity, but just as often because of its moments of artistic brilliance, scholars have been drawn into rigorous intellectual formulations of horror cinema, thereby investing the genre with a seriousness of purpose that had long been absent in discussions about vampires, monsters, and alien creatures from outer space. While always of interest to fantasists, popular culture scholars, and film critics specializing in genre work, in the past thirty years horror cinema has received its fair share of mainstream critical attention—unlike its dark sibling, horror fiction, which still remains relegated to bastard-child status in the literary pantheon. Film history has never had to contend to the same extent with the essentially false dichotomy that literary scholars have employed to distinguish high (serious) from low (popular) literary art, nor has film scholarship felt the compulsion to justify the horror genre as a serious art form, since horror has made steady and significant contributions throughout cinematic history. Cultural critic James Twitchell notes this curious distinction between film and literary criticism when he observes "critics of the gothic novel have, with the exception of [Montague] Summers, been academics trained in the rigors of literary scholarship, while critics of film have been aficionados who usually don't care about the provenance of the images they view" (9).

Film critics have recently discovered in the cinema of terror a tendency to repeat core themes and tropes that bear important cultural relevancy. For example, the issue of the horror monster—a staple representational figure throughout the genre's history—is now invested with an array of conflicting signifiers and symbolic interpretations. The horror monster is alternately viewed by critics in the field as a rebel-outsider against the social mainstream and as a re-enforcer of the social status quo, as an aggressive feminist archetype and the embodiment of a postfeminist backlash, and as a symbol of sexual liberation and repressive patriarchal control.

Additionally, for the past three decades, many film and cultural studies critics have directed their attention to the horror film as a vehicle for discussing, among other topics, gender distress, social transgression and transformation, psychoanalytic reactions to repression, homoerotic anxiety and indulgence, and various examinations of the human body under physical and psychological assault. Individual books as well as a variety of edited essay collections focus on these and other topical concerns. This chapter seeks to summarize several of the major theoretical positions constructed over the past thirty years—paralleling the emergence of horror as a legitimate and multileveled postmodern film genre.

Defining the Beast

Much of the contemporary horror film's critical attention originates in the writing of film critic Robin Wood. Throughout the 1970s and 1980s, Wood published several essays—some of the most important of these collected and republished in his book *Hollywood from Vietnam to Reagan*—providing a social context for interpreting American horror films. Not only were Wood's interpretations among the first serious scholarly investigations into the cultural relevancy of the genre, his Marxist orientation also revealed a "political subtext" at work in many of these films that served, in Wood's opinion, to indict "monogamous heterosexual bourgeois patriarchal capitalists" (71). Just as Leslie Fiedler argued for the accuracy of reading popular literature as a means for understanding the particular culture that produced it in his 1966 book *Love and Death in the American Novel*, Wood likewise felt that the youthful popularity and supernatural phenomena of the horror film disguised the genre's "dangerous and subversive implications" (78). Indeed, Wood insists persuasively that the horror movie, by virtue of its self-conscious distancing from reality and frequent flaws in technique and purpose, "can be far more radical and fundamentally undermining than works of conscious social criticism, which must always concern themselves with the possibility of reforming aspects of a social system whose basic rightness must not be challenged" (78). Thus, the best horror films possess a subtext that delivers a serious social commentary cleverly masked as escapist entertainment; in Wood's view, these movies present a critique of the symbolic order, particularly the social institutions of heterosexuality, family, church, government, and corporate capitalism.

Wood employs the phrase the "return of the repressed" (77) to describe the horror monster's intimate and conflicted relationship with the social mainstream. Because monsters are always positioned as social outcasts, or Other, they represent a force which "bourgeois ideology cannot recognize or accept" and therefore must either reject by annihilating the Other, or render it safe by assimilating it (73). The forces of normality present in the horror genre feel a quasi-hysterical compulsion to destroy or negate the Other because it represents what these forces are most secretly afraid of in themselves individually and in their collective culture. While we all feel the need to capture and eliminate the threat posed by serial killers such as *Red Dragon*'s Hannibal Lecter and Francis Dolarhyde, Wood would argue that we are also unconsciously (and sometimes not so unconsciously) attracted to the power these psychopaths maintain over their victims. We want to know more about them and the design of their plans, and not only because we need this information to help facilitate their capture. Their violence secretly stimulates antisocial impulses that the audience has been taught to repress. Wood understands that this contentious relationship between normality and monstrosity "constitutes the essential subject of the horror film" (79). The monster is, after all, the central figure in most horror movies, and he is the one around whom all the other characters adjust their actions and reactions. The monster is also the object of the audience's attention, and this is the main reason that he is kept out of sight—even as his violent presence or reputation is acutely felt through the other characters whom he affects—for as long as possible. From the vampire Nosferatu to Jack Torrance, the distressed father and husband in *The Shining*, the monster "both horrifies us with his evil and delights us with his intellect, his art, his audacity; while our moral sense is appalled by his outrages, another part of us gleefully identifies with him" (80). The horror monster, then, according to Wood, is that part of ourselves that we collectively repress, "the monster as normality's shadow" (80). Central to the popularity and purpose of the horror film is "the [monster's] fulfillment of our nightmare wish to smash the norms that oppress us and which our moral conditioning teaches us to revere" (80).

Freudian critics of the genre following Wood have tended to emphasize the psychoanalytical potential of the monster as emblematic of the liberated libido, but Wood's own interest in horror art goes beyond merely viewing it as a source for personal and sexual rebellion. He sees "the genre's real significance" in offering "the possibility of radical change and rebuilding in a period of extreme cultural crisis and disintegration" (84). In other words, Wood was first to recognize that the horror film threatens the political and cultural status quo; the monster, in his role as out-sider and challenger of social rules and mores, is a violent protest against ideolog-ical repression: "One might say that the true subject of the horror genre is the struggle for recognition of all that our civilization represses or oppresses" (75). By extension, the monster's attractiveness to the audience (because his violations are often the wish fulfillments of our darkest urges) is that he presents an alternative vision—as destructive as it is transformative—that extends beyond the limits of what society permits and condones.

Viewing the film *Blade Runner* as a prototypical example of his thesis, Wood maintains that the replicant rebel monsters are actually not nearly as monstrous as the oppressive forces that capitalism summons to subdue their rebellion: "hero and villain change places, all moral certainties based upon the status quo collapse" (187). Thus, while the horror film typically ends in the subjugation of the mon-ster and the reaffirmation of the status quo, a subversive energy has nonetheless been unleashed; the audience has witnessed the punitive consequences that accom-pany nonconformity as well as the potential—albeit ephemeral—range of alterna-tive political possibilities. Because of the audience's evolving identification with the monster (this varies, of course, depending upon the level of the monster's behavior and suffering) and our growing disaffection for the oppressive forces that first isolate and then violently dispatch the creature, the death of the horror mon-ster often hails no real catharsis. In fact, because the audience establishes such deeply sympathetic bonds with pursued and persecuted outlaw-others, quite the opposite occurs in representative films such as *Blade Runner*, *King Kong*, and *Edward Scissorhands*, to name only a few of the many possible examples.

Like Wood, Noel Carroll's *The Philosophy of Horror or Paradoxes of the Human Heart* is especially interested in cataloguing the various monsters that populate the horror genre. However, where Wood seeks to contextualize these monsters, read-ing them primarily as sociological phenomena, as the unconsciously repressed desires of the American bourgeois mainstream, Carroll's approach is less politicized and historically based. Although he understands that horror art often "violates the culture's standing concepts and categories, presenting figures that cannot be (can-not exist) according to the culture's scheme of things" (176), this transgression does not, as it does for Wood, pose a corresponding impulse to examine that which we marginalize in ourselves and our culture—our personal and collective perpetrations of, for example, greed, sexism, racism, and violence. Carroll essentially dismisses reading horror art as a self-reflective vehicle for viewing critically ourselves or our political institutions: "Indeed, many horror fictions seem too indeterminate from a political point of view to be correlated with any specific ideological theme" (197). He consequently undervalues the fact that the genre often calls attention to the limitations and collective anxieties of the culture from which it emerges.

For Carroll, monsters may invite psychoanalytical readings (he cites, for example, the value of Ernest Jones's *On the Nightmare*), but mostly he views the horror monster as a decidedly *aesthetic* violation: The creature repulses/attracts us because it is physically grotesque, in possession of elements "typically adjudged impure or disgusting within the culture" (49). Deliberately eschewing Wood's positioning of the monster as a cultural and political entity, Carroll necessarily limits his analysis even as he assembles a comprehensive survey to accommodate and categorize a great majority of the creatures of the horror genre. He establishes a generalized discussion of horror art and its deathless fascination for the generations that have always been attracted/repulsed by the genre, but Carroll insists that this response is and always has been based on a universally accepted sense of transgression and violation. All horror art, in other words, possesses elements that consistently inspire similar reactions in every audience. Whether it be the art of the eighteenth-century Gothic novel written as a reaction against the Age of Enlightenment, or the contemporary horror cinema with its emphasis on graphic displays of intimate assault and bloodletting, the same sensations of confusion and fright, violation and excess remain the common denominators of all horror art.

Although Carroll's argument is diminished by his failure to provide close readings of the many horror texts he references, *The Philosophy of Horror* nonetheless raises important questions about the genre in general and the impact on its spectators. "Normally, we shun what causes distress; most of us don't play in traffic to entertain ourselves. So why do we subject ourselves to fictions that will horrify us?" (159). For Carroll, this is a question that has always been relevant for the genre, not just a contemporary by-product of recent American publishing and Hollywood entertainment priorities. His ruminations center on issues of aesthetic theory, what he calls "the paradoxes of horror," namely the attractions of the horror mode that continue to represent universal elements of the human legacy. The hunger for the bizarre, the occult, the grotesque, and the attraction to pain is fundamentally rooted in human nature. Horror is an existential reminder that we live in an uncertain and terrifying world, "a deep-seated human conviction about the world, viz., that it contains vast unknown forces" (162).

Referencing several texts, including Lovecraft's *Supernatural Horror in Literature* and Rudolf Otto's *The Idea of the Holy*, Carroll constructs formulations that link horror art to the religious experience. The horror film puts the spectator in a vulnerable position, taking her out of her own immediate and mundane experience and into a situation that inspires *awe*, the paralyzing sense of fear, of being overpowered by forces larger than the self. This process holds its closest analog to the *numinous* religious experience of encountering God: "Another way of explaining the attraction of horror—one that may be connected with elements of the religious account—is to say that horrific beings—like deities and daemons—attract us because of their power. They induce awe" (167). This formulation is especially help-ful when considering monsters aspiring to God-like status, such as Dracula or Francis Dolarhyde in *Red Dragon*.

Gendering Horror

Many of the illustrations Robin Wood proposes in defining the subversive discourse of the horror film center upon women and their threat to patriarchal control. Focusing on the job of specifically categorizing this threat resulted in Barbara Creed's book *The Monstrous-Feminine*. Like Carroll and Wood, Creed also under-stands that the monster is the ultimate figure on the landscape of the modern hor-ror film, but for her the monster is a gender-specific creation. The female body is itself considered a perpetually worthy subject of horror art. This is why the horror film—delving always into the abject as a means for terrorizing audiences with every-thing from bodily excrement (blood, sweat, vomit) to sexual perversion as sexual-ized, violent death—relies so heavily on the female character, be she in the role of besieged heroine or monster, in order to subvert further the comfort level of the viewer.

While the horror film has tended to represent the monster as a gendered male creation and most women who are present in the genre as his victims, Creed reminds us that the inverted image of woman as monster is neither new nor infre-quently represented. The monstrous-feminine, as Creed defines it, occupies sever-al categories: woman as possessed body (*The Exorcist*), woman as animal (*Cat People*), woman as witch (*Carrie*), woman as vampire (*The Hunger*), woman as pri-mal mother (*Alien*), and woman as castrating mother (*Psycho*). "The concept of the monstrous-feminine, as instructed within/by the patriarchal and phallocentric ide-ology, is related immediately to the problem of sexual difference and castration" (2).

Creed posits that the terror inspired by the female monster is most often asso-ciated with her body. Males find themselves faced with the *difference* of the female form, and this physical difference suggests several forms of abjection: corporeal decay and death; excess and uncontrollable fluids, bodily wastes; and, of course, the feminine body as site of mystery and fear: "Abjection is constructed as a rebellion of filthy, lustful, carnal, female flesh" (38). Most horror films construct some kind of border that is threatened or violated by the monster's behavior. When the mon-ster is a male, "it is man's phallic properties that are frequently constructed as a source of monstrosity" (83). In horror films that feature female monsters, the vio-lated border is defined in terms that are significantly feminized: blood that cannot be appropriately contained or controlled, bodily organs—especially the vagina and mouth—that threaten the male with castration.

Julia Kristeva's book *The Powers of Horror: An Essay on Abjection* posits a definition of the abject in terms that are particularly relevant to discussions about horror art. Kristeva views the abject as terrifying because it threatens to disrupt our conventional understanding of "borders, positions, rules" (4). The horror monster signifies abject terror because it violates cultural categories, disrespects organizing principles, and generally serves to present a chaotic alternative to the place of order and meaning, socially as well as biologically. The abject is what is set in motion by the monster, the terror that his disruptive actions inspire. When Creed applies Kristeva's range of psychoanalytical formulations specifically to the physical bodies of women in horror films, she discovers that the monstrous feminine is centered within a woman's reproductive and mothering functions when they cross beyond their normal range of meaning and appear out of control. In other words, abject terror as found in the excessive blood imagery that is associated with Carrie's menstruation and symbolic prom-queen sacrificing; it is located in the open maw of the Alien creature that continually secretes a toxic saliva; and it is likewise in the various horrific wombs of horror cinema that give birth to nonhuman offspring (*Demon Seed*, *The Fly*, and *Rosemary's Baby*), as well as in the ghostly visitations contained and vented inside physical dwellings (the haunted house as symbolic womb). The abjection associated with and created by the feminine monster is therefore closely aligned with the rebellious mother insofar as her rebellion against the paternal order is what produces both the film's chaos and monstrosity: "What is common to all these images of horror is the voracious maw, the mysterious black hole that signifies female genitalia which threatens to give birth to equally horrific offspring as well as threatening to incorporate everything in its path" (27).

Consequently, Creed views the science-fiction creature in *Alien* as "the archaic mother," and the film's dominant imagery centers on "scenes which explore different forms of birth" (17). Similarly, the body of the female child in *The Exorcist*, Regan, becomes the battleground for expressing the film's themes of social alienation, religious skepticism, and marital divorce. Most of all, Regan's demonic possession embodies all of the profane rage that the girl's mother feels toward the absent husband-father, and the demon manipulates an adolescent female body on the cusp of womanhood to represent and coalesce these conflicts: "But while the theme of spiritual decline is central to *The Exorcist*, it is secondary to the film's exploration of female monstrousness and the inability of the male order to control the woman whose perversity is expressed through her rebellious body" (34).

In the essay "When a Woman Looks," Linda Williams continues Creed's emphasis on the links between woman and monstrosity. While Creed maintains that the monstrous-feminine is monstrous because it represents a threat to patriarchal control over the feminine, Williams complicates Creed's split along clear-cut gendered dichotomies by positing that often horror films encourage a cross-gendered identification between the typically male monster and female characters and female spectators of these films. Since the "monster's power is one of sexual difference from the normal male"—provoking comparisons of excessive, inadequate, or deviant sexuality—"he is remarkably like the woman in the eyes of the traumatized male: a biological freak with impossible and threatening appetites" (20). Citing evidence from *Psycho*, *Dressed to Kill*, and *Peeping Tom*, Williams argues that women are punished for "looking"—i.e., expressing their sexual desire literally and symbolically. Their punishment is that they are forced into an identification with the monster's persecuted and outsider status and then, typically, are mutilated by the figure with whom they share "a flash of sympathetic identification" (21). Because the monster and the woman in horror films share a similar existence insofar as they exist "to be looked at" by the audience's shared male-gaze, the "woman is both victim and monster" (28). Trapped in the traditional role as object of the gaze, she finds herself unconsciously aligned with the monster as the movie's object of disgust. However, horror monster and woman seldom establish a bond of mutual dependency or an open alliance against the patriarchal order that both intimidate. Instead, female and monster remain in opposition until either the woman is destroyed or rescued in the monster's destruction.

The identification that Williams suggests between women in the horror film audience and on-screen female protagonists under siege is a core element of Carol Clover's thesis in *Men, Women, and Chainsaws: Gender in the Modern Horror Film*. Primarily interested in those horror films that fall under the category of the "slasher" variety—*Halloween*, *The Texas Chain Saw Massacre*, *Friday the 13th*, *Nightmare on Elm Street* (and their relentless sequels)—where a serial psychopath "propelled by psychosexual fury" (127) preys upon teenagers with various weapons—such as a chain saw, finger blades, ax, and knives—the most provocative elements of Clover's book concern the volatile gender dynamics set in motion by these films, including the audience's shifting identification with cinematic characters. Just as Linda Williams sees a cross-gendered identification between woman victim and male monster in horror films, Clover insists that this, as well as more radical and fluid identifications co-exist, including those that take place within the "largely young and largely male majority audience" (23) that pays to see these films. Bonding initially with the misogynist killer in his rampage against sexually active teenage men and women, the audience—males and females alike, as Clover seldom makes a distinction—eventually reverses its allegiances. Clover claims that our response to terror on the screen shifts from a desire to see innocent victims—especially females—pursued and violently opened, to an insistence that their random deaths be revenged and the monster destroyed. We tire of the monster's unimaginative stalkings, grow increasingly repulsed at his random and accumulated carnage, and come to appreciate and identify with the Final Girl, Clover's term for the last teenager whose intelligence and stamina keeps her alive to do battle against the psychopathic monster: "Observers stress the readiness of the 'live' audience to switch sympathies midstream, siding now with the killer and now, finally, with the Final Girl" (46). An attractive person who is imperiled on-screen—and in the Hollywood world the actresses in slasher films are always attractive—inspires the audience's desire to see her survive. Women are more closely aligned with children in these movies, thereby increasing their vulnerability, but likewise the audience's wish for them to endure. While the horror audience may enjoy seeing a beautiful woman tortured, it does not necessarily want to see her destroyed.

Although physically striking and equally as imperiled as the other women around her, the Final Girl combines the functions of suffering victim and avenging hero, and as the slasher genre evolved through the 1980s, Final Girls became more and more violent. She "is the first character to sense something amiss and the only one to deduce from the accumulating evidence the pattern and extent of the threat" (44). She appropriates the phallic symbols of the male killer, and in the course of her struggle to stay alive she finds the strength and the will to "stop screaming, face the killer, reach for a weapon, and address the monster on his own terms" (48). Clover believes that the male audience for the slasher film supports and identifies with the Final Girl because "she is not fully feminine—not, in any case, feminine in the ways of her friends," that is to say, those female victims who try to cope with the monster by "crying and cowering because [they are] women" (13). In contrast, the gender of the Final Girl is "comprised from the outset by her masculine interests, her inevitable sexual reluctance, her apartness from the other girls . . . her exercise of the 'active investigative gaze' normally reserved for males and punished in females when they assume it themselves" (48). As Clover envisions her, the Final Girl is not necessarily a particularly feminist development, since she assumes so many gendered masculine qualities—violence, a proactive stance, the male investigative gaze, and athleticism—in her quest to survive. Thus, her endurance requires her to co-opt the position of the masculine hero: to vanquish the monster and survive through acts of violence.

Clover's thesis is, in part, a response to film theory's fascination in the 1980s with the concept of *viewer identification*; that is, how point of view, camera angle, montage, and mise-en-scène shape our perception of an on-scene personality. Laura Mulvey's argument that the audience is aligned with the camera's exploitation of the female as an object of glamour is called into question by Clover's insistence that viewer identification with the male gaze is less static and solid. Indeed, it is evident that in postmodern film criticism regarding gender and the horror genre the scholarship reflects a movement away from Mulvey's reductive victimization of woman at the hands and eyes of the dominant male monster-spectator and towards a more proactive assertion of female independence and survival skills. Clover's Final Girl is a long way from the helpless Gothic maiden merely a generation removed who awaits rescue at the hands of the hero male, the latter arriving in time to dispose of the monster and eventually marry the besieged maiden. In contrast, the contemporary horror heroine often finds herself out on her own; she must confront the monster with an independent resolve. As Clover concludes: "By 1980, the male rescuer is either dismissably marginalized or dispensed with altogether; not a few films have him rush to the rescue only to be hacked to bits, leaving the Final Girl to save herself after all. . . . Abject terror may still be gendered feminine, but the willingness of one immensely popular current genre to re-represent the hero as an anatomical female would seem to suggest that at least one of the traditional marks of heroism, triumphant self-rescue, is no longer strictly gendered masculine" (60). A generation of feminism has given birth to a female hero who refuses to remain trapped in her gendered victimization; her own capacity for enduring violence in addition to engaging in it herself (e.g., Stretch in *Texas Chainsaw Massacre 2*) tends to make her nearly as intimidating as the monster in pursuit of her.

Arguing the point that Clover's "powerful female is underneath it all a male in drag" (81), Isabel Christina Pinedo's book *Recreational Terror: Women and the Pleasures of Horror Film Viewing* takes a more progressive and pro-feminist stance regarding the Final Girls that have emerged from horror cinema. Linking them to the transgressive sexuality of film noir heroines, Pinedo insists that heterosexual women in the audience are not necessarily following Clover's paradigm that situates pleasure only in regarding the Final Girl as a male-identified construction of the boy in drag. Instead, she maintains that aggressive women in horror art can still maintain their status as women, and this action, far more than Clover is willing to admit, "subverts [the] binary notion of gender that buttresses male dominance" (83).

What is especially interesting about the recent proliferation of critical work and theoretical dialogue about horror cinema is how much of it is being written by women film scholars. Long viewed exclusively as objects inspiring salacious behavior from the horror monster, or at least as the object of the monster's victimization, the status of women in the horror film has been markedly upgraded because of the efforts of critics such as Carol Clover, Barbara Creed, Linda Williams, Julia Kristeva, Vera Dika, Isabel Christina Pinedo, and Judith Halberstam. These scholars have enlarged the critical discourse to include questions such as: What are the reasons the horror genre centers such negative energies on issues of gender conflict and distress? What kinds of bonds do the monster and female protagonist share in their common positioning as peripheral "outsiders"? Is it possible to read women's roles in certain modern and postmodern horror films as challenges to the traditional place women occupy in the genre?

It is no exaggeration to point out that feminists have written the most original as well as the most exciting interpretative criticism of horror cinema over the past three decades. There is something of a poetic irony in this fact, as it might be said that women have finally reclaimed for themselves a place in a genre that has for so long abused their gender; in fact, women scholars in the field have actually set out not merely to reiterate the facts of feminine exploitation at the hands of misogynist men and monsters, but to move beyond this position by pointing to those places where it is possible to recognize resistance and empowerment, such as in the *Alien* cycle or in the Final Girl of the slasher film.

Recent feminist interpretations of horror cinema, however, go beyond merely carving out a place for women in a genre that has typically been interested only in their capacity for indignities and pain. Their interpretations have helped to elevate and legitimize the importance of horror as a film genre. Too often held as a suspect art form by "serious" scholars of film and literature, the work of these women critics insists that horror art cannot be so easily dismissed, even if the interpretative theories applied to them are sometimes more sophisticated and engaging than the primary film texts themselves. Feminist scholars who write so persuasively about these films have required the rest of us to view horror movies not only as representative samplings of genre art, but as more fully achieved artistic expressions.

Horror and Psychoanalysis

While arguably the most excitingly innovative contemporary scholarship on the horror film has emerged from feminist critics, gender is not the exclusive area of interest for those analyzing the genre. Some of the more interesting theoretical discussions of horror art grapple with psychological and identity formulation issues that propel the discussion well beyond the boundaries of gender theory: For starters, why are we even attracted to an art form that celebrates the aesthetics of the ugly, indulging in images of repulsion, nightmare, and disgust? What can a genre predicated on the unreal and supernatural possibly reveal about the human psyche and the realities of everyday life?

Perhaps the first true theoretician of terror was the philosopher Edmund Burke, who in his eighteenth-century treatise on the beautiful and the sublime, insisted, in terms that were decidedly antineoclassical, that horror produces "the strongest emotion which the mind is capable of feeling. I say strongest emotion, because I am satisfied the ideas of pain are much more powerful than those which center on pleasure" (39). Noting the relevancy of Burke's observation in their patients' maladaptive behavior, psychoanalysts have also tried to explain the human fascination with horror imagery and its connection to the antisentiments of psychological aberration, specifically neurotic behavior. As early as 1913, Freud began his own investigation into the connection between horror, what he called "the uncanny," and psychological neurosis. The monstrous projections of horror stories, fairy tales, and nightmares are all interwoven in the mind's tapestry as projected urges (both as extensions of wish fulfillment and self-destructive impulses). For Freud, we are drawn to horror's imagery because it provides an important release mechanism for repressed emotions and projections that threaten the psyche. Without indulging such a release, these negative emotions, Freud speculated, might manifest themselves as neuroses. Ernest Jones, a disciple of Freud, in his book *On the Nightmare*, concurs with the latter in his assessment that our fascination with supernatural creatures—witches, vampires, werewolves, and the devil—is a manifestation of unconscious anxiety; indeed, that it is sexual in its origin: "The real cause of the Nightmare . . . is of mental origin, a sexual wish in a state of repression" (343).

Freud, Jones, and especially Carl Jung were highly influential sources for James F. Iaccino's more recent efforts to assemble psychological archetypes and apply them directly to horror films. His book, *Psychological Reflections on Cinematic Terror*, builds on historical archetypes in arguing that there exists a "striking correlation between these archetypes and the content of many horror film story lines" (x). Citing several of Jung's archetypes—among them, the persona/shadow, mother/father, wise man/magician, and anima/animus—Iaccino argues that most horror films rely on the inability of horror protagonists to resolve their conflicts with one or more of these archetypes. The failure to integrate the archetype into their personalities results in both personal conflict and varying levels of terror. For example, the film versions of *Dr. Jekyll and Mr. Hyde* rely upon Jekyll's struggle to integrate his Jungian shadow, i.e., the Hyde part of his personality. The shadow archetype, according to Jung, is the most powerful and dangerous of them all because it contains those avatars of a primitive and bestial nature that defy rational boundaries and restraints. Using the Jekyll and Hyde story as his illustration, Iaccino concludes that "Within the medium of the horror film, one message is continually expressed: The dark shadow cannot and perhaps should not be repressed" (7).

Although Iaccino is not faithful to exploring thoroughly either the archetypical categories he presents in this text or the films that illustrate their conflict, interpreting horror cinema from a Jungian perspective is nonetheless an extremely rich theoretical approach. It allows us, for example, to view Sarah Connor in *Terminator 2* as an embodiment of an *Amazon-warrior archetype* or to appreciate that Norman Bates in *Psycho* suffers from a severe *mother complex*; the latter persuasively explains the fact that while Norman desires to be with an adult female, his obsession with his mother (both as sexual taboo and parental voice of repression) undermines his masculine identity, producing "a severely disturbed adult who can never find satisfaction with himself or another" (6).

A more disciplined and persuasively argued Jungian analysis of horror cinema is found in Janice Hocker Rushing and Thomas S. Frentz's book, *Projecting the Shadow: The Cyborg in American Film*. Centered specifically on the image of the machine serving as a shadow archetype for the human society that created it, *Projecting the Shadow* insists that several recent horror films center on the problem of integrating the machine (shadow) into the collective psyche of the society that has produced it. Films such as the *Terminator* series, *Blade Runner*, *Jaws*, and *Deer Hunter* feature machines that, although created by humans to perform their will, have suddenly turned against man, "usurping the sovereignty of its creator" (5). As the machine is often initially constructed by man as a weapon to help him subdue nature, Rushing and Frentz argue further that these films create an association among machine, nature, and the concept of the horror monster as alien outsider—"the feminine, the dark Other, the beast" (76)—setting up a conflict where the humans approach these archetypes "as either an enemy they must control or as a part of themselves that they must reclaim" (74). Following closely the Jungian imperative for assimilation with the shadow, postmodern man as he is portrayed in these selected horror films is forced to "integrate the subjected elements of himself that he has rejected. This process of centering . . . [can occur] only for the heroes who have the anima or the animals on their side" (76).

Relying heavily on hunter archetypes as they have filtered down through the myths of the American wilderness and Jungian analyses of heroic journeying, *Projecting the Shadow* argues for a unique juxtaposition of past and future myths. The American hunter tradition in literature and film has always been a sort of initiation ritual, whereby a naïve (often civilized) male must make his way into the wild to encounter its violence and primitivism. In the process of engaging this rite of passage, the protagonist must also confront his own dark shadow, sometimes located in the wild (Quint's pursuit of the shark in *Jaws*), and sometimes located within the protagonist himself (Deckard's role reversal and identification with Batty at the conclusion of *Blade Runner*). Applying this paradigm to techno-horror films set in a dystopian future, Rushing and Frentz argue that similar initiation rites emphasizing an integration with the hunted Other/monster/machine are still operative and affective principles that serve to create a continuum between past myths and archetypes and a postmodern technological future. As postmodern man confronts the horror of his own technology turned against him, his survival depends on his ability "to realize that the Other is part of the Self" (74).

Less committed to psychoanalytic models for interpreting the relationship between horror art and the individual psyche, Mark Edmundson posits in *Nightmare on Main Street* that our fascination with horror in all its popular manifestations, from film and television to rock music and fashion, is symptomatic of the spiritual malaise that characterizes American social life at the beginning of a new millennium. For Edmundson, an appreciation of horror art "is antithetical to all smiling American faiths. . . . Horror films [are] for misanthropes, for people who live in the cellars of their own minds" (x, 5). Furthermore, we are drawn to the horror film because it confirms many of our darkest feelings about the "estranging, brutal society" (16) Americans have created. Edmundson has a deep appreciation of America as a culture of the Gothic, citing many insightful and original examples of the ways in which the tropes of horror pervade postmodern society and especially its entertainment industries (e.g., the afternoon talk show as populated by "the husband or son who has persecuted the family" [57] forced to confess his monstrous acts of depravity).

Although instructive in detailing the cultural permutations of contemporary American Gothic, Edmundson's split between the pessimism of horror art and what he argues is its Manichean flip side—the visionary hopefulness of Ralph Waldo Emerson and his descendants, contemporary New Age optimists—appears overly reductive and polarized. It is beyond Edmundson's ability to appreciate, for example, that horror art is not always entirely pessimistic and fatalistic; indeed, that many horror films present alternatives to their images of excess and destruction: "Dead-end, no-fault, paranoia: our current Gothic modes invite us to be afraid, but not, in general to fight back. . . . They counsel us to despair about political change and social reform. They offer us only the satisfaction that can come from complete fatalism, from giving up" (62). However, this depiction is clearly not always accurate. Horror films as diverse as *The Exorcist, Jaws, The Day the Earth Stood Still, Alien, Misery, The Lost Boys, The Terminator 2, Last House on the Left,* and *Blade Runner,* to offer only a partial list, present the opportunity for an audience to experience a similar level of public catharsis and spectacle that is similar to witnessing classical tragedy; many horror films, like many of Shakespeare's tragedies, ultimately confirm harmony and social order through the conquering of delirious fears that must be defeated. While Edmundson is partly right in his assertion that the horror genre contains strong elements of negation and violation, many of its texts also possess contrasting elements of transformation and transcendence that are deeply wedded to the meaning of the films. The endings of the aforementioned movies suggest that the genre they represent can be as much about survival and moral advancement as it is about fatalism and giving up.

The Horror Body

Since the 1980s, much has been written about the physical body in horror—its various transformations, alterations, and assaults. The image of the transforming body—ranging from Hyde's literal emergence from within Jekyll's skin, to the insect hybrid that the scientist watches himself become in *The Fly*, to the desire to penetrate and mutilate flesh in the slasher film—is a central trope in the horror genre. Images of the body's metamorphosis dominate various subcategories of horror film, such as those dealing with vampires, werewolves, and alien creatures that usurp the human body completely or use it as a vehicle for furthering the self-expression of a monstrous life form (as in *Alien* and *The Exorcist*).

In her tracing of nineteenth-and twentieth-century horror film and fiction, Judith Halberstam suggests in her book *Skin Shows* that nineteenth-century monstrosity consisted of a combination of class, race, and gender affixed to a single deviant body: "the deviant body—Dracula, Jekyll/Hyde, and even Frankenstein's monster before them are lumpen bodies, bodies pieced together out of the fabric of race, class, gender, and sexuality" (3). Thus, interpreting the Frankenstein monster must delve into discussions of the creature as an embodiment of "class struggle, the product of industrialization, a representation of the proletariat; the monster is all social struggle" (29). Dracula's monstrosity is located in what Halberstam believes is the anti-Semitic subtext of Stoker's novel, feasting upon Western wealth and health, and in his body's outsider status established in his unique blending of masculine and feminine traits. Stevenson's Jekyll and Hyde likewise reveals a monstrous body that emerges out of control. Halberstam posits further that Hyde is representational of the homosexual body that Jekyll needs to keep secret as well as the maternal body that is equally repellent: "Since he moves in an almost exclusively masculine world, Jekyll, as divided and dividing, becomes different from his colleagues and friends by becoming woman and alien, feminine and foreign" (76).

In postmodern film, however, Halberstam argues that the horror text exhibits the markings of a crisis of sexual identity and gender, but not so much the distinguishing signs of class or race. In contrast to nineteenth-century horror, which tends to coalesce within the single hideous body of the monster, the postmodern horror film rejects this neat identification and alignment. Contemporary monsters no longer coagulate into a single, recognizable face or skin. In contrast to the Frankenstein monster or Dracula, they do not "scare us from a distance, [as] they are us, they are on us, and in us" (163). "The birds themselves in Hitchcock's film are a good example of the transference of horror from a specifically unnatural body to nature itself embodied within the myriad form of a flock of aggressive birds" (24).

Halberstam's final chapter, dealing with the film version of *The Silence of the Lambs*, insists that postmodern horror "has cannibalized nineteenth-century Gothic, eaten its monsters alive" (177), by constructing in the film's serial killer, Buffalo Bill, a figure as obsessed with skin and the body's appearances as Victor Frankenstein and Dr. Jekyll. However, what distinguishes Buffalo Bill from these earlier monsters is the level of his gender distress. He is involved with what he believes to be a transcendent process. He cuts gender apart and then reconfigures it as a "woman suit" designed to forge a connection back to his mother and forward to a new and radical gender identity. In this way at least, the serial killer in *Silence* maintains a closer parallel to Norman Bates in *Psycho* than he does to nineteenth-century conceptions of the monster. In his need to kill what he most wishes to become, Buffalo Bill is a postmodern monster: a creature that defies easy categorization. In appropriating the feminine body, Buffalo Bill seeks to circumvent his own body, pointing the way to a more glamorous world. However, his dream of refashioning himself female must ultimately leave Bill suspended in a nether realm where he remains neither male nor female. As Halberstam reminds us, "Buffalo Bill is prey to the most virulent conditioning heterosexual culture has to offer—he believes that anatomy is destiny" (167). Where Hyde, Frankenstein's monster, and Dracula bear the *symbolic* trappings of gender transformation and blurring, Buffalo Bill takes their quests to the furthest, *literal* extreme: He is lost in a way that no scientific potion or surgical realignment can hope to reconstruct happily.

Discussions of the physical body in horror art are, as might well be imagined, an important facet of criticism dealing with the slasher film. This subgenre's emphasis is on the open wound of the broken body, the resplendently appointed corpse that opens out, to display itself as a visual feast. Our public fascination with torn and open bodies and torn and open persons prompted critic Mark Seltzler to proclaim America a "wound culture," and to argue that the spectacle of the wounded body has helped to birth the serial killer and a series of Hollywood horror movies that center on him as a central character: "The spectacular public representation of violated bodies, across a burgeoning range of official, academic, and media accounts, in fiction and in film, has come to function as a way of imagining and situating our notions of public, social, and collective identity. These exhibitions make up the contemporary pathological public sphere, our wound culture" (21). Because the body is the object of assault in films such as *The Texas Chainsaw Massacre* and *Friday the 13th*, by the end of these films teenage victims are indistinguishable from one another. Even as dissections of the body are central to the violence of these movies, it is as generic corpus—gendered slabs of meat—rather than individualized human beings. As Jonathan Lake Crane notes, "Only when inscribed with Jason's signature do bodies acquire any meaningful or notable mark of difference. Only in death, reduced to shattered viscera, do victims become truly worthy of our undivided attention" (148).

Vera Dika has likewise written extensively about bodies and violence in the slasher film. Her position is that the victims in slashers occupy essentially "feminine positions because their narrative and cinematic enfeeblement has rendered them functionally castrated . . . they are the helpless objects of the film" (90). In spite of this, Dika also views the postmodern horror film as an exercise in survivalism. As Bruno Bettelheim interprets the most disquieting elements of fairy tales imparting important lessons to children about what to avoid and how to cope with threatening situations, Dika likewise views the horror film as a morality tale: imparting warnings to teenagers about avoiding excessive self-absorption, assuming responsibility for their actions, and learning survival skills in a world where adult authority is conspicuously absent.

Pointing Toward the Future

As the future of the horror film pushes the perimeters of its traditional themes and forms, reinventing itself even as it cannibalizes its own history of monsters and fearful locations, increasingly the genre appears to focus, as *Projecting the Shadow* prophetically anticipates, on the technological bodies of cyborgs, robots, and simulated contrivances that threaten any and all established definitions of what it means to be truly human. As we enter into a new century of terror on celluloid, the body has become increasingly mechanized; the technology of monstrosity is central to films as diverse as *Blade Runner, Twelve Monkeys, Minority Report,* and the *Terminator* series. According to cultural critic Christoph Grunenberg, "The industrial Gothic of contemporary film and fiction reflects an increasing weariness about the alienating power of technology and its disastrous social consequences" (197). The monsters of the future appear to be less about flesh and blood and more about machinery and computer chips. Indeed, in films such as *Videodrome, Poltergeist,* and *The Ring,* television technology has assumed an infernal life of its own, bringing some sort of unexpurgated evil directly into the living rooms and lives of innocent strangers who are then forced into confronting what they have unwittingly unleashed. The horror film and its not-so-distant relative, the science fiction film, have been steadily merging into one another (creating the techno-horror subgenre examined in chapter 5), making it virtually impossible both to distinguish where the science is fiction and where either genre—horror or science-fiction—begins and the other one ends. The winged seductions of the vampire film are giving way to the corporation as vampire; an unbridled capitalism and its scientific technology have replaced Victor Frankenstein as the indirect source for suffering due to ventures that threaten the limits of human comprehension and morality.

As we will see in chapters to follow, the horror film has always been interested in exploring sites of uneasiness that lurk just beneath the collective and personal consciousness. Whether the film's subtext speaks to teenage angst about sexuality, as it does in the slasher film; or the collapse of the home as a safe refuge for bourgeois patriarchy, as it so often does in the demonic possession film; or our cultural anxieties about moving too fast into an uncharted and ungoverned technological marketplace, as in the techno-horror film, horror cinema remains one of the great barometers of popular culture for measuring the cultural advances and the anxieties that attend these advances at any given moment in time. No longer concerned with the production of grand and majestic terror themes, the horror film we have inherited today reflects a hesitant and apprehensive state of mind obscured by a deep fear of the unfamiliar future (Gruneberg 160). Not merely a genre for exploiting pure sensationalism and sensory induration, at its best the horror film is perhaps most like a visit to a trusted psychoanalyst: We reveal something of what is troubling us, and in return we get the opportunity to explore its meaning to our lives—and maybe, if we are lucky, to leave less anxious than when we arrived. If nothing else, future horror films will continue to provide us with insights about what it means to be human.

In her ruminations on what she calls the art of the grotesque, Joyce Carol Oates believes that we are compelled to experience horror quickly, "with a rising sense of dread, and so total a suspension of ordinary skepticism, we inhabit the material without question and virtually as its protagonist; we can see no way out except to go forward" (307). While Oates's commentary certainly contains the breathless spirit of an adrenaline rush attendant to good horror art, it also suggests that we should not think too much—if at all—about the experience itself, as though it were exclusively an emotional, rather than also an intellectual activity. Like all good cinema, however, the horror film also demands a certain thoughtfulness, a critical appreciation of its form and meaning as *art*. For too long the horror aesthetic has been dismissed as juvenile, hideous, and lowbrow. Horror art may be this, but it is just as often something more, as the various theoreticians introduced in this chapter have argued. The best horror films offer us cautionary tales, abject lessons in terror that we may not necessarily wish to hear—as horror themes typically take us to places that are both disquieting and uncomfortable—but, then, isn't the truth often what we try hardest to repress?

2.

Stark Terrors

The Cabinet of Dr. Caligari,
Nosferatu, Metropolis, Frankenstein,
The Bride of Frankenstein

The first horror movies were not coincidentally also some of the first products of the nascent European film industry. It is certainly no exaggeration to posit that the history of motion pictures began in the shadowy world of the nineteenth-century Gothic novel. The very earliest European films—*The Raven* (1915) [which is lost], *The Cabinet of Dr. Caligari* (1920), *Korkarlen* (Swedish: *The Phantom Carriage* [1921]), *Nosferatu* (1922), *The Phantom of the Opera* (1925), *Metropolis* (1927), and *The Fall of the House of Usher* (1928)—shared some important similarities with the next generation of horror pictures produced the following decade in the United States by Universal Studios. Although Universal's efforts were designed, in part, to capitalize on the immediate success that had attended the German (*Caligari, Nosferatu,* and *Metropolis*) and French (*The Raven* and *Usher*) forays into horror, it was also an effort, as David Skal notes in *The Monster Show,* to awaken the American motion picture industry to the full possibilities of their art: These early films were "a kind of cultural sputnik launched from out of nowhere by Europe, a gauntlet not thrown down, but projected up on the shivering screen of America's insecurities" (43).

The American response came in the productions of *Frankenstein, The Bride of Frankenstein, Dracula, Jekyll and Hyde,* and *The Werewolf of London,* among others, all released in the 1930s. Universal Studios made several impressive silent horror films in the 1920s—*The Hunchback of Notre Dame* (1923) and *The Phantom of the Opera* (1925) were definitely the most notable in terms of critical appraisal and commercial success—but these early productions notwithstanding, the American cinematic response to horror is typically considered to have arrived with the advent of sound. As film historian Ian Conrich reminds us, "Universal, the most European of the American studios of the 1920s, constructed a horror film legacy, which was conveyed from its silent to sound productions" (40–41). Like their earlier silent European predecessors in horror, the American films relied upon literary sources, and these sources were the dominant European literary monster myths of the nineteenth century: an evolving Frankenstein story line, Mr. Hyde, and the vampire.

While much of the modernist movement—specifically in literature, painting, architecture, and music—generally eschewed the previous century in its desire to create art that represented a radical new departure from what came before it, modern cinema, in contrast, embraced the gothic fiction of the nineteenth century for at least its thematic inspiration. *Nosferatu* and *Dracula* were both based on Stoker's novel, a text that has always maintained a strong popular allegiance, never falling out of print since its 1897 publication. The fascination with transforming novels of Mary Shelley, Robert Louis Stevenson, Victor Hugo, Gaston Leroux, and Edgar Allan Poe's work into film, as well as *Dracula* itself, suggest a recurring pattern in horror that continues even today: The genre is constantly revisiting and readapting its core myths. Like the deathless vampire who must repeat its stalk-and-kill cycle in order to satisfy a recurring blood hunger, the earliest film horrors cannibalized its literary ancestry again and again. The surrealists of the 1920s, for example, sensed a strong kinship with Gothic art, recognizing that the horror monster was very much a projection of the unconscious mind that was key to the movement's commitment to the overthrow of repression and the indulgence of subconscious impulses. So it is not surprising that Salvador Dali and Luis Bunuel's film *The Andalusian Dog* (1929) owes as much to Gothic horror as it does to the tenets of surrealism.

In addition to capitalizing on the enduring popularity of nineteenth-century literary texts, the early horror film industry was not required to pay permission fees for interpreting them into celluloid, as Poe, Shelley, and Hugo had published the original source works nearly a century earlier. The notable exception, of course, was Murnau's *Nosferatu*, and the reader should consult Skal's thorough and fascinating investigation of the convoluted struggle between the film's director and Stoker's estate detailed in his book, *Hollywood Gothic* (43–63). The nineteenth-century literary texts that supplied the inspiration for early horror cinema also came with a built-in set of characteristics that were enticing to Hollywood's evolving dream-machine. Stoker's *Dracula* highlights the sexuality of the vampire with its subtle blurring of the distinction between blood and semen. Bela Lugosi's filmic rendition of the Count merely builds on the sexual subtext of Stoker's graphic novel. Poe's literary vision further lent itself perfectly to the black and white chiaroscuro of early cinema. In "The Raven," "The Fall of the House of Usher," "The Black Cat," and "The Tell-Tale Heart," some of the earliest film adaptations from Poe's canon, the shadowy world of interior rooms lit by candlelight and suffused with melancholic gloom lends itself perfectly to a black-and-white mise-en-scène. Moreover, Poe's fascination with the underworld and with giving vent to an interior psychopathology paralleled and indirectly inspired the expressionistic milieus of early German and American horror cinema. While Hollywood required a sequel to *Frankenstein* in order to explore the pervasive social critique inherent in Mary Shelley's tale of rejection and alienation, all of Universal's permutations of the *Frankenstein* plot still retain a cautionary status that warns against the dangers of prideful individualism. In an era when totalitarianism was reshaping the world's political landscape and attaining its form primarily through the ambitious expressions of individual megalomaniacs such as Hitler and Mussolini, the subtext of the Frankenstein films released from 1930–45 detail the devastation that comes when an individual chooses to pursue domination fantasies and ignore moral prohibitions.

In the Gothic literary texts that were most attractive to the nascent horror film industry, it is often difficult for the reader to establish clear distinctions between reality and dream, trapped as she is in a fantastic narrative that seeks to render an interior psychological state of consciousness that borders the landscape of dream. In Stevenson's *The Strange Case of Dr. Jekyll and Mr. Hyde*, for example, the sleeping Jekyll is unable to control the Hyde that lurks just beneath his skin, indicating that the monster is not only conceived and most fully realized in the subconscious, but that he is also as much about a psychological state of being as he is about physiological transformation. The world of cinema, replete with visualized images flickering across a darkened theater, became, of course, the perfect medium for illuminating such concerns, the dreamscape of the mind so central to understanding the interior microcosm created in the narrative texts of Poe and Stevenson. The exterior exists, in both Poe's poems and fiction as well as in a film such as *The Cabinet of Dr. Caligari*, to illuminate an inner landscape, a fantastic voyage visualized expressionistically. Cinematic art has always been about the projection of dreams—individually and collectively. The first directors of horror cinema understood that these dreams could be compelling when projected as nightmares.

Inside Caligari's Cabinet

In keeping with the atmospheric dreamscape that characterizes the whole of the cinematic experience, German expressionism in the movies is delineated by phantasmagoric experience, bizarre and distorted cinematography, and a thematic predilection toward portraying degrees of madness and obsessive acts of evil. The techniques of the German directors centered around chiaroscuro lighting effects that emphasized the polarities of light and dark, distorted and surreal backdrops, angular claustrophobic spaces, extreme camera angles, and shadows inappropriate to the object that produced them. All of these techniques were designed to heighten the spectator's appreciation for the psychological or psychopathological crisis being projected on the screen (Kavka 215).

The painted sets of Robert Wiene's *Dr. Caligari*, designed by Hermann Warm and fellow members of Berlin's expressionist *Der Strum* group, feature sharply sloping inclines, slanted rooftops, swirling colors, and angular walls and ceilings. The passage of time has not lessened the heightened effect of this film's bizarre, highly unstable worldview; if anything, the history of cinema's reliance on realistic settings and atmospheres now makes *Caligari* appear all the more unnerving. The film's mise-en-scène has much in common with a deeply personal, hallucinogenic experience where external appearances mirror the rabid flux of a distressed—and perhaps, more specifically, a diseased—psyche. Just as the walls of buildings and the frames of windows and doors attain a surreal quality in *Caligari*'s sets, the film is distinguished by its attention to abnormal pursuit and motivation; indeed, the action of the picture radiates from a country carnival. In his role as a carnival barker encouraging the crowd to witness the reawakening of Cesare, a somnambulist who has been asleep in a cabinet for twenty-five years, Dr. Caligari introduces himself as a man in possession of dubious scientific credentials.

In waking Cesare, Caligari releases the first celluloid monster. He murders men in their sleep and kidnaps a beautiful woman, Joan. Just as Cesare is the first movie monster, Joan is the prototypical Gothic maiden, abducted against her will by a monster both smitten by her beauty (Cesare cannot bear to kill Joan) and frustrated by his inability to possess her. Caligari's monster thus continues the literary tradition of the eighteenth-century Gothic villain as a morbidly sensitive and ultimately misdirected wretch. At the same time, his destructive energies also anticipate the Frankenstein monster—himself as much sinned against, as he is himself a sinner. Like the Frankenstein creature, Cesare dies as miserably and as isolated as he has lived, and both monsters are manipulated victims of misguided science experiments.

Later in the film, it is revealed that Dr. Caligari is also the director of a mental facility. He is a man of science gone bad—the first in a tradition that will include Rotwang in *Metropolis*, Dr. Jekyll, and Frankenstein—obsessed with releasing a monstrous psychology that lurks submerged within himself, even as this release comes through the sublimated actions of a monstrous Other (e.g., Cesare, Mr. Hyde, the cyborg Maria). The abruptly awakened or scientifically constructed Gothic monster, regardless of the shape it assumes, always closely resembles in some crucial way, and often even poses a distorted mirror to, the psychopathology of the human scientist that created it. It is also interesting that these creations, born as they are from men of science, never turn out to be of positive benefit to the scientist and the society in which they are unleashed; scientific experimentation in the horror film always produces the anarchic monster, never the benevolent philanthropist. Thus, Hyde embodies all the repressed energies of Dr. Jekyll's id and gives vent to them in the shadowy alleyways late at night. Cesare, in turn, embodies the destructive spirit of Dr. Caligari, as the doctor is ultimately responsible for manipulating the somnambulist he has awakened and directing his violence against others. For example, Cesare only pursues Joan after she encounters Caligari and the latter is clearly excited by her beauty and his own maddening desire to possess her. The film is unclear whether Caligari employs the monster as a surrogate killer to avoid direct responsibility for committing acts of murder himself or if he simply enjoys the evil power that comes in dictating his will through another being. In either case, *The Cabinet of Dr. Caligari*, as the first horror film, uses psychological terror to permeate the entire atmosphere of the work. Thus, the highly subjective perspective of Caligari's madness extends beyond both himself and his monstrous companion and into the distorted landscape that surrounds them. The walls of the mental institution that Caligari directs, like those of Cesare's cabinet, are impossible to distinguish from the rest of the film's exteriors.

Visual Terror: *Nosferatu*

The main and most important contrast between *Caligari* and Murnau's *Nosferatu* is their degree of consciously imposed artificiality. *Caligari*'s lavishly painted sets, elaborate makeup on the actors, and sharp-angled camera creates a work that is studio-bound. This is not to say that its haunting atmosphere is any less effective as a result; if anything, its acute levels of claustrophobia and psychological disorientation are heightened in such a restricted milieu. *Nosferatu*, however, uses real sets and places—its camera is allowed to travel outdoors. Thus, Ellen is posed on the edge of the ocean awaiting the return of her husband and/or a visitation from Count Orlock. Hutter travels through the blasted landscape of Transylvania. The deserted streets of Wisborg reflect the devastation wrought by the introduction of the plague. *Caligari* relies on static and painterly images, *Nosferatu* on supernal energies that pervade and haunt the surfaces of everyday life. Although quite different in their means of production, the two films eventually complement each other in their end results: to create environments that transcend reality, investing the objective ordinary with a subjective sense of the extraordinary.

Strongly influenced by the emerging art movements of its time—cubism, surrealism, expressionism—*Nosferatu*'s grainy black and white mise-en-scène is a perfect vehicle for evoking the distorted, nightmarish atmosphere of the vampire. Like the pictorial art of the early twentieth century that helped to shape Murnau's vision, the film vacillates between the macabre and the lyrical, underscoring in its mise-en-scène the horror of modern life. Because of the absence of sound, Max Schreck's portrayal of the undead relies exclusively on visualized terror; Nosferatu is an angular abomination; all his extremities are elongated to the point of disquieting distortion—skull shape, nose, ears, fingers, and especially dual front teeth. The first in a long lineage of monstrous grotesques, Murnau's vampire is the cinematic patriarch to variants as diverse as the *Alien* creature and Freddy Krueger; indeed, a direct line of descent connects these creatures in physical appearance as well as monstrous propensities. Nosferatu's physical distortions underscore his outsider status from all things human. Thus, he is deliberately made to resemble more the angular stone archways and vacant high-rise edifices of the city he invades, the shape of the doorways he opens without touching in his castle, even the long coffin he carries in the night. *Nosferatu* remains such a disturbing picture for reasons similar to the *Alien* series: These films all feature exotic monsters that inspire awe in the audience because they are so far detached from all things recognizably human.

The sequence that may best highlight the otherworldly nature of *Nosferatu* occurs when Graf Orlock (the vampire) picks up Hutter and transports him up the mountain to his castle. Before the vampire actually arrives, the gypsy villagers deposit Hutter in front of a bridge that they themselves refuse to cross because they "will go no further into the land of the phantoms." When Hutter crosses the small bridge alone—interestingly, emphasizing the exercise of his own free will and thereby posing a parallel to the myth of the vampire requiring permission in order to enter into the domicile of a potential victim—he is essentially turning his back on both a rational world and the dire warnings the gypsy peasants tried to impart the evening before at the inn. He is "crossing over" into a uniquely alien landscape. Murnau continues to emphasize this transition through the appearance of the black-hooded horses, the heavily draped conveyance they draw, and the muffled coachman that arrives to pick up Hutter. In the scene, lasting less than a minute, where Hutter is driven up the mountain, Murnau signals the transition into a horror realm through negative film photography, so that the entire countryside—although shot in bright daylight—appears to reverberate silver-gray, the carriage and horses gaunt and ghostlike. In addition, the horse-drawn carriage appears to stutter and sometimes nearly to float, dreamlike up the side of the mountain. It is a highly dramatic cinematic effect that manages to strip the film—and Hutter's psyche—of rational balance and clarity, while also highlighting the unstable boundary between dream and reality, the banal and the monstrous.

The technique of using negative photography is an apt metaphor for the fact that Hutter's formerly complacent worldview is being literally and psychologically turned inside out. As he proceeds up the mountain, Hutter appears to lose himself in the massive, exotic landscape. His former patronizing attitude toward the gypsies at the inn and his scorn for their *Book of Vampires* suddenly appear tragically shortsighted. When the brief journey up the mountain is concluded and Hutter is deposited outside the castle, nothing remains the same for him; he enters into a realm that challenges him physically, psychologically, and morally. The inverted (negative) filming mirrors this transition into the land of the phantoms. Moreover, it represents the first time, but certainly not the last, that the horror film will employ startling special effects in the evocation of audience terror. Murnau's technique may appear unsophisticated by today's filmic standards of special effects, and David Skal reminds us "that Murnau and his crew were working with extremely limited technical resources" (*Hollywood Gothic* 51). As such, this sequence is really quite remarkable in terms of invoking a nightmarish condition that symbolizes the exact break between the normal world of commerce—where Hutter is in control—and the phantom world of Orlock.

In *Skin Shows: Gothic Horror and the Technology of Monsters*, Judith Halberstam posits that the vampire in Stoker's *Dracula* is a symbol for the stereotyped representation of the Jew: "his parasitical desires, his aversion to the cross and to all the trappings of Christianity, his blood-sucking attacks, and his avaricious relation to money, resembled stereotypical anti-Semitic nineteenth-century representations of the Jew" (86). Murnau's 1922 adaptation of Stoker's novel provides several additional features that expand Halberstam's anti-Semitic encoding. Nosferatu's thin elongated body might be viewed as adding to the obvious stereotyping Halberstam details, but it is in shifting the locale from Stoker's London to Wisborg, Germany, that Murnau's film begins to confront more seriously the pressing issue of anti-Semitism and its relationship to the German populace.

Halberstam views Dracula as a supernatural variant of the moneylender who lives off the blood and labor of the London masses, a "parasitism linked specifically to Jewishness" (96). Murnau's Nosferatu is likewise interested in acquiring property, which is why he summons Hutter in the first place, but in the film it is specifically *German* property that is acquired. The invasion of the German homeland by an outside force associated with rootlessness and exploitation and that exists solely to undermine the health of the nation poses disquieting parallels to the anti-Semitic atmosphere festering in Northern Europe in 1922. Just as important, Nosferatu's arrival in Germany is signaled by an outbreak of the plague, a parasite that infects and feeds on German blood. Throughout the film Orlock is linked to vermin—in his own physical appearance (the two hyperextended front teeth and clawlike fingers) and in the nervous, high anxiety he evinces around humans. Rats emerge from the coffin on board the ship where the vampire reposes, and Nosferatu transforms himself into rats that quickly disperse in order to escape detection when the ship docks in Wisborg.

All of these associations encourage further the nexus between Nosferatu and European stereotyping of the Jew. There is, however, no evidence to suggest that Murnau, himself a homosexual and thereby presumably more sensitive to the persecution of a subgroup inside the larger German society, meant to establish these anti-Semitic parallels on a conscious level. Indeed, they appear especially disturbing to us now mainly because we possess sufficient historical distance to trace the progress of anti-Semitism to its tragic consequences during Hitler's Third Reich. Conversely, the horror film, as discussed in the introduction and chapter 1, often speaks to us most effectively on an unconscious level and about subjects that the filmmaker and his audience do not necessarily seek or intend to expose. In an interesting—and ironic—reversal of Nosferatu as Jewish metaphor discussed here, Siegfried Kracauer maintains that the vampire Orlock is a foreshadowing of Nazi tyranny—that the vampire, paralleling Hitler's rise to power a decade later, preys on the life-spirit of the German people in his obsessive quest for violent domination. It would do well for the reader to remember that modern art, viewed as decadent and degenerate, was one of the forms of civilization that Hitler's Germany set out to destroy. While Hitler admired the political possibilities of motion picture technology, he was no fan of German expressionism or any of the other artistic movements associated with modernism that influenced the making of Nosferatu. In either case, the vampire as Semitic stereotype or precursor to Hitler, the final scene of Nosferatu features a ruined building, and its vacant windows appear as if bombed out by war. It is both a prophetic and historical image from a German filmmaker whose work in terror art was caught between the devastation left by one war (whose horror Murnau experienced firsthand as a pilot in the German Air Force during World War I) and the even greater destruction of another still to come.

A Tour of Hell: *Metropolis*

The horror film has always spoken to us of societal and cultural concerns. The horror genre reminds us continually of the dangers inherent in our well-intentioned efforts to progress—individually and culturally. Since its inception, Gothic art has focused on the avatar of sin that is humankind's legacy and above which we can never hope to rise completely. We work hard at convincing ourselves that we are evolving—spiritually, materially, and culturally. We are products of radical individualism, of a century that has argued for the abandonment of limits set on human knowledge, and accordingly our lives are better off than those of our grandparents, aren't they? Gothic art, however, persists at undercutting such faith, that this optimistic premise is at best misleading, at worst, a lie. The genre insists on calling attention to the stain on the dress that looked so beautiful when we tried it on at the store; it is a sudden bloody nose in the middle of a promising job interview. Horror is, in short, a reminder that all things human are necessarily flawed, that bad things happen despite good intentions, that our greatest ambitions are tainted by a price we will have to pay to attain it, and that we ignore such realities only at the expense of dire peril. The genre does not always confront our fears and inadequacies directly; it sometimes speaks to us more subtly, through symbolic codes that suggest the limitations of the human and the social relationships we have created. As we have seen, a film such as *Nosferatu* may be read as something more than a dark supernatural fantasy; the vampire's journey through the streets of Wisborg, if we care to interpret the film as such, carries strong historical and ideological implications.

The earliest horror films, occurring at the height of modernism, frequently explored issues relevant to the advent of the machine age. Although the machine is a highly relevant and constant component of the modernist landscape (futurism, for example, saw itself as a movement committed to social advancement through the advent of new technologies), many artists during this era were highly skeptical of the ways in which the products of industry were irrevocably altering urban life. Animated by electricity and a hybrid assembly of miscellaneous body parts, the Frankenstein creation is more machine than human. David Skal posits that "Like a gargoyle on the Chrysler Building [completed in 1930] the Frankenstein monster is yet another inevitable culmination of the machine aesthetic: a looming and unforgettable piece of vernacular architecture" (*Monster Show* 133). Indeed, the monster's connection to the machine is suggested in his hard-edged facial expressions; his birthing from the now classic mad-scientist laboratory apparatus of coils, generators, and electrified tubing; his limited linguistics; the very manner of his locomotion, as he lurches rather than walks; in the boxlike size and shape of his head; and in the metal electrodes that protrude from either side of his neck enabling his animation. He poses a direct threat to an agrarian village that is no more open to accepting the monster's physical differences than it was to the first motorcar that rode through its cobblestone streets.

In *Metropolis*, Fritz Lang's quasi-Marxist exploration of class inequality, the machine age is the vehicle used to highlight the chasm that separates workers from managers and capitalists. The sterile beauty of the underground machine city with its reliance on giant cogs and wheels and pistons is nothing less than a modern inferno replete with plumes of steam, searing electric lights, and the tortures of the damned. The machine age is exposed as a nightmare, a series of endless assembly lines where soulless laborers are exposed to unsafe working conditions and the mindless repetition of performing the same dreary task without respite. Although the film eventually suffers from the attempt to reconcile its oppositional ideological forces under an awkwardly imposed Christian mysticism, Lang's political divisions are so effectively rendered because they occur within the backdrop of a highly visualized Gothic milieu. In scene after scene, oppressed workers appear, backs facing the viewer, arms outstretched in simulated crucifixion postures, toiling over pressure valves and clocklike devices on various steaming machines until the humans either drop from exhaustion or the behemoth machine malfunctions and explodes. Heads down, looks of grim determination on their faces, the black-suited workers resemble zombies or the undead more than human beings. Their saintly blonde benefactor, Maria, who is as lovely as she is inspirational, preaches patience and tolerance in the face of their dehumanization, but constant interaction with machines have stripped the laborers of their dignity, and their desire for violent revolution appears to foment just beneath their lives of quiet desperation.

Science in *Metropolis*, particularly in the form of the wild-eyed inventor, Rotwang, works not to enhance the lives of the workers, but to oppress them further by making their labor and lives expendable. As Rotwang tells his capitalist patron: "I have created a machine in the image of man that never tires or makes a mistake. Now we have no further use for living workers." Rotwang also serves the interests of capitalist oppression by creating a robot in the image of Maria who sows the seeds of proletariat disunity, rebellion against the machines, and a nearly suicidal effort to flood the underground city. Rotwang is the Gothic villain modernized, the first in a long line of cinematic mad scientists who misuses his knowledge to create a new race of human robots. The line of descent is clear: Rotwang's secluded laboratory of electrified apparatus employed to bring the inanimate to life anticipates Frankenstein's quest; his artificial hand (Rotwang = rotted wing?) looks forward to Kubrick's Dr. Strangelove, another madman whose science is as out of control as the prosthetic arm that keeps delivering Nazi salutes; his unethical mixing of science and corporate politics poses similar problems in the *Alien* series; and, finally, Rotwang points the way toward Tyrell's morally tainted goal, a century later in *Blade Runner*, to manufacture a race of cyborgs "more human than human."

"It's Alive!" Horrible Birthings in the Frankenstein Saga

The influence of the German expressionist directors on the American horror films that followed was not only conscious, but also direct. According to David Skal, James Whale had studied carefully *The Cabinet of Dr. Caligari* in preparation for directing *Frankenstein* (*Monster Show* 132). In the late 1920s and early 1930s, many of these pioneering German directors—Fritz Lang, F. W. Murnau, Robert Siodmak, and Edgar Ulmer, among others—came to the United States where they helped to transform the nascent American cinema and the emerging shape of the horror film. The two classics to emerge from early Hollywood Gothic cinema are Tod Browning's *Dracula*, which will be considered in the next chapter, and Whale's *Frankenstein*, both released by Universal Studios in 1931. These two films initiated a "golden age" of American horror, where for more than a decade Universal capitalized on sequels to these two classics as well as extending the possibilities of the genre by including films about more monsters, such as *The Wolf Man* and *The Mummy* (Kavka 214). The result was a truly "gothic" phenomenon where creatures and themes and settings tended to be revisited and reemployed in subsequent films, even to the point where monsters were forced to encounter one another in the same picture, such as the regrettable *Frankenstein Meets the Wolfman*. This intermingling (and interbreeding) highlights once more that no individual Gothic film or novel truly exists on its own, but instead reaches back to draw on the tradition that simultaneously feeds and constrains it. By marking the Gothic as cannibalistic, as an essentially consumptive genre that feeds parasitically upon the tropes and traditions that constitute the genre itself, Judith Halberstam views the intertextuality of the Gothic in distinctly Frankenstein-like terms: "as a genre, itself a hybrid form, a stitched body of distorted textuality" (33). Thus, the earliest renditions of *Dracula* and *Frankenstein* cast their shadowy cinemyths deep into the future, shaping the serious Hammer remakes in the 1960s and 1970s, the self-conscious horror-humor parodies of *Young Frankenstein*, *Blacula*, and *The Rocky Horror Picture Show*, as well as postmodern progeny hybrids such as *Interview with the Vampire* and *Pet Sematary*.

Whale's *Frankenstein* begins with Henry Frankenstein in the role of an adventurous scientist probing the perimeters of knowledge, willing to risk everything, including both his status in the community and his potential as a husband, to "discover the great ray which first brought life into the world." The monstrous hybrid he animates is fashioned from a defective brain, stolen by mistake and reanimated by Frankenstein despite the fact that the jar Fritz brings back from the laboratory is clearly labeled, "Dysfunctional and Abnormal Brain." When the monster proves intractable and murders Fritz, Frankenstein's attitude toward his creation changes abruptly. What began as an inspiring experiment to explore the mysteries of life and death becomes a curse that is unleashed on the unsuspecting village and the naïve scientist who brought it to life.

Correspondingly, the main protagonist in the film is a divided personality, as much in possession of a bifurcated self as Henry Jekyll. Frankenstein has always been portrayed as a "split" personality: In Mary Shelley's novel he mirrors the creature he abhors in his chronic melancholia and willingness to resort to violence (especially in destroying the female creature the scientist eventually decides to abort); even in *The Rocky Horror Picture Show*, which will be discussed in a later chapter of this book, the transvestite parody of Herr Frankenstein, Frank N. Furter, is split between traditional concepts of masculine and feminine in his attire and sexual preferences. In Whale's film, the murder of Fritz appears to reawaken the domestic side of Henry's personality, perhaps because it offers empirical evidence that supports the moral condemnation first leveled by Frankenstein's former university professor, Dr. Waldman. Although Henry deliberately isolated himself from his fiancée, Elizabeth, in the beginning of the film, once the monster turns out to be a criminal, his creator seeks refuge in the woman and community he formerly spurned. There is an interesting moment after the distraught Frankenstein is removed from his laboratory and brought back to recuperate in his father's mansion. In contrast to the hyperactivity that characterized his scientific personality, he is pictured at the Baron Frankenstein's house (almost as if it were a photograph or an eighteenth-century portrait) in leisurely repose: Elizabeth seated by his side lighting his cigarette, family dogs sleeping comfortably in front of the couple, a gentle pastoral summer scene as a backdrop behind them. Here is Frankenstein, the bourgeois gentleman, heir to the Baron's fortune, tasting the blessed fruits that "have always been here" awaiting his claim. This is the world of domestic bliss that stands in sharp distinction to the harried scientist in the first half of the film. The Baron speculates that the distractions keeping his son from marriage are based in Henry's interest in another woman. While we share Elizabeth's understanding that this is not true, there is something insightful about the Baron's reasoning. Henry is interested in how women function biologically—specifically, in usurping the feminine by creating life himself. This "work" takes him into a dark and barren realm where he is associated with desolate graveyards and gallows and where the humpbacked Fritz—the prototype for the horror genre's Igor—is his only trusted companion. When engaged in this unholy quest, Frankenstein inhabits a drafty and sullen stone castle that intimidates Elizabeth and makes the Baron wonder if it wouldn't be better just to burn it down. Setting and location in this film thus become symbolic indicators to the state of Henry Frankenstein's mental disposition.

In order to rejoin society, to rediscover his place back in the community of civilized men and women—a position, by the way, that never really motivates Shelley's fictional protagonist to any great degree—the mad scientist in Whale's movie must transform himself into the domesticated husband by surrendering his id (the monster) to the dominance of his ego (the role of the good husband). Thus, in the second half of the film Henry is an entirely different man from what he is in the first half, assimilated back into society and appreciative of its values, even leading the mob he once scorned in its search to destroy the rampaging monster he is responsible for unleashing. This sequence of events also represents an interesting inversion of the occurrences that take place in Shelley's source work, where Frankenstein himself grows ever more estranged—mirroring the monster's plight—from social intercourse as the creature's violence against Frankenstein's family and friends push the scientist into deeper spheres of guilt. Although Frankenstein created the wretched creature, in both novel and film his loyalty to it is fleeting. In order to establish his position as Elizabeth's husband, however, Whale insists that Henry must engage in a symbolic act of self-destruction in the ritualized slaying of his creation. He is made to pay dearly for his desire to "know what it feels like to be God." Accordingly, Henry's body is crushed in his fall from the windmill at the climax of the film, creating a parallel to the monster's own demise when he is trapped beneath the wooden support beams of the burning windmill.

It is not surprising that the monster comes to center his most destructive energies on disrupting the intended family that the betrothed Henry and Elizabeth pursue. In Whale's film and in Shelley's novel, the monster wants to be recognized as the legitimate heir, "the son" that the Baron yearns to grandfather and that Henry turns elsewhere to procreate. Mary Shelley's novel is all about various constructions of "family"—from the book's early recollections of Frankenstein's parents and childhood, to the creature's interactions with the De Lacey family, to the obvious father-son bond that the creature seeks to impress upon the reluctant Frankenstein. Although Whale's movie does not provide as thorough a deconstruction of family as what exists in Shelley's novel, the direction is likewise drawn to the issue of the monster's birthing as an immediate threat to the familial union and a patriarchal line of descent. The monster disrupts the festivities that are taking place throughout the town on the day when Henry and Elizabeth are to be married. Instead of consummating their marriage, the murders of Dr. Waldman and Maria and the attack on Elizabeth force Henry to admit, "There can be no wedding while this horrible creation of mine is alive."

Henry understands that he must accept responsibility for destroying what he has birthed; he can no longer expect that the matter will be resolved by someone else or continue to hope that the monster will simply go away. Elizabeth senses this in her premonition just before the monster's attack that "something is coming between us." Shelley's Frankenstein maintains the secret of his "illegitimate creation" from Elizabeth, and it ends up costing him his betrothed on their wedding night. In Whale's film, the secret "son" also rises up after Elizabeth, and the violence that is directed at her barely masks the fury that the monster feels in being excluded from their intended union. However, early Hollywood took advantage of nearly every occasion to blunt the severity of Shelley's criticism toward Frankenstein and her radical sympathy for his creature. Not only does Elizabeth survive her attack in the film, Henry Frankenstein appears destined to a better life now that he has been sufficiently chastened and is willing to submit to his own domestication. While the monster dies a horrible, isolated death, Henry is shown recovering from his fall and has earned a new life that is as far removed from both his initial scientific madness as it is from Mary Shelley's somber ending. For no such happy resolution is available in the novel, as creature follows the self-destruction of his creator, while exactly what kind of "moral lesson" Frankenstein has learned from his experience is left very much in doubt.

The Bride of Frankenstein certainly takes its time getting to the birthing issues that are so central to Frankenstein. First, the story takes us back to Mary Shelley and a specious attempt to expand the narrative story line. Next, director James Whale covers ground that explains the survival of the monster after the windmill burns down. Finally, forced by the evil Professor Pretorius after he kidnaps Elizabeth, Henry Frankenstein creates a monstrous bride in his castle laboratory. The angry villagers, motivated by fear and ignorance, play a much more substantial role in Bride as well, as they are even more obsessed with the monster than Henry himself. This sequel argues emphatically that the monster's violence is inspired not by an abnormal brain, which appears to be the problem in the original, but rather by the unwillingness of violent humans to tolerate the very existence of a creature desperate for affection. In Frankenstein, there are hints of the monster's humanity in his attraction to Maria (her death is an accident; the result of the monster's innocence as much as the child's inability to swim). In Bride, however, the monster wanders the earth searching someone to befriend. The creature's isolation is underscored in the parallels that are frequently established between the monster and Christ: When the villagers first capture him, the creature is bound to a long wooden pole in a mock crucifixion pose; when he establishes a bond of friendship with the blind man in the forest, a crucifix is pictured on the wall hanging over the monster's bed; and in the cemetery, trying to avoid being recaptured by the angry villagers, the monster hides in a crypt marked by a huge statue of Christ on the cross. All of the film's allusions to the crucified Christ are meant, of course, to suggest the similarities between the two outsiders condemned by their respective societies as monstrous. Only the blind man, because he is blind, is open to the monster's humanity; everyone else flees in terror at his approach.

It is the sincerity of his friendship bond established with the blind man that makes the monster yearn to possess a female "friend." Once brought to life by Frankenstein, however, the woman monster is a reluctant bride, as she, too, spurns her male mate. With tears streaming down his face, the monster concludes that "She hate me—like others," and pulls a destruction lever that reduces the castle laboratory to a heap of stones. The conclusion of Bride may prove less than satisfying, but it does underscore the major theme of the film: The monster possesses a much deeper level of humanity in this sequel than in the original Frankenstein, and, in contrast, the humans who either seek to manipulate him or shoot him, in failing to sympathize with the monster's plight, emerge as the true monstrosities. In this way, at least, *Bride* holds more in common with Shelley's source work than does Whale's first film. Thus, the Frankenstein monster that appears in this sequel joins other Hollywood horror creatures from the 1920s and later 1930s, such as the Phantom of the Opera, the Hunchback of Notre Dame, the Werewolf, and Mr. Hyde. All are victims of ignorance and prejudice—turned into estranged outlaws whose random acts of violence cannot be separated from their own social persecution.

In the 1920s and 1930s, Hollywood recognized the inherent value in creating monsters that were fear-invoking yet somehow sympathetic in their excessive suffering and desperation. Certainly some of this effort can be explained by virtue of the studios' wishing to avoid potential conflict with the officious censors. David Skal posits that the horror movies from this epoch "offered an instinctive, therapeutic escape" from the realities of unemployment, the devastation of the First World War, the economic collapse of the Western world, and the rise of totalitarian states (*Monster Show* 115). Given the stark realities of the period from which they emerged, however, it seems just as likely that the early horror monsters were also distinct projections of their particular place in time.

Just as the Frankenstein monster, the Phantom, the Hunchback, the Werewolf, and Mr. Hyde inspired fear in a social era that was particularly fearful for the movie-going public, these individual creatures also solicited from this audience a strain of sympathy in their relentless suffering and persecution. They were, after all, lost in a world where there was neither support nor compassion for their plights. The earliest monsters were complex, bifurcated figures embodying the spirit of their age—the emblem of all the modern terrors set loose upon the earth—and, simultaneously, unwitting victims of their historical epoch. Their madness and irrational violence were symbolic of a world no longer governed by rationality and authority. Many of the earliest monsters were products of the same Gothic science that had created shrapnel bombs and mustard gas.

The horror monster became at once the inexplicable engine of destruction bearing down on the masses, and the individual standing out from the mass, the man and woman besieged by forces beyond their ability to understand or to control. Figures such as Cesare in *Caligari* and the Frankenstein monster emerge as common soldiers stumbling their way through a blasted landscape ravaged by war, encouraged to commit atrocious acts in order to survive the aggression and manipulation of others. The fact that both Cesare and the Frankenstein monster are intimately linked to coffin boxes and cemeteries only encourages the interpretation that both are zombielike walking dead, symbolic protests to the dehumanization of World War I. Indeed, this war maintained such lasting and dramatic reverberations on all levels of society for so many years after the Treaty of Versailles that it is impossible not to consider its influence, however indirect, on early horror art. The physical deformities of the Hunchback, Jekyll, and the Phantom of the Opera suggest a similar parallel to the returning soldiers from the trenches of war whose maimed bodies and devastated faces were the lasting legacies of man's inhumanity to man and the more recent effectiveness of science as a weapon. Like the average world-weary citizen caught between wars and economic uncertainty, the horror monster of the 1920s and 1930s lacked a clear identity and purpose. Seemingly rejected by man and God alike, the monster's final utterance was always one of despair. The essential suicides that most of these creatures bring upon themselves serve as nothing less than a mirror to the darkest inclinations of the audience watching them.

Stark Terror's Legacy

The most enduring legacies associated with the earliest horror films have little to do with plot narrative. Like the majority of eighteenth-century Gothic novels and their nineteenth-century heirs, the penny dreadfuls and the German shocker tales, horror film's prototypes featured themes that were, at the time of their production, unsettling displays of disruption and distortion. The shock value of horror art, however, has a very short shelf life; what terrorizes one generation, does not necessarily translate very well to the next. The degree of exaggerated acting and abrupt conclusions to plot conflicts represent some of the major liabilities of early cinematic art. Thus, the fact that the depraved Dr. Caligari is left in control of both the narrative and the fate of the film's protagonist, Francis, at the end of *Caligari*, no longer unnerves a postmodern audience long accustomed to viewing films where malefic forces are not always neatly contained, much less vanquished; similarly, the horror of *Metropolis's* irreconcilable ideologies is in the end diluted by the movie's sentimental and artificially imposed Christian resolution of class conflict.

What inspires the requisite awe that is a constituent element of all great horror art centers primarily on atmospheric effects: the immortalized images established in these early films. These black and white, highly stylized productions, featuring elaborate sets of bold lines and jagged shapes that are often more interesting than the actors who worked in front of them, present a world stripped of color, where shadow and form consequently take on mysterious and monstrous size and influence. While the birthing sequences in *Frankenstein* and *Bride of Frankenstein* may no longer inspire the same level of terror that they did for their original audiences (actually sending spectators running from theaters), the interior of Frankenstein's dark castle laboratory continues to enflame the imagination, and it points the way to infernal birthing chambers in *The Fly, Demon Seed,* and *Alien.* The dystopian urban backdrops for *Metropolis* and *Nosferatu* establish a bleak milieu that feels exactly right for the domination of the machine and the vampire, respectively; their haunted cityscapes still resonate in films as diverse as *Blade Runner, Don't Look Now,* and *The Tenant.* In a final analysis, the dark children spawned by the film industry's earliest efforts grew up to be monstrous adults. Horror's reign of terror, at least when traced through cinematic history, is an unabated continuum that connects past and present.

3.

Vampiric Terrors

Dracula, The Hunger, Interview with the Vampire, Bram Stoker's Dracula, Buffy the Vampire Slayer

Film noir is a genre of seduction. Its evocative music, atmospheric imagery, and excursions into criminality point toward mystery and a primal desire for the forbidden. A central character in film noir is the femme fatale who is, traditionally, as untrustworthy as she is sexually potent. Most film genres feature similar stock characters, a consistent personality type born from and readily identifiable with the genre in which we find them: the marshal in the Western, the mob boss in the gangster film, the amoral bad guy in the action thriller, the good-natured but bumbling buffoon in the screwball comedy.

In the long and shadowy history of the vampire film, the vampire—typically, the figure around whom the action of the narrative revolves—has been neither a consistent personality nor a stable point of reference, at least not in the prescribed range that we might use to define the Western's sheriff or noir's femme fatale. The cinematic vampire is as slippery to characterize as he is to kill; in fact, even the procedures necessary for slaying him alter slightly from generation to generation. The first vampire film, *Nosferatu*, featured a toxic being so self-absorbed and focused on his quest for human blood that, in the end, his affiliations are more bestial than human. Many of the cinematic vampires that have followed Murnau's Orlock—Barlow in *'Salem's Lot*, the bloodsucking barflies in *From Dusk till Dawn*, the majority of the Hellmouth revenants who populate episodes of *Buffy the Vampire Slayer*—show a bloodlust motivated by a similar animalistic compulsion.

As the vampire subgenre evolved, however, conceptions of the undead have expanded accordingly. In more recent manifestations, the vampire has come most to epitomize the worldly flaneur as described by Baudelaire in *The Painter of Modern Life*, a being whose sensibilities are often superior to those of his human prey, and whose deep appreciation for life sometimes compromises his welfare as a vampire. His never-ending search for new access to blood markets links the vampire to consumer culture and capitalist imperialism, and his global search makes him, at the same time, a world citizen. His multiculturalism, ironic detachment, and appreciation for multiple points of view born from his ancient longevity have provided the vampire with the essence of a postmodernist sensibility. Bernadette Lynn Bosky suggests that, historically, the most obvious trait that distinguishes vampire narratives is the difference between the "latent sexuality" of the nineteenth-century vampire and the "explicit sexuality central to many recent vampire stories" (217). Accordingly, the vampire's roles—his very inclusion as a figure of monstrosity—have expanded accordingly, from an Old-World Count in search of new plasma markets, to crime-solving vampires, lesbian vampires, extraterrestrial vampires, dominatrix vampires, prostitute vampires, redneck-cowboy vampires, and motorcycle gang vampires, to name only a few of their cinematic representations. The year that Francis Ford Coppola made *Bram Stoker's Dracula* (1992), for example, saw either the release or the continuation of work on twenty-five other vampire films. Finding new plotlines in the horror film has become increasingly difficult; finding them in the vampire film has become nearly impossible. Jörg Waltje argues that so many vampire storylines and historical settings have interconnected to the point that "there are by now more differences than similarities between the films that make up the genre. Yet, in a way they are all interdependent, and like the figure of the vampire itself, the genre can find no rest, transmogrifies constantly, and lives on forever" (63).

Like most of the monsters considered elsewhere in this book, the vampire presents a problem in gender identification. Because the mouth represents the site of pleasurable (and hence, erotic) experience for most vampires, within that orifice we find both masculine and feminine traits. Christopher Craft has located a fusion of gender polarities in "its soft flesh barred by hard bone, its red crossed by white . . . compelling opposites and contrasts into a frightening unity" (445–46). The vampire penetrates with phallic teeth at the same time as its mouth then becomes an orifice used for extracting fluids. Further complicating easy definitions of stable gender coding, the vampire's mouth serves a similar purpose for both male and female vampires. Moreover, the vampire film creates a whole other level of gender ambiguity in blurring the lines separating homo- and heterosexualities. The lesbian vampire film, for instance, constitutes a rather extensive subgenre of the vampiric cinematic history, and even those movies that feature heterosexual vamping (e.g., *Interview with the Vampire*) often suggest an implicit homoeroticism. The vampire thereby connects to many of the other monster figures to be considered in forthcoming chapters of this book. His gender and sexual ambiguities link him with other images of abjection ranging from the Alien creature to the serial killer in the slasher film genre.

The Vampire Goes Hollywood: *Dracula*

The vampire in *Nosferatu* never manages to elicit much sympathy or identification from the audience. At least Stoker's literary prototype is provided a brief moment of somber introspection when he tries to defend himself against the accusations of the three vampire sisters with his plaintive, "Yes, I too can love" (43). Murnau's Orlock, though, never manages a similar moment, to impress us with his humanness; even his physical appearance precludes his claim to manhood, as the monster most resembles a rat or a bat. Tod Browning's *Dracula* is the first cinematic attempt to humanize the vampire, and it is interesting that this is accomplished primarily by sexualizing him. At the symphony, when Lucy is first introduced to the Count, his mysterious and exotic nature captivates her and leaves her disposed to the vampire's will even before he actually ravishes her. Despite Mina's good-natured attempt to mock him when she is alone with Lucy later that night, the latter reveals her susceptibility in her fantasy wish to become "Countess Dracula": "Laugh all you like," she responds to her friend, "I think he's fascinating." Bela Lugosi's portrayal of Dracula is the prototype upon which many future vampire men and women—from Christopher Lee's Hammer Studio *Dracula* movies to Frank Langella's Latin lover version of the Count to the elegant Catherine Deneuve in *The Hunger*—based their seductive allure. Even the *Dracula* parody, *Love at First Bite*, features the Count as a disco charmer, a snappy dresser and dancer as adept as Tony Manero in *Saturday Night Fever* at sweeping women off their feet.

Unlike the expressionistic settings and characters in Murnau's *Nosferatu*, Browning's *Dracula* is more romantic in nature and design. Like many of the literary vampires who originated in the nineteenth century, Browning's version of the Count portrays the vampire as a Byronic hero capable of mesmerizing others with his imperious glare and quick to express his anger at the slightest provocation. Comparable to other romantic-Gothic villains in literature, Lugosi's Dracula possesses a tyrannical spirit that demands compliance. Throughout the film, Renfield professes his loyalty to "Master," but Dracula reciprocates by driving him mad and then murdering Renfield after he has served the Count's design in helping to procure Mina.

Lugosi's Count is foreign and sophisticated; he is the product of civilization's refinements, a far cry from the fanged rat creature that slinks along darkened buildings and through the misty shadows of *Nosferatu*. Certainly one persuasive explanation to account for the difference is that Murnau was strongly influenced by the dark aesthetics of German expressionism while Browning's *Dracula* is a shining product of the nescient film industry in Hollywood, the Count's foreignness notwithstanding. When he first arrives in London, Dracula saunters leisurely along the streets dressed in formal attire on his way to the symphony (a scene that Coppola will effectively revisit decades later in *Bram Stoker's Dracula*). He wishes others to gaze at him as much as he wishes to see others. Eyes are very important in Browning's movie. The newspapers supply eyewitness evidence attesting to Dracula's "red eyes," and each time Lugosi wishes to cast a spell, small white spotlights artificially highlight the area around the vampire's eyes. Van Helsing first notices that the Count is a revenant when the latter fails to cast a reflection in the mirror of Dr. Seward's cigarette box. Later, when Dracula battles Van Helsing, it is a contest of wills that centers on the gaze of the vampire and the scientist's ability to withstand it. Cynthia Freeland argues that Lugosi—with his pale skin, eyes outlined in kohl, and darkened lips—is a parody of the era's female screen goddesses. In his tuxedo and cape "this vampire is above all a monster to be looked at, or gazed upon . . . the vampire is shown as both subject and object of the gaze" (*Naked and Undead* 129). In the most important way, Lugosi was not only the father of modern Draculas, the actor also gave birth to the vampire as an urbane sophisticate. It is worth noting that nowhere in Browning's film do we see evidence of Dracula as primal beast. He turns into a bat but never into any of the other animal shapes we find him assume in Stoker's novel: lizard, rat, or wolf. Lugosi turned the Count into an object of attraction, even desire; he made the vampire into an agent of romantic seduction bearing an image for others to consume, on the screen as well as in the audience.

Consuming Vampires: *The Hunger*

The figure of the vampire as object of the cinematic gaze is never more fully realized than in *The Hunger*. The elegant Catherine Deneuve, who, at the time of the film's release was the featured model for Chanel perfume advertisements, dresses in fetish garments designed to highlight the role of vampire as fashion icon: form-fitted black leather skirts and matching leather gloves, stiletto heels, tight corsets, hats with veils, and dark sunglasses that contrast her bright crimson lips and nails. Like Lugosi strolling the London streets at night, Deneuve is a figure of immense self-confidence, and she wishes to call attention to herself as an object of fashionable desirability. By the time we get to *The Hunger*, the vampire's monstrosity is far removed from the physical abomination uncovered in *Nosferatu*; instead, Deneuve's monstrosity is found in her spiritual coldness that finds a suitable parallel in the artificiality of her heavily made-up face and sculpted chignon. Resembling a noir femme fatale, Deneuve plays a vampire who uses her beauty and clothes to entice her prey. Her extreme use of cosmetics—particularly dramatic eye makeup and lipstick—is the mask behind which she both hides and projects to the nocturnal world as she pursues men and women in urban bars and clubs (see Figure 4, p. 193).

The Hunger, as its title suggests, is about desire and consuming out of an effort to quench that desire, but not just in terms typically associated with the conventional vampire narrative. Casting Deneuve and musician David Bowie as the central vampires in the film is entirely appropriate to its theme of consumption, as their real-life roles as fashion model and rock star represent two of the most blatant figures of libidinous energy and consumer identification in Western culture: Both occupations rely on images with which their respective audiences identify. In the essay "Fashion and the Homospectatorial Look," Diana Fuss makes the connection between advertising and vampirism explicit when she argues that the act of looking at fashion photographs in magazines encourages women "to *consume*, in voyeuristic if not vampiristic fashion, the images of other women, frequently represented in classically exhibitionist and sexually provocative poses. . . . [W]omen themselves are invited to actively consume the image—female spectators constrained to assume the position of lesbian vampires" (210, 222). It is a complex exchange: Through the recollection of her highly stylized Chanel advertisements as well as the image Deneuve assumes on the screen as Miriam the vampire, the viewer simultaneously desires and consumes the composite image Deneuve projects via her clothes, her makeup, her panache as a glamorous fashion model/movie star/ vampire. Like the fashion model, whose "look" is a compilation of the model's own beauty, makeup, clothes, and photographic background (setting, lighting, associated objects and products, and so on), Deneuve's success as a vampire relies on a similar combination that produces a comparable effect upon the viewer. The vampires in The Hunger create a screen representation so alluring that it translates into a consumer hunger: the desire to possess the elegance of Catherine Deneuve or the rock-star cool of David Bowie. We therefore purchase the objects they wear or with which they are affiliated, be it perfume or Bowie's music, because we have been double-vamped by both the products they are selling as well as by their flamboyant and famous personae. As a vampire, when Deneuve prowls through a nightclub dressed in the clothes of a leather dominatrix, men and women are drawn to her for similar reasons that couture fashion advertising is an effective strategy for selling high-priced clothes: She is an extension of a fantasy image others desire to possess, or be possessed by.

Fuss's allegorizing the activity of viewing fashion photography as an act of lesbian vampirism is particularly relevant to a discussion of The Hunger because Miriam is a bisexual vampire. According to Fuss, when a woman looks at another woman posed in a fashion magazine photograph, the spectator identifies with and actively consumes the image on the page in transposing herself from viewer onto object. In order to identify with the image Catherine Deneuve projects, then, she must necessarily dress like her, smell like her, consume all the essences of her stylized femininity—and this can only be accomplished by spending money to accumulate the many fashion artifacts which are linked to Deneuve's marketed persona (all contingent on the purchasing of material objects, of course, that eventually go out of style, necessitating that the process repeat itself deathlessly, resembling the vampire's own feeding cycle). In this way, the consumer is likewise vamped by corporate capitalism (Marx often invoked the image of a vampire when describing capitalists) even as she is, initially, merely consuming the representational female carefully configured in the magazine advertisement.

The Hunger was released in 1983, during the era of Ronald Reagan, whose presidency elevated consumer consumption of the type just described, especially for the rich, into a means for defining social status. Luxury retailers such as Neiman Marcus and Saks Fifth Avenue sold $200 leather gloves, $300 sunglasses, and $700 boots resembling Miriam's outfit when she goes out to seduce her prey. In this film, the vampiric life is synonymous to the pursuit and glorification of expensive consumer goods. It is not only that the vampire is beautiful and sophisticated, "European," as Sarah attributes Miriam's inimitable style, she is likewise a representative of her historical moment (even as Miriam's vampirism is ageless) extolling the virtues of conspicuous consumption: an objectified woman constructed to be consumed by others as much as she seeks to consume them.

It is Miriam's projection as a fashion icon and sophisticated woman that Sarah longs to vamp, the latter positioned in a role similar to how Fuss interprets the female spectator identifying with a fashion model's photograph. In other words, while Miriam, as a vampire, aggressively seduces Sarah, the seduction is mutual. Perhaps that explains why the vampire desires to make Sarah her new mate, rather than just another disposable source of nourishment. Miriam seeks a marriage with Sarah because she has recently lost her husband (Bowie's character, John) and desires a new vampire partner. At the same time, it is also clear that Sarah wishes to consume Miriam considering that the erotic attraction between the two women is evident whenever they look at one another. Sarah is thus vamping Miriam even before their exchange of fluids takes place, unconsciously working, as in one of Fuss's fashion photographs, to incorporate Miriam's glamorous image and persona into herself. The most prophetic line in the film occurs when Miriam tells Sarah, "I'll teach you how to hunt, how to be like me." In the final scene of the movie, it is obvious that Sarah has completed her education by displacing her instructor. As the new vampire queen, Sarah is shown in possession of her own concubine, surveying the city from atop her high-rise perch, wearing Miriam's earrings and blood-red lipstick, and lost to the mortal world forever. As Barbara Creed points out in her discussion of lesbian vampires in *The Monstrous-Feminine*: "Once bitten the victim is never shy. She happily joins her female seducer" (61). Sarah ends the film vamping Miriam: She does not wish to "join her female seducer," to share power with her; instead, she has taken over Miriam's place as the monstrous queen mother, presumably suckling her children only to betray them, leaving them, as Miriam once did, devoid of love and blood in a dry, dusty attic.

Beginning with Samuel Taylor Coleridge's *Christabel* (1800) and J. Sheridan Le Fanu's *Carmilla* (1872), the lesbian vampire has a long lineage as a subgenre of vampire fiction. Because vampire tales explore forbidden and repressed sexual themes, homoeroticism is a frequent subtext found in many vampire narratives. The lesbian vampire film, which evolved primarily during the 1960s and 1970s (although *Dracula's Daughter*, released in 1936, is an important precursor), represents a continuation and development of its literary predecessor. Bonnie Zimmerman has speculated that the popularity of lesbian vampire films such as *Vampyres: Daughters of Darkness*, *The Velvet Vampire*, *Countess Dracula*, and *Twins of Evil* in the 1970s grew out of the emerging feminist movement, where women began to bond with one another and express a "sexual attraction [that] threatened the authority of the male-dominated society" (382). In both films and prose, the lesbian vampire maintains her allure as a figure "on the margins of activity, dissipating rigid structures of gender and received identity . . . exposing the insubstantiality of the barriers that separate men from women, death from life" (Auerbach 181, 183).

Lesbian vampires emphasize elements of seduction and sensuous communication between women rather than the forceful physical display bordering on rape that typifies the hunger of a male vampire. The female vampire tends to welcome her victim into a sisterhood; male vampires, however, are seldom endowed with similar sensitivities or sophistication in the bedroom. Moreover, the vast majority of vampire movies feature male vampires. Women most often appear in victim roles, and when they are present as revenants, their characters, like the three sisters in *Dracula*, continue to reflect gender subservience to the alpha male vampire. The lesbian vampire film represents one of the few avenues available to actresses in vampire art finally to assume a position of dominance, even if it is over other women.

There are also other reasons to explain the genre's popularity. The lesbian vampire, on the one hand, in distinct contrast to male homoeroticism in the genre, is attractive to a broader audience base; her erotic sexuality appeals to many heterosexual women and men, as well as to lesbians. On the other hand, it is difficult for the vampiric lesbian to separate herself from a pornographic context. Society's attitude toward female homoeroticism has always been more permissive than it is toward the threat of male homosexuality. In the latter case, acts of vampirism that include overtly sexual homoerotic behavior between men potentially alienate a straight audience. Thus, a major reason the lesbian vampire film has retained its popular allure is because of its erotic attraction for predominately heterosexual viewers.

A film such as *Interview with the Vampire* contains a strong male homosexual undercurrent—one man feeding from the throat of another man while they float suspended intimately joined together in the air—but the specifically sexual implications are more cautiously rendered, particularly in light of Rice's more graphic treatment of the topic in her novel. It is interesting, for example, that in the film adaptation of *Interview*, based on a screenplay written by Anne Rice, Louis does not sleep in the same coffin with Lestat. Their sleeping arrangements stand in sharp contrast to those in Rice's novel, where the two males sleep face-to-face on top of one another, and can only be explained as an effort to downplay the homoerotic subtext of the film. The dangerous threat of male homosexuality is especially relevant to this movie in light of the fact that Louis and Lestat are played by Brad Pitt and Tom Cruise, respectively, whose box office appeals have always been deeply associated with their heterosexuality. Accordingly, the majority of the vampire scenes in *Interview* are aligned with heterosexuality: Louis and Lestat vamp women, not men. Moreover, when Lestat bites male children, the vampirism either occurs off camera or is discretely rendered (mouth to wrist, rather than mouth to neck) in an effort to preserve the status of Cruise and Pitt as icons of straight masculinity. As such, they are permitted to indulge in the sexual eroticism and promiscuity of being vampires while steering clear of the specter of homosexuality.

Many lesbian vampire films, in contrast, and *The Hunger* is among them, are far more explicit in portraying acts of vampirism as an overtly sexual experience. When Miriam and Sarah embrace in an orgy of blood—a scene that is particularly feminine in its primal associations—it is hard to imagine two male vampires engaged in a similar exchange of fluids. The level of abjection is strong enough when two women allow blood to flow and intersect; when it occurs between two men, the homoerotic subtext, and its inevitable link to AIDS, violates a whole different realm of abjection.

The five-minute bedroom scene between Miriam and Sarah, when it was first released, caused a minor controversy because of its highly sensual blurring of vampirism and lesbian sex. Indeed, the scene is more an explicitly sexual encounter than it is the initiation passage for a non-vampire crossing over into the vampire world. The first part of the montage is wholly sexual, as the two women engage in languid stares and deep, open-mouthed kisses; it also emphasizes Sarah's willingness to join with Miriam in a consensual act of lovemaking. Only as the scene gradually progresses does lesbian sex unfold into an act of vampirism: The music darkens with ominous strings that slowly cut across and displace the gentle voices of the soundtrack's operatic aria; there are two subliminal flashes of a thin red line or ribbon that appear beneath the white gauze netting above the bed and between the two writhing, naked female bodies pictured below so quickly that the viewer is apt to miss them entirely; and, finally, Miriam concludes their assignation by cutting Sarah's arm with a scalpel hidden inside her ankh, turning the erotic encounter into an overt act of bloodsucking. In a film that is as much about a monstrous materialism as it is about vampirism—as we have seen, the two concepts are conjoined—it is extremely relevant that Miriam chooses to kill not with her mouth, the method most vampires traditionally employ, but with her jewelry.

The Vampire Existentialist: *Interview with the Vampire*

Transformed into a vampire by force and without the freedom of choice, Lestat conducts himself as though seeking revenge for the violation he has personally undergone. Becoming a vampire allows Lestat the opportunity to indulge his most decadent fantasies, including the savoring of aristocratic blood for his last kill of the evening. He revels in the God-like power that attends his daily decision regarding which mortals are to live and which are to die. His appetite knows no bounds, and he is amoral to the point of making the child Claudia into a vampire to manipulate and preserve control over "the little family" he has constructed with Louis. In this way, Lestat adheres to the tradition of the vampire as a monster, a figure as evil as he is abject. He is attracted to Louis as a companion and as the "object" of his creation, but Lestat is also clearly frustrated by Louis's incapacity to appreciate fully his transformation into a vampire. As Lestat confesses to the interviewer he has just bitten in one of the few comic moments in this somber film, living with Louis has required him to listen to his "constant whining—for centuries."

His deathless "whining" notwithstanding, Louis offers a far more complicated response to vampirism. Although he is immortal and must feed on blood to sustain his existence, Louis's persistent qualms over the sacrificing of human life elevate his moral stature to a position that is certainly superior to those of the other vampires found elsewhere in *Interview* and, for that matter, throughout the genre as a whole. More philosopher or spiritual seeker than killing machine, Louis is disgusted by the vamping of the young female victim in the theater of vampires' performance, and dismisses it as "monstrous." Even Claudia appears deeply intrigued by the metatheatrics of "vampires who pretend to be people pretending to be vampires," but not Louis. He sees through their avant-garde sophistry to the brutal core the participating vampires cannot disguise.

While he eventually learns to prefer human blood to vamping rats and chickens, Louis never comes to savor murdering, as do Lestat and the French vampires; although metamorphosed into a vampire, Louis never loses touch with the human he once was. In fact, becoming a vampire only serves to make Louis more aware of his humanness—issues of life and death, guilt, morality, and responsibility burden him to the point of obsession. Louis longs to understand the nature of his new being, to answer the questions: "What are we? Who made us what we are? The source." His quest takes him to Europe where he discovers ancient vampires who are more similar to Lestat in their pursuit of decadent pleasures. The philosophical issues that plague Louis link him not to other vampires but, instead, back to the human world with which he still feels intimately connected. Although Louis claims to be haunted by the memory of Claudia, who is destroyed by the French vampires, it is really the love he maintains for her—the very essence of a human, and certainly not a vampiric, emotion—that fills him with regret and, in his own mind, isolates him further still from both the living and the undead. All he ever discovers, however, as man as well as a vampire, is that "the world was a tomb to me." He sees himself as a being "at odds with everything. I always have been." Before becoming a vampire, Louis was an affluent plantation owner in New Orleans who also owned slaves. Although he sets the slaves free before burning down his mansion, as a vampire Louis acts like one of William Faulkner's guilt-ridden Southerners, perhaps a cousin to Quentin Compson in *Absalom, Absalom!*, a man haunted by the knowledge that he is an integral part of a history that has caused the suffering of others. Like Faulkner's tortured Compson, Louis hates himself, and wishes for nothing more than to escape his own skin, to find peace in some other identity, which is why he elects to become a vampire in the first place.

Perhaps his existential despair is the real motivation for the "interview" Louis is compelled to pursue and that frames the narrative of his life and the film itself. It is, after all, less an interview than a confession, a chronicle of Louis's quest to uncover answers to the nature of his being and the ontology of good and evil. In the end, the interview is not really about sharing his nocturnal journey with a human or even dispelling the stereotyped superstitions the world associates with the nature of the walking undead (Louis likes the sight of a crucifix), so much as it is an opportunity for the vampire to wrestle with his own history, to create a kind of psychotherapeutic monologue wherein he confronts and reveals the essence of his most vexing problem: existence. Louis's introspection ends up captivating the interviewer, as the latter already thinks of his occupation as a journalist in vampiric terms: "That's what I do. I am a collector of lives." After listening to Louis's personal history, the interviewer yearns for Louis to make him a vampire, as he sees the revenant's immortality and sensual nature as a counterpoint to modern despair. In disgust, Louis dismisses the human with the remark, "you haven't been listening," but it is really Louis who has not been listening closely enough to his own words. His long and deathless narrative as a vampire is a compelling journey, more human than supernatural. His constant "whining," however, has made it impossible for Louis to recognize that the dualities embodied in the vampire—violence/arousal, repulsion/attraction, and terror of death/freedom from pain—also represent the core experience of what it means to be human. His vampiric history leaves him only with regret and loss, but these are likewise intensely human emotions that distinguish Louis not only from Lestat and the French vampires, but also, as the interviewer labors to tell him, from most human beings, whose lives are so fleeting and unexamined that the opportunity for true meaning too often passes us by.

Claudia represents daughter, wife, and companion to the alienated Louis. His love for her is about the only thing in his life that he ever appreciates fully, that he can explain in unqualified terms. However, even his relationship with Claudia is morally tainted because the vampire must live with the fact that he is responsible for helping to curse her: She is doomed to remain a woman trapped in the body of a child. As Diana Reep points out, "Claudia can never quite be a full companion to Louis because her body cannot match her emotions, and she needs him to take care of her in a world that sees her as a child" (130). All through this film, vampires search for a psychological intimacy that is missing in their lives: life-long companions, children, parents, and a God to believe in. *Interview* offers an interpretation of vampires in the most human of terms: They desire power, feel regret, and need spiritual nourishment that can come only from contact with others. In contrast to most vampire narratives, however, Louis's supernatural condition turns out to be more metaphysical than physical; his personal crisis allows for us to view the vampire not as alien Other, but as one of us. Susan Ferraro has observed that Rice's vampires are trapped, "lonely prisoners of circumstance, compulsive sinners, full of self-loathing and doubt. They are, in short, Everyman Eternal" (67). There have been hundreds of vampire films made since the release of *Nosferatu* and *Dracula*; of them all, *Interview* is the best illustration of the vampire's struggle with his humanity. It is the motion picture that most forcibly depicts the vampire's ironic return—if it can be said that Louis ever really leaves—to its human origins.

Coppola's *Dracula*: A Love Story

When director Francis Ford Coppola and screenwriter James Hart decided to revisit the mother lode of all vampire stories, they ostensibly set out to recreate a version of *Dracula* so dedicated to its source that it would deserve the title *Bram Stoker's Dracula*: "Mainly, it was that no one had ever done the book. . . . [W]e were scrupulously true to the book" (Coppola and Hart 3). Alas, the vampire is always an elusive figure, and Stoker's Dracula is arguably the most elusive of all vampires. Coppola's rendition actively pursues the veiled ambiguous sexual imagery contained in Stoker's novel, and exploits it—to the point of exaggerated distortion. Thus, Lucy and Mina are erotically titillated by sexually explicit drawings they discover in the *Karma Sutra*, and Lucy impresses the viewer as a promiscuous woman even before Dracula vamps her, ready and willing to take on multiple male lovers. Coppola filmed his own postmodern interpretation of *Dracula*, not a version true to Stoker's novel. It is, however, in the depiction of Mina's character that the director indulges his greatest liberties with Stoker's text. In the novel, Mina remains a chaste, conservative Victorian woman, a repository of the Western values for which the men with whom she is affiliated are willing to sacrifice themselves in their battle against the Count. Although forced against her will to partake of the "vampire's baptism of blood" (280) as part of Dracula's plan to corrupt Mina, she never capitulates to his design; in fact, she successfully resists the vampire's influence throughout the final third of the book, even to the point where she demands of the men "that, should the time come, you will kill me . . . when you shall be convinced that I am so changed that it is better that I die that I may live" (287).

Stoker's Mina is brave enough to articulate the fear that over time she may unwittingly be "leagued with your enemy against you" (288), but she is rescued and Dracula destroyed before Mina is forced to betray either herself or the men she so respects who comprise the Crew of Light. Coppola's cinematic version, however, projects Mina's hypothetical betrayal into a full-blown reality: The horror of *Bram Stoker's Dracula* is that the film is a love story between Mina and her vampire; her husband and the Crew of Light mean very little to her when compared with her love for the Count. The novel shows her struggling against becoming another version of the lascivious Lucy and her true feelings of terror regarding an out-of-control female sexuality. The film, on the other hand, pushes her into the realm of the abject: violated and violating, insatiably linked to the monstrous in choosing to reject Jonathan for the love of Dracula.

Screenwriter James Hart has vaguely suggested that the "movie was meant to portray a woman's story" (Coppola and Hart 69) by which he may intend that Mina is more central to the film than she is to the novel and, further, that in the film Dracula is more a romantic hero than a monster. Coppola's Dracula continues the process we have been tracing in this chapter of complicating—by humanizing— the figure of the vampire. Indeed, Coppola's Count becomes a wounded refugee from the Lifetime television channel, a lost man in a deathless search for the wife stolen from him epochs ago, and for whom he still continues to pine. His marital fidelity and gentleness as a lover stand in marked contrast with the predatory, wanton animal featured in Stoker's novel. The fact that both Dracula and Mina are pictured wearing fashionable leather gloves during the seduction sequence in the movie theater is meant to emphasize the soft potential of Dracula's touch. In this scene, the Count is represented as the white wolf, a creature capable of inflicting great violence one moment, but likewise possessing the capacity to restrain himself and become a tamed beast beneath Mina's gentle hand. Like Louis in *Interview*, Coppola's Dracula is more man than beast; this also explains why he refuses to vamp Mina when he has her trapped in the cinematograph: Dracula does not want her as a helpless victim but as a willing lover. There are certainly numerous possibilities for interpreting Stoker's *Dracula*: as a narrative of reverse imperialism, as a journey-quest, as a Manichean battle of good versus evil, even as a daring erotic thriller featuring deviant sexualities. To read the novel as a love story, however, is perhaps the least plausible of all likely analyses, especially when Stoker's imperious Count is interpreted as a monogamous and wistful romantic whose "love never dies," which is the subtitle of Coppola's film. In Stoker's novel, after Mina is forced to drink Dracula's blood, the Count crows that he has usurped the Crew of Light's "best beloved one," and projects a future for them together, where Mina will serve "later on [as] my companion and helper" (252). Although this future scenario is abhorrent to both Mina and Stoker, it is obviously a pivotal moment for Coppola and Hart, and they project the basis for their love story upon it. The director and screenwriter have conveniently forgotten that the possibility of a future together is Dracula's fantasy; it is never Mina's.

In Stoker's novel, Mina proves very adept at employing the modern technologies introduced in the book—a typewriter, train schedules, Dr. Seward's tape recorder, and a manifold on her typewriter that allows reproduction of multiple copies in three. Her obvious comfort level in using modern technology contradicts the disdain she harbors toward modern cinema in Coppola's film version. When Dracula first seduces Mina inside the cinematograph it is clear that she feels awkward surrounded by this new and mysterious medium. When the Count professes his admiration for the "science" of motion pictures, Mina differs and responds, "How can you call this [cinema] science?" Indeed, it is Dracula who is most enthralled by the various emerging technologies, especially cinema, that he finds in London. His embrace of and association with modernity represents quite a break from the superstitious traditions to which he adheres in Stoker's novel.

The question is why does Coppola's film reverse Dracula's and Mina's perspectives on technology? One possible explanation may be related to Dracula's awareness that the new technologies that surround him—particularly those associated with the emerging science of cinema—are essentially focused on acts of reproduction. A camera records and reproduces moving images. The camera, as Jennifer Wicke effectively points out, produces a "celluloid analog of vampirism in action, the extraction out of an essence in an act of consumption" (176). In playing back these images in a darkened theater, reality is effectively duplicated or mirrored by the technology of cinema. This is precisely what occurs when Dracula drains life from one of his victims: The vampire is reproduced, duplicated in the transforming of a living human into another undead being. Furthermore, the special effects that are possible in the filmic medium also correspond to the supernaturalism Dracula is capable of summoning. In the film montage, the two bite marks Dracula leaves in Lucy's neck transform into the eyes of a wolf, which, in turn, give way to the images of an erotic movie playing on the screen at the cinematograph. As the Count begins his seduction of Mina in the movie theater, the two appear to float together magically off the floor, surrounded by black and white projected images of lingerie-clad dream women who appear and abruptly disappear off the lap of a man in a movie. When Dracula holds Mina down and his eyes redden as he is preparing to vamp her neck, it occurs literally behind a movie projection screen, so that her seduction is juxtaposed with a pornographic subtext of various women screened in the theater and the Freudian symbolism of a train speeding down the tracks. The world of modern cinema appeals to Dracula in Coppola's picture because the vampire recognizes, as Ken Gelder argues, that "film is an erotic medium which splits the audience in terms of gender: while women are 'carried away,' men are positioned voyeuristically. And Coppola's film, generally speaking, reproduces the split" (89). Dracula's manipulation of the scene places Mina in a submissive position, where she is overcome by the fantasy technology of film suddenly interfacing with real life, while Dracula materializes as the auteur director of the sequence, capable of shaping events (the huge white wolf in league with the vampire prowls the theater terrifying bourgeois patrons) or stopping them altogether.

Coppola's *Dracula* manages to capture well the reproductive technology of the nascent "dream" industry, where images are born out of the darkness and reality is reproduced and/or superceded by the magical possibilities of film. Just before he enters the cinematograph, Dracula is literally filmed walking along the street through the lens of an early motion picture camera, suggesting that his presence is capable of transcending spatial constructions of memory and recognition, present and past time frames. From this point on, the entire sequence is conscious of its meta-construction as film, reflecting the difficulty of defining real-time from the manufactured version of reality projected via filmic experience. During Mina's seduction, it is as if she and Dracula enter into their own film where no one else in the theater is capable of observing, intruding, or altering their encapsulated moment. As such, the connection between the vampire and the business of making movies is entirely appropriate. Only through the medium of film is it possible for us to "see" and learn about the activities of the vampire, as we learn in the scene when Dracula is reading a newspaper on the street and only the paper's reflection is visible in a storefront windowpane. Just as a film is typically made in one geographical locale and then crosses international borders during the history of its distribution, the vampire, as discussed earlier in this chapter, is also a figure that moves freely around the world with little or no respect for global law or borders, a nomadic boundary crosser that is at least as reliant on a human audience as is the release of a motion picture.

Staking Her Claim: *Buffy* and the Vampire Tradition

There are several reasons why a chapter on vampire film should conclude with a discussion of the television series *Buffy the Vampire Slayer*. Originating in 1997, *Buffy* has, according to Golden, Bissette, and Sniegoski, authors of *Buffy the Vampire Slayer: The Monster Book*, "had perhaps the most significant impact on the presence of vampires in present-day popular culture" (160). The series has spawned bi-monthly magazines, trading cards, Web sites (e.g., www.slayage.tv), graphic novels, script books, short story collections, a boxed DVD collection of the 22 episodes from each individual season, the scripts for the show assembled and published in a book collection, video games, musical CDs, a television spin-off (*Angel*), and a plethora of other fan-based memorabilia. Most interestingly, the series is distinct from the tradition we have been tracing throughout this chapter. In *Buffy*, most of the vampires and other supernatural monsters are seldom humanized, much less treated as introspective, self-conscious philosophical beings inspiring viewer sympathy or in need of varying degrees of psychiatric counseling. Only Angel, Buffy's part-time boyfriend, and Spike, her one-time nemesis who later becomes her ally, appear as vampires in the series who possess conflicted souls, but they remain notable exceptions in a universe of the undead featuring monsters with feral brows and noses that furrow into deep ridges at the scent of delectable human prey. In most of the episodes I viewed, the vampires portrayed are typically common thugs united in a similar quest: the physical destruction of Buffy and her teenage allies. With the exceptions of those special demons from the underworld, such as Moloch the Corruptor, the vampires Spike and Drusilla, and The Master, the majority of vampires in *Buffy* are aligned with the typical, nondescript hordes of bad guys found in most action thrillers and spy movies. The series, then, returns the vampire to its mythological and folkloric base denominator—as a mindless creature, more akin to a zombie than a philosopher—and spiritually not very far removed from the dust it crumbles into after being dispatched by one of Buffy's phallic wooden stakes.

The popularity of *Buffy* is due in no small measure to the fact that the series reverses the general trend in vampire films over the last seventy years. *Buffy* does not romanticize the undead—anthropomorphizing the vampire into a unique, if frequently misunderstood, essence—but, instead, details the everyday world of a teenage girl whose greatest preoccupation is neither dating, shopping, nor getting good grades so much as protecting the oblivious citizens of Sunnydale by keeping its revenant population in check. In this way, Buffy is also a kind of superhero without typical supernatural capabilities (her only physical weapons are her kickboxing skills and a set of omnipresent wooden stakes)—the first and last line of defense separating the malefic supernatural forces that emerge from the Hellmouth from the small California community that has no idea of their existence. It is important to highlight the fact that in addition to the Slayer's athleticism and always evolving knowledge of how to kill demons and vampires, Buffy also relies on her sense of humor as a form of self-protection. The endless puns and verbal jokes that Buffy and her human sidekicks level against the evil forces they encounter is more than just campy sarcasm designed to appeal to the program's adolescent fan base; the humor in the show is also a serious weapon that emboldens the Slayer, often operating as a kind of battle charge that serves to separate Buffy from her supernatural enemy and helps to initiate her physical attack. In addition, as long as Buffy is able to make fun of her monstrous adversary, mocking his physical grotesqueness or her demonic fashion sense, the human female is able to conceal and redirect her fear. Perhaps this explains why in those episodes where Buffy is captured she is frequently tied up, but never gagged: To silence the Slayer would likely render her impotent.

The stereotypes associated with her name notwithstanding, Buffy Summers is no mere ex-cheerleader bimbo. In fact, the series frequently sets up stereotyped behavior and images, particularly those associated with being a beautiful female teenager, and then dispels them through Buffy's emotional, intellectual, and martial abilities to take command over crisis situations. Although her resplendent hair has turned blonder each season, her attire steadily tighter and more revealing, and her black boot heels higher and thinner, Buffy has earned the designation queen of the vampire hunters; her only rivals in the art of dispatching the undead are all males: Stoker's Van Helsing, Seth Gecko in *From Dusk till Dawn*, Jack Crow in John Carpenter's *Vampires*, and the cinematic action hero Blade are her likely brethren and competition. Like these other vampire slayers, Buffy is surrounded by her own Crew of Light: Rupert Giles, trained to be Buffy's Watcher, possesses a vast understanding of supernatural lore and magical properties; Willow Rosenberg, Buffy's best friend, is highly skilled in both magic and computer knowledge; and Xander Harris and Cordelia Chase are two of Buffy's closest allies despite their sometimes contentious relationship with her. Faith, Anya, and Dawn, women in possession of supernatural powers who are sometimes torn between good and evil, but typically found in Buffy's camp, join her other allies in later episodes. In fact, in the sixth and final season of the show, all the major characters are tempted by evil; none remains pure, and they all exit the series with checkered pasts.

Perhaps Buffy's greatest asset, however, is her uncanny ability to keep cool in the midst of the most nightmarish circumstances. The viewer would be hard pressed to find an episode where Buffy follows the plight of most horror genre heroines and screams her way to rescue or weeps in the face of horrific danger. While securely bound in chains attached to the wall of a dungeon or suspended over the fires of hell, she may object to the foul breath of her hideous revenant tormentors, but Buffy would never give them the satisfaction of watching her beg for mercy, much less surrender to their evil machinations. The television series offers an interesting balance of campy humor and dialogue, adolescent relationship situations, ominous monsters that are convincing constructions of makeup and special effects, and a unique heroine who is as much a product of feminism as she is *Cosmopolitan* magazine. Buffy is capable of uttering lines such as "I need to find something slutty to wear tonight" ("The Initiation") at the same time as her independence is never much in doubt, as when she acknowledges in the episode entitled "Primeval," "I don't jump through hoops on command. I've never really been one to toe the line." *Buffy* is a distinctive blend of teenage melodrama, such as *Dawson's Creek* and *Beverly Hills 90210*, and the slasher horror genre discussed in chapter 8. In essence, Buffy is perhaps the ultimate illustration of Carol Clover's Final Girl, insofar as she has managed to survive a wide variety of hellish beasts that have appeared over successive seasons through her combination of wits, athleticism, and endurance. Similar to the paradigm Clover defines, Buffy, while not a virgin and at times truly in love, has still evaded romantic commitment to remain an independent entity befitting her role as a Slayer-heroine.

In the first episode of the series' fifth season, "Buffy vs. Dracula," the Slayer finds herself in battle against the legendary Count. This particular episode is an excellent example of the entire series, as it embodies the spirit of the show in delineating the complex relationship Buffy maintains with the forces of evil aligned against her. Her nocturnal encounter with Dracula initially produces mixed feelings in Buffy. When she meets him in the graveyard, her first reaction is that of the Slayer: She tries to kill him. However, Buffy is simultaneously attracted to the Count, in part because he is "famous," but also because she is drawn to his charm, as the Dracula in this episode returns the vampire to the Lugosi prototype of the handsome figure that seduces women with his "dark and penetrating eyes." Indeed, best friend Willow is transfixed by Buffy's encounter, and when she calls Dracula "sexy," Buffy concurs. Unlike her attitude toward the typical vampire she must vanquish on her nightly patrols, Dracula affects the Slayer deeply. She allows him to call her his "kindred," she is flattered by his obvious interest in her, having "searched the whole world over for you," and she even allows the dangerous vampire to bite and leave puncture holes on her neck. It is not only Buffy and Willow, however, who find themselves so favorably disposed toward the vampire: Xander is hypnotized into becoming the Count's slave, eating insects and operating in a comic role that parodies Renfield from novel and film versions of *Dracula*; even Giles finds himself "nuzzling" the three vampire sisters in the basement of Dracula's castle and is reluctant to leave them.

The narrative strategy of each *Buffy* program is to pose a particular problem from the underworld that threatens the stability and welfare of Buffy and her friends, and then has Buffy resolve the crisis. Thus, just as Buffy appears ready to drink from Dracula's wrist in her own baptism of blood scene, the Slayer reasserts herself and defiantly puns, "I think the *thrall* has gone out of our relationship," as her cue to throttle the Count. While drawn to the invitation to drink the transformative blood of the vampire, Buffy ultimately resists following Mina in Stoker's novel and Coppola's film and finally ends up staking Dracula herself. That Buffy is capable of doing what Mina could not and dispatches the Count without any help from her boyfriend, Riley, and Giles, who are both attempting ineptly to rescue her, is a sign of exactly how progressive *Buffy the Vampire Slayer* is as a vehicle for expressing themes of female empowerment. Buffy's Crew of Light often comes to her assistance, but in this series the survival of Sunnydale and its citizens is usually dependent upon Buffy herself—her skills, her moxie, her powers of resistance. Violent females, particularly those who are expert in the martial arts, are difficult both to pigeonhole and to identify with. There are many possible explanations that might go far in interpreting this difficulty, including that culturally there remains something disturbing and disorienting about a teenage girl who insists on walking—or stalking—through nocturnal graveyards alone. Perhaps this is why the feminism inherent in the series is handled so deftly. Buffy may be quite capable of vanquishing on her own the sons of darkness—even Dracula himself—but she also retains her feminine wiles, gazing up into the anxious face of her boyfriend, and gently assuring him that despite the seductive allure of the Count, "I'm still your girl."

One way in which we recognize the vampire is as a shape changer. It assumes the form necessary to survival: transmogrifying from debonair count, to bat, to wolf, depending on its needs or desires. The celluloid vampire is also a shape changer, morphing from the rat-like Nosferatu of Murnau's early film, to the chic urbanity of Miriam in *The Hunger*, to the creature things that populate films such as *From Dusk till Dawn*. Nina Auerbach notes that "ghosts, werewolves, and manufactured monsters are relatively changeless, more aligned with eternity than time; vampires blend into the changing cultures they inhabit" (6).

Over the years, the vampire has attained a ubiquitous presence within the horror cinescape. In addition to those films that feature them in easily recognizable roles, vampiric metaphors can also be found animating sources of monstrosity far removed from the traditional figure of the cinematic bloodsucker. In horror films as distinct from one another as *Poltergeist*, *The Brood*, *The Silence of the Lambs*, and

The Ring, the evil that pursues and covets human life is certainly vampiric in nature. The ghostly agents in these movies may not lust after human blood per se, but the monsters in them engage in a kind of psychic vampirism, displacing human beings from their homes, their families, and the stability of their own psyches. In the majority of films adapted from Stephen King's prolific canon, to argue the point further, a form of vampirism frequently represents both the motivation and the consequence of stalkings, hauntings, and supernatural involvement in human affairs. Although the traditional image of the vampire is absent from the hotel in *The Shining*, the mansion in *Rose Red*, the car in *Christine*, the Wendigo spirit in *Pet Sematary*, the shape-shifter in *IT*, the collective will that directs the townspeople in *The Tommyknockers*, the violent alter ego in *The Dark Half*, and the laundry machine in *The Mangler*, all these inanimate things and supernatural agencies are nevertheless possessed of a vampirelike hunger that either literally feasts on human blood or seeks to channel directly its malefic influence through a human host. Even many of the interpersonal relationships in King films that do not feature excursions into paranormal phenomena—e.g., *Apt Pupil* and *Misery*—are most accurately defined in vampiric terms.

In order to explain the proliferation of the vampire in modern and postmodern horror art, we must recognize the deathless attraction they have come to represent. Beginning with the Romantics and stretching unabated to our own era, vampires have evolved into tremendously seductive figures. Perhaps it is the freedom with which they conduct their lives, existing simultaneously in and out of the flow of human affairs; perhaps it is the erotic pulse that so often quickens when their incisors drop and they swoop down to kiss, then to bite the neck from which they feed; perhaps it is the lure of immortality, to be "free of pain" as Armand reassures the frightened girl facing death in *Interview*'s theater of vampires. Cinema keeps returning to a deathless fascination with the vampire because of all the monsters in horror cinema, the vampire most resembles us, or at least that romantic part we sometimes fancy ourselves to be—the nomadic spirit devoid of serious commitments and mundane responsibilities alike—unfettered to wander the earth in the quest to satisfy our most selfish urges. This projection may provide the best explanation for why movies have felt compelled to romanticize vampires. In contrast to the other aliens that populate the horror genre, the motion picture industry has made the vampire more attractive than repulsive, more an intimate acquaintance or even a lover than a figure of abject terror.

4.

The Terror of Hitchcock

Vertigo, Psycho, The Birds

In Alfred Hitchcock's film *Rear Window*, adventure photographer L. B. Jeffries (called "Jeff") finds himself confined to his urban apartment with a broken leg. Bored and restless, he spends hours observing the neighbors who live in the building across the courtyard from his own. Although Jeff doesn't realize it, at least not consciously, each of the apartments he watches—from the newlyweds, to "Miss Lonelyhearts," to the unhappy couple with a dog, to Lars Thorwald himself, the husband who murders his nagging, invalid wife—are projections of Jeff's own unconscious anxieties about women, and marriage in particular. His glamorous girlfriend, Lisa Fremont, who wants nothing more than to settle down with him and raise a family, pursues Jeff romantically throughout the film. The murder of Mrs. Thorwald represents the most extreme projection of the anxiety Jeff harbors about his own impending marriage decision: that someday he may likewise grow to detest the woman who demands his freedom in exchange for matrimony.

In Hitchcock's cinematic universe, heterosexual coupling always comes with its own inimitable terrors. More specifically, women—and particularly mothers—are simultaneously the adored love objects and feared agents of destruction in Hitchcock's universe. The director was profoundly attracted to powerfully independent women—the cool blondes played by Ingrid Bergman, Grace Kelly, Janet Leigh, Eva Marie Saint, Tippi Hedren, and Kim Novak—who threaten the safety of the men they choose to pursue with a rapacious romantic hunger and relentless will. As Hitchcock confessed to Truffaut, indicating the exact (and exacting) degree of his awareness in creating a particular type of female character: "You know why I favor sophisticated blondes in my films? We're after the drawing-room type, the real ladies, who become whores once they're in the bedroom" (167). Lisa Fremont, Melanie Daniels, Marion Crane, Frances Stevens, and Madeleine Elster are the archetypical Hitchcock heroines whose lethal combination of stunning beauty, fierce sexuality, and determined personal resolve anticipate the femme fatales of future horror-thriller films such as *Fatal Attraction*, *Basic Instinct*, *Bound*, *Body Heat*, and *The Last Seduction*.

Although Hitchcock's men are disquieted by Hitchcock's women, it is, ironically, the women who are most often victimized and made to suffer—physically as well as psychologically. A pattern typically emerges: Early in many of his pictures, especially the later work, the male protagonist finds himself under the romantic spell of a woman so beautiful that she appears unworldly. At first, he is nearly overwhelmed by her uniqueness, but midway through the film the dynamic shifts, placing the main female character under siege, in a position of crisis. Sometimes this crisis comes from a source outside the woman herself, such as in the attacks of the birds in the film with the same title or in a husband's desire to murder his wife in *Dial "M" for Murder*. In other films, however, such as *Vertigo* and *Marnie*, the Hitchcock female inherits a psychological burden—often imposed upon her from a maternal source—so debilitating that it warps her personality and imposes her self-destruction. While often idealized as romantic icons of beauty and inspiration, Hitchcock's women are as much a nightmare as a dream come true.

Hitchcock liked to quote nineteenth-century playwright Victorien Sardou's inspiration to "Torture the women," although Hitchcock was also known to amend this advice by adding, "The trouble today is we don't torture the women enough" (Fawell 88). The auteur did more than merely cite this line as opportunity to foment scandal and draw more attention to his cheeky sense of humor. Part of Hitchcock felt that "torturing women" created moments of artistic tension that heightened spectator identification with women in jeopardy and the imperiled situations in which they were cast. It is, for example, only when Lisa puts herself deliberately in danger by entering Thorwald's apartment in search of evidence of his murderous deed that Jeff as well as the audience begins to view his girlfriend as a brave adventurer and not just a mere fashion icon.

It is, moreover, only at this point in the film that Jeff begins to desire Lisa sexually; Hitchcock understood that sexual desire is often based—especially for men—at the intersection where the visual becomes dangerous. Similarly, Melanie Daniels in *The Birds* grows in status after she suffers a terrible bird attack while trapped alone in an upstairs bedroom. The goal of many of Hitchcock's films was to place a haughty and beautiful female protagonist in a position where she was reduced to a disheveled and imperiled victim-hero. Such a reversal made her more attractive to the male hero in the film as well as the spectator in the audience. Her involvement in dangerous situations helped to crack the cold exterior of her blonde aloofness, simultaneously revealing her humanity. Additionally, it provided Hitchcock's men and his audience the opportunity both to admire the attributes of female endurance while reaffirming the absolute importance of a male in the role of a rescuing hero.

The imperiled female-hero is an archetype that recurs throughout the horror film genre. Early versions of the horror heroine placed her in situations where she was totally helpless against whatever monster pursued her and totally reliant on rescue from her male lover or husband, as is the case with Elizabeth in Whale's *Frankenstein*. As the horror genre evolves and is influenced by feminism in the 1970s and 1980s, however, female imperilment remains a staple, but the potential for varying responses to her situation—extending even to the point of self-rescue—become available to horror heroines. Hitchcock's films should be viewed as residing at a "middle way" on the continuum of feminist evolution: While not quite ready to allow women to rescue themselves from monstrous circumstances (indeed, in Hitchcock's cinema, sometimes independent women are themselves the monster), the auteur nonetheless invests his unconventional and antitraditional women with a steely self-resolve that points the way to the emergence of Clover's Final Girls, the latter rewarded for their independence instead of punished for it.

At the same time that his male protagonists are made uncomfortable by assertive women, and especially their pronounced and open sexuality, Hitchcock's men cannot pull away from them; the director's portrayal of feminine power, as Tania Modleski notes, "is both fascinating and seemingly limitless" (1). However, despite Modleski's provocative thesis that in Hitchcock's movies "the strong fascination and identification with femininity subverts the claims to mastery and authority of the male characters" (2), Hitchcock's males are seldom willing to accept women on their own terms. Instead, they seek to confront and alter their perceived monstrous femininity to the point that if the women cannot be dominated, perhaps they can at least be made tractable enough to marry. To this end, the director's male protagonists seek somehow to "remake" threatening women into less independent and certainly less predatory beings; Norman Bates in *Psycho* is merely the most overt manifestation of male terror in Hitchcock's canon that manifests itself in the paradoxical need to destroy exactly what it most desires.

Despite Mitch Brenner's reassurance to his mother in *The Birds* that he "knows what [he] wants" and "can take care of [himself]" in pursuing his liaison with Melanie Daniels, the personal worlds of Hitchcock's once complacent men—reflecting the director's own gender phobias—are abruptly and severely undermined by the presence of women. The crisis in masculinity that develops at the core of so many of Hitchcock's films brings with it the impulse to "tame" women, but, should that fail, resorting to murder is sometimes the last available means to reaffirming male sovereignty. Gender conflicts in Hitchcock are never wholly reconciled in his films until the woman acknowledges and submits to the logic of the patriarchy (which, for example, occurs in the endings of The Birds and Marnie, but not in Rear Window). All these elements, of course, only serve to complicate a clean definition of the monstrous in the director's canon: Does the terror in Hitchcock reside more in the women who have rejected traditional constructions of feminine behavior, or in the men who demand that fulfillment of desire—what Freud termed a female's "masculinity"—be repressed in women?

Projections of Male Fear and Desire: *Vertigo*

In "Visual Pleasure and Narrative Cinema," Laura Mulvey's famous exegesis of Hitchcock films, she argues that both Rear Window and Vertigo are tailored "to the measure of male desire" (17), exploring, in other words, the fears and desires of both the male protagonists and, by extension, the spectator (both males and females in Mulvey's paradigm) watching in the audience. Because of the anxieties associated with castration posed by the woman's image on screen, Mulvey posits, Hitchcock accommodates the male desire to see her fetishized and controlled in the course of the narrative.

Mulvey's analysis raises several issues vital to any discussion of fear and desire and attraction and repulsion in Hitchcock's males. Certainly central to her reading of the director's later films is the bifurcated role of the woman; she is at once a stunning image of beauty and a terrifying enigma. In Vertigo, Madeleine Elster's character is essentially defined by her elegant femininity (mostly projected via her clothes) and suicidal obsession. Her personality, trapped as it is in her association with a tragic grandmother, Carlotta Valdes, both terrifies and fascinates John "Scottie" Ferguson, the detective who is hired and then duped by Madeleine's husband. Her personal nightmare becomes Scottie's when he falls in love with the image of a romantic heroine who is as mysteriously doomed as she is resplendently attired. For it is impossible to separate the haunted and lonely Madeleine—who wanders through a misty forest of giant Sequoias wearing a snow-white trench coat, high heels, and long black gloves and scarf—from the image she projects via her clothing. Although sharing the same name with the Usher sibling in Edgar Allan Poe's "The Fall of the House of Usher," Hitchcock's Madeleine also shares much in common with Poe's Ligeia, who is likewise known to the reader primarily through the narrator's obsession with her feminine body parts: hair, eyes, hands, and supernal footfall. This is precisely what Mulvey means when she suggests that

Madeleine Elster is a fetishized object of male desire in *Vertigo*. The image that she projects—of platinum blonde radiance and articles of designer clothing—is what makes Scottie fall for her; he doesn't know her long enough to love anything else about her. Robin Wood notes this as well with the remark "Scottie has not been in love with a woman so much as with—almost in the Platonic sense—an Idea" (*Hitchcock's Films* 94). Thus, when he accidentally encounters another woman who resembles the dead Madeleine (because this woman, Judy, had in fact duped Scottie by her earlier impersonation of Madeleine), the detective sets out to transform her into his lost love by fetishizing her hair, lipstick, and clothing—right down to duplicating Madeleine's hairstyle and color, tailored suits, long gloves, and stiletto heels.

It is a very bizarre courtship, as Scottie appears as much obsessed with Madeleine's wardrobe as he is with the woman who wore the clothes. In the suicidal Madeleine, Scottie wishes to subdue a feminine force that terrifies him because it is out of control of itself—and particularly because it proves also to be out of his ability to control. Like the vertigo he suffers from each time he looks down from a great height, the feminine principle embodied in Madeleine entices him at the same time that it makes him feel nauseous. Scottie remains convinced that he should be able to "beat" these hyperbolic sensations, as when he practices standing on chairs in Midge's apartment early in the film. He is, however, no more capable of exerting his will over the acrophobia than he is able to thwart the murderous deception that Judy Barton and Gavin Elster perpetrate against him. Scottie's response to Madeleine is essentially masochistic; her self-destructive impulses and his own powerlessness to counter them enflame him psychosexually. His reaction to the devoted but unexciting Midge poses the problem explicitly: Her maternal love for Scottie—more a chaste friendship than a traumatic challenge to his sanity—cannot compare to the masochistic pain that Madeleine inspires in pushing him to the nadir of psychological humiliation.

Just as the doomed Madeleine develops an obsession over reanimating the past by sacrificing her life in the present, Scottie is also haunted by a figure from the past that he cannot escape. After her suicide, Scottie assumes Madeleine's curse. This is why Scottie watches himself fall into Carlotta's empty grave and plunge to his death from the mission bell tower during his long dream sequence following Madeleine's death. The dream sequence indicates that he is not only beset with guilt over Madeleine's loss, he is likewise personally identifying with her. In the course of the film, Scottie gets to indulge his masochism most fully by psychologically turning himself into Madeleine, even as he seeks to recreate her persona in another woman. In discussing the relationship between masculine desire and feminine attire, Iris Marion Young makes an argument that helps to define Scottie's unconscious self-identification with Madeleine: "Woman serves as the mirror for masculine subjectivity and desire. She reflects back to him his self . . . this function of femininity is the mirror in which man sees himself reflected" (202). In the second half of the picture especially, Scottie resembles the traditional eighteenth- and nineteenth-century Gothic maiden—tortured by a past that will not stay dead, unable and unwilling to abandon his internalized and passive state of being, and desperately seeking rescue from an outside source against circumstances over which he has no control.

Indeed, once Scottie is released from psychiatric care, where he is treated for the Poe-esque disease "acute melancholia," he most clearly resembles one of Poe's protagonists, wandering the streets of San Francisco tormenting himself deliberately with recollections of the lost Madeleine. Poe's famous observation in "The Philosophy of Composition" that the death of a beautiful woman is the most poetic of all topics, especially when experienced vicariously through her bereaved lover, represents the storyboard that guides all of Scottie's actions, especially in the second half of Vertigo. He experiences a double take when he notices an elegantly dressed blonde in a restaurant; his heart soars when he notices Madeleine's car in the driveway of the apartment building where she once lived; he hopes to find her in a blonde stranger gazing at Carlotta's portrait in the art gallery; and, eventually, he recreates a simulacrum of Madeleine out of Judy. The murderous subplot constructed by Elster and Judy notwithstanding, Scottie would have been forced to reanimate the ghost of Madeleine in some other woman if she had not already existed in the duplicitous Judy. This is exactly why he is so offended at Midge's face superimposed upon Carlotta's portrait. His guilt and his grief have become so self-reflexive that Scottie has completely lost the ability to laugh—either at himself or anything associated with his love object.

Although I will have more to say about the elaborate connections that link Hitchcock and Poe later in this chapter, Scottie owes much to the mysteriously haunted and driven narrator of Poe's "Ligeia," whose obsessive efforts center on reincarnating his beautiful and dead first wife into the convenient body of his equally prosaic and reluctant second spouse. (Appropriate to a director trying to reflect the atmosphere of the American 1950s, however, Hitchcock has merely reversed Poe's nineteenth-century association of the exotic and sexual with a dark-haired heroine, as the brunette Judy of Vertigo is transformed into her era's ideal of romantic sexuality: the platinum blonde.)

Vertigo's opening credits appear in white letters over a series of ever-changing geometric designs. The common variable all these varying shapes retain is their link to circles and spirals. Each geometric image revolves around, or is itself a circle or spiral. These shapes, coupled with the image of Madeleine's circular eyeball that also opens the film, connects most immediately to Scottie's reoccurring problem with vertigo. However, the circle and spiral also extend to become defining metaphors for the major themes of the movie—from Madeleine's compulsion to keep returning to sites associated with her dead grandmother; to Scottie's obsession with circling back to his memories of Madeleine; to the reappearance of Madeleine herself in Judy; to the physical locations and objects of feminine attire that are continually revisited and duplicated throughout the film, such as the haunting church bell tower and stairs (another spiral image), Carlotta's ruby pendant that finally reveals Judy's true identity, and Scottie's compulsive need to reconstruct an image of Madeleine out of Judy. Most importantly, of course, the circle is the operative metaphor for Scottie's own life. True to the romantic tradition, he is trapped in a spiral of guilt and longing, from the opening scene where his vertigo ends up sacrificing a policeman's life, to his obsessive need to rediscover Madeleine. Only in the last five minutes of the film does Scottie break out of his solipsistic circle and triumph over the past—"There's one final thing I have to do, and then I'll be free of the past"—but even here he echoes the exact words he once spoke to Madeleine and then proceeds to reenact her suicide.

Psychoanalytical Horror: *Psycho*

The plot premises of *Vertigo* are flamboyant and heavily reliant upon circumstantial juxtapositions. As Robin Wood points out, "No one would ever set about murdering his wife in *that* way" (*Hitchcock's Films* 72). It is not just the bell tower substitution that appears so far removed from reality, but also the accidental "discovery" of Madeleine/Judy in a city containing millions of people and Scottie's remarkable ability to discern, more than a year later, the resemblance to Madeleine in spite of the fact that Judy has taken great pains to alter her appearance dramatically. Hitchcock is uninterested in sharing with us how Scottie manages to escape the opening scene left dangling from the gutter of a high rooftop where his vertigo is triggered by the fact that he inadvertently caused a policeman's death when he tried to save him. What is clear in much of Hitchcock is that objective reality is always subordinate to individual psychology, so that *Vertigo* must be appreciated for its exploration into the interior terrors of the human mind far more than its reliance upon a balanced rendering of realism or rational coherence. In this way, then, *Vertigo* shares much in common with the mysterious milieus of the films that follow it in Hitchcock's canon. In *Psycho* and *Marnie*, for example, the viewer is likewise trapped in dysfunctional worlds that reflect less on the workings of the everyday and more on the highly personal and subjective realms of dream and aberrant psychopathology. In the context of this discussion, it helps to keep in mind Hitchcock's profound appreciation for the surrealists—the paintings of Salvador Dali and Giorgio de Chirico, in particular. They influenced the topography of

Hitchcock's mise-en-scène (recall the Chirico-inspired heavy shadows cast by looming white columns at the Spanish mission in *Vertigo*) as well as the director's fierce commitment to liberating the workings of the subconscious through the disruption of modern surface-reality.

As each of his pictures continued to explore the perimeters of the unconscious, madness—its lure, threat, and terror—evolved into the subject of Hitchcock's greatest films. Because of the director's attention to visualizing the workings of diseased psyches, it is neither a surprise nor an exaggeration to suggest that *Psycho* altered irrevocably the landscape of the horror film. While horror was certainly a well-established cinematic genre for decades before Hitchcock's movie, *Psycho* turned the genre's focus inward, providing the horror film with an intellectuality and deadliness of purpose formerly missing by emphasizing the psychological over the physical. Whereas earlier horror monsters were readily identifiable via their outward otherness in exaggerated bodies and corporeal identities (e.g., Universal Picture's creature feature parade from the 1930s and 1940s and the various science fiction oddities from the 1950s), Norman Bates bears little in common with his horror cinema ancestry; in fact, he is a harbinger of the monster of the future: the serial killer. Each rendition of the Frankenstein monster, the werewolf, and the gelatinous creatures from outer space or under the earth, original fear-invoking intentions notwithstanding, always carried with them an unwitting level of self-parody in their overstated filmic presence, making them a perfect subject matter for drive-ins and the ridiculous slapstick of Abbott and Costello.

There has, however, never been anything silly about Norman Bates. Half a century later, he is still a disturbing figure, surrounded by his stuffed aviary and tortured by his transgendered Oedipal distress. Hitchcock and the movie's production company, Paramount Studio, seemed to sense the seriousness of their material content in publicizing the film differently when it was released in 1960; specifically, the director's terror disclaimer in the beginning of the movie and the refusal to allow patrons late entrance into the theater once the picture commenced. Speaking to Truffaut about *Psycho*, Hitchcock said, "My main satisfaction is that the film had an effect on the audiences. . . . I don't care about the subject matter; I don't care about the acting; but I do care [that we were] able to use the cinematic art to achieve something of mass emotion" (211). The unique edginess and intensity of *Psycho* contribute to the impact the film had on the popular consciousness of its immediate era as well as those to follow, as sales of glass shower stalls skyrocketed immediately following the picture's release, while the diminutive term "psycho" is still employed in popular parlance to describe an individual whose behavior has transgressed beyond the range of what is socially acceptable. Norman is the prototype in a long line of normal-looking, boy-next-door psychopaths. While resembling one of us on the outside (Norman = normal man, the norms of man),

Norman seethes on the inside. His monstrosity is neither the result of abnormal body shape nor wild special effect; rather, he is the product of an abnormal psychology—of the wildness within—the terrifying consequence of bad parenting. Norman is the first horror monster who is wholly and unholy human. Thus, his filmic introduction anticipates a generation of boy-men serial murderers obsessed with their mothers as much as they are with murdering mother-surrogates: Michael Myers, Jason, Leatherface, and Jame Gumb are all Norman's cinematic descendants.

Psycho's musical score is an important part of the movie. During the credits that begin the picture, jarring and intrusive strings accompany alternating vertical and horizontal white lines on a dark background. These white lines rapidly close in from the perimeter margins of the frame only to stop abruptly at the center of the picture to reveal each individual credit. Thus, even before the picture—filmed in black and white instead of the ubiquitous Technicolor that had revolutionized the movie industry for the past decade—presents its first visual image, the audience is already assaulted and unnerved, sensitized to the fragmented nature of the music and hyperkinetic white lines traveling against a black backdrop. The opening strings are restated throughout the film—as Marion makes her way out of Phoenix and whenever Norman-in-mother-drag flashes his knife. Bernard Herrmann's score in Psycho does not employ violins in the melodious and rhythmic movements of his later work in Marnie. Instead, the strings of Psycho emphasize discord and disunity; throughout the first half hour of the picture, the music almost appears to be chasing Marion, much like the cop who persists on following her in his cruiser, or the way in which the voices of her boss and Cassidy, whose money she has stolen, pursue her down the highway haunting her guilty imagination. In a manner that will be repeated in later horror films influenced by Psycho, such as Carrie and Halloween, Hitchcock pioneered the relationship between cacophonous music and the unfolding of narrative surprise and suspense. Moreover, the particular stringed assault of Psycho is most appropriate to the subject matter of the film itself: Norman Bates is a "highly strung," neurotic character. At the climax of the picture when his attempt to murder Lila Crane is foiled by Sam, and mother is revealed to be son, Norman's gnarled facial and body expressions become the emotive embodiment of the tortured and fragmented musical score we have heard throughout the picture.

The Bates house and motel have come to occupy an archetypal position in the long, nefarious history of gothicized American places. They take us back especially to Poe's Usher mansion and Shirley Jackson's Hill House, while also anticipating the disturbing edifices of the Amityville horror and the Overlook Hotel. Jackson's influential novel appeared the year before Hitchcock's film, in 1959, while the director's life-long obsession with Poe's fiction is aptly and amply documented in Dennis R. Perry's book, Hitchcock and Poe: The Legacy of Delight and Terror. Although Perry avoids any specific discussion of Psycho—a frustrating as well as glaring omission—on the opening page of his analysis, he cites Hitchcock's comment that "without wanting to seem immodest, I can't help but compare what I try to put into my films with what Poe put in his stories: a perfectly unbelievable story recounted to readers with such a hallucinatory logic that one has the impression that this same story can happen to you tomorrow" (1).

What is surprising, given this degree of influence, is that the director never attempted to interpret in a feature-length film one of Poe's tales or poems, leaving the job—for the worse—in the hands of his contemporary, Roger Corman. (Although the first two episodes of Hitchcock's television series, as Dana Brand notes, were relatively straightforward adaptations of Poe's "The Premature Burial" and "William Wilson" [123].) Poe's influence on Hitchcock may have been subtle, but it was also pervasive. I have already alluded to the profound impact that Poe's protagonists, caught as they are in a ghostlike aura between past tragedy and present-tense doom, had on Hitchcock's portrayals of Madeleine Elster and Scottie Ferguson in *Vertigo*. As obsessed as both artists were with romantically haunted females, they likewise shared something in common in their mutual fascination with torturing them. Poe was the first writer to tell the tale of terror from the point of view of the monster. In doing so, he placed the reader of "The Tell-Tale Heart" or "The Cask of Amontillado" in a highly uncomfortable position, trapped inside a disturbed psyche that willingly shared both his homicidal plans and actions in a conspiratorial intimacy. As such, we become the unwitting confessor and historian of psychopathic behavior. Hitchcock's use of point of view through a camera liberated enough to go anywhere it wants—across the Phoenix skyscape and into a hotel bedroom, or even into the small peephole of Norman Bates's office—forces the film spectator into a complicit relationship with the camera as voyeur. As in Poe, we are privy to the most private acts, such as viewing Marion in her white underwear in a postcoital position. For perhaps the first time (but certainly not the last) in cinematic history, we are taken to places where we are neither invited nor are particularly eager to visit. Perhaps the best example occurs when an attractive woman's shower erupts into a slaughter, but more about this scene later.

Both Hitchcock and Poe are masters of manipulation, putting spectator and reader, respectively, into disturbing situations that are fraught with tension. Each artist sets up shots of surprise or dramatic situations deliberately designed to control how the audience will react. Just before the last brick is plastered into place sealing his immolation in "The Cask of Amontillado," the unfortunate Fortunato cries out in anguish, "For the love of God, Montressor!" The reader also wants to cry out the same warning, realizing, even if Montressor does not, that his game of revenge has gone far enough; now, it becomes an irrevocable act of murder. We are similarly shocked and terrified in *Psycho* when we view a gnomelike white blur rush through the framed doorway of a second-floor bedroom to slice the unsuspecting detective, Arbogast, as he makes his way up a set of carpeted stairs. The omniscient point of view of Hitchcock's suspended overhead camera puts the spectator in a position to witness everything—the sudden but unclear emergence of the Norman-mother figure from the bedroom, the raised knife, and Arbogast's shock and backwards fall into oblivion. In fact, through the camera's moving eye, we literally follow the detective as he falls down the stairs. In both instances we are made to experience Fortunato's imminent terror as well as Arbogast's stunned surprise. Moreover, we are just as helpless in stopping Montressor from inserting that last brick as we are in arresting Norman's arm or cushioning the detective's backward plunge. We want to cry, "Look out!" but it's already too late. Poe and Hitchcock were the first masters of their respective mediums capable of transcending their mediums—that is, in making us experience horrific moments that cannot be dismissed as sensational fiction or allowed to occur discretely off camera. The terror in their work is so effective because it is uncensored and rendered without remorse.

Just as Poe invented the first literary detective, there are a number of his descendants that populate Hitchcock's films. Hitchcock's detectives are nowhere near as infallible as Poe's Dupin, as they merely complicate the situation in *Rear Window*, or are dispatched unceremoniously in *Psycho*. Additionally, officials of the law in Hitchcock are always as ineffectual as the policemen and the prefect of police in Poe's detective tales. The sheriffs in both *Psycho* and *The Birds*, for example, can barely process the most obvious evidence presented to them, much less make an attempt to solve the problem. As representatives of narrowly defined investigative approaches based upon previous casework, the police in Poe and Hitchcock are always unable to think beyond the details and facts supplied by the evidence and thereby fail to allow the nature of the individual crime to reveal its own inimitable pattern. It might be argued, though, that many of Hitchcock's male protagonists operate in a way that at least suggests the detective genre that Poe invented insofar as they are all trying to solve a problem by unraveling a mystery. Often, in the detective genre, the problem to be solved is complicated by the detective's inability to view the mystery as an intimate reflection of something within his or her personality. As Robin Wood notes in *Hitchcock's Films*, this same level of blindness coexists in Hitchcock's male protagonists: "The Hitchcock hero typically lives in a small, enclosed world of his own fabrication, at once a protection and a prison, artificial and unrealistic, into which the 'real' chaos erupts, demanding to be faced" (69). This self-designed environment likewise bears much in common with the artificially imposed Parisian world that Dupin and his narrator sidekick inhabit in "The Murders in the Rue Morgue" and "The Purloined Letter."

Clearly, however, the most obvious and maybe the most important line of descent that connects the twentieth-century film director to the nineteenth-century writer is in a mutual fascination with abnormal psychology, particularly aberrant psychopathologies, and a recognition that physical place both mirrors and symbolizes inner psychology. In *Psycho*, each shot of the Bateses' Victorian mansion is viewed at an upward camera angle forcing the spectator to stare continually up at the house, making it appear larger than life and in possession of a power that looms over the landscape below. Moreover, we are only ever permitted a fractured view of the mansion: the left front half and its adjacent side dominates, again suggesting that the *whole* of the building is ultimately unknowable. The Bateses' mansion simultaneously mirrors and contrasts the motel beneath it: Each structure contains multiple rooms, murders are committed in both places, secrets are maintained, and Norman moves freely between both structures (see Figure 2, p. 192).

Truffaut was perhaps the first to draw attention to the fact that the architecture contributes to the atmosphere of *Psycho*. His observation "that the architectural contrast between the vertical house and the horizontal hotel" (205) is one of the more distinctive contrasts that the movie offers between the two dwellings. The house is clearly identified as Mother Bates's domain; while the grounds in front of the mansion have grown unkempt and weedy, its interior is spotless. When Norman is speaking with Marion, Mother Bates's voice appears to resonate from inside the house; we see mother's silhouette in a rocking chair on the second floor as if she is still presiding over the house (and, indeed she is); and the house's interior still reflects mother's choice of furnishings and fabrics. In contrast to the Victorian opulence of the house's interior, replete with elegant statuary, stained-glass windows, and richly appointed woodwork, the motel located on the street-level below epitomizes contemporary Americana, with its Spartan-like furnishings, cheap lamps and nightstands, and plastic shower curtains (see Figure 2, p. 192). The outside of the motel—in contrast to the unassuming but clean interior of its rooms—is in near disrepair, needs a new coat of paint, and crates of garbage and the rusting shell of a discarded automobile are located just around back. Hitchcock told Truffaut that he wished to be "accurate" in making "the motel an authentic reproduction of the real thing" (205).

While these two structures appear to be contrasting studies in aesthetic form and meaning, both places are no longer "functional" according to the purposes for which they were originally constructed. The motel fails to bring in money because it is so far removed from the highway and thus is no longer frequented by guests. "This place looks like it's hiding from the world," Arbogast remarks when he is introduced to Norman and, indeed, it is, as Norman sometimes even fails to illuminate the sign that advertises its existence. The Victorian mansion is just as void of meaning as a *home* to Norman: While Mother Bates's presence still looms over its interior, she has, after all, been dead for ten years. We can only imagine the Oedipal torments that tortured Norman daily to the point where he finally resorts to murdering his mother and her lover in their bedroom. Her room is still impeccably maintained by Norman as a kind of shrine or sanctuary to her memory, and when Lila pulls down the bedcovers the two lumpy indentations in the mattress eerily suggest the ghostlike silhouettes of the murdered corpses that Norman poisoned years earlier.

As one might imagine, given the subordinate role that Norman plays in his relationship to his mother, her bedroom remains centrally located and is the biggest in the house, while his is off to the side. Inside, Lila discovers furnishings that underscore a case of arrested development. Although an adult man, Norman's room speaks to a crisis in masculinity. The interior is cluttered with dolls, comic books, toy cars, a stuffed bunny rabbit, and the objects of childhood games, indicating that Norman has not developed normally; in contrast to his mother's double bed, Norman still sleeps on a plain cot in the corner of his room too small for his height. All of these childhood mementos indicate that he inhabits a border world of perpetual infantilism ironically subverted by a copy of Beethoven's "Eroica" symphony on the record player. The "Eroica" may speak to the repressed sexual desires Norman evinces toward both his mother and Marion when the latter visits the hotel, and he watches her undress through the peephole in his office.

In Poe's "The Fall of the House of Usher," the vertical fissure that runs down the center of the mansion and essentially splits the house in two is suggestive of the split that separates Madeline and Roderick Usher, a set of twins, brother and sister, who may have joined as one in an incestuous union. At the end of the tale when Madeline returns from the grave to embrace her brother and to bear "him to the floor a corpse, and a victim to the terrors he had anticipated" (335), the house collapses in on itself burying the unfortunate pair. Similarly, in *Psycho*, the dissolution of Norman's personality is mirrored in the oppositional physical structures he inhabits. The distinctions that we have been tracing between the Bateses' motel and mansion are meant to underscore Norman's schizophrenic self: the contrasting elements in his psyche that compel him to fluctuate between the personae of Norman and Mother Bates. As Frederick Frank has noted in his study of Gothic settings, "Gothic architecture is imbued with the character and will of its former owners. Place becomes personality" (14). The motel represents that part of him that has managed to present some kind of "social" veneer to the world, that part of Norman that longs to connect with other people, such as Marion. While stationed behind the desk in the motel's office, Norman assumes the air of a bourgeois businessman in both demeanor and conversation. After his mother-self kills Marion, Norman the ever-meticulous innkeeper works hard to remove her bloodstains from the white bathroom floor and to straighten up the room that Marion rented. The mansion on the hill, on the other hand, embodies that aspect of Norman that will never be anything more than a boy—his mother's son, trapped, like one of the stuffed animals that populate his office and bedroom, in a psycho-dynamic correspondence within the parallel terrains of his mother's tyrannical will and Victorian living quarters. Similar to the male narrators in Poe's tales of terror, Norman Bates simply cannot and does not subsist for long outside the physical sphere of his childhood. It is clear that just as house and motel no longer function as either a viable home or business, Norman inhabits a personal chaos world where he is not child, man, or mother—even as he tries to be all three.

Which brings us, finally, to the swamp. Somewhere behind the motel, or off to its side, or perhaps in back of the house itself, lurks a very deep swamp. Norman employs it for the disposal of at least two bodies and two automobiles, and the film concludes with one of the cars being dredged from its depths. *Psycho*'s audience is provided a fairly accurate awareness of spatial relationships on the set of the film. We know, for example, that the Bateses' mansion is perched up on a hill and that the motel is located in front of the house at the base of the hill and to the immediate right of the mansion itself. What remains totally unclear throughout the film, however, is where the swamp is located in relation to the rest of the property. I think this is not to be overlooked—the swamp's spatial ambiguity—for it corresponds to that part of Norman that is unrealized in the course of the picture: his unconscious. The mansion, with its clear invocations of Victorian maternal authority, is most obviously linked to Norman's superego; it is the place where he is most repressed. The motel, as I have already alluded, corresponds to Bates's ego, as he struggles in his role as the hotel's manager to present some kind of acceptable social persona, as ineffectual as it may be, for operating in the world. The invisible swamp, on the other hand, contains all the destructive and impulsive energies associated with the Freudian id. Here is where Norman deposits the nude and plundered body of Marion, the money she has stolen, and the officious detective. The swamp hides and is associated with all the libidinal and self-destructive impulses that compel the Norman-mother amalgamation into tumultuous action throughout the film.

Raymond Durgnot's psychoanalytical reading of *Psycho* poses a provocative association between "Marion's dead face settled upside down below the toilet bowl [and] her car, her surrogate body, sinking into the black ooze. To cite a popular idiom, she's in deep shit" (140). What Durgnot does not make clear, however, is how the affiliation among excrement, swamp, and wet female nakedness is specific to Norman's peculiar psychosexuality. The "ooze" of all three certainly underscores Norman's inability to deal with Marion as a sexual being, but in psychoanalytic terms it may also underscore his failure to evolve beyond the anal stage. Moreover, the choice of selecting to kill her in the shower raises many interesting questions, such as: Why the shower when there are other opportunities? Why not murder Marion when she is alone in her room wearing black lingerie, or later, when she will be asleep? There appears to be something about Marion's nakedness—her ultimate vulnerability inside a warm shower—that motivates Norman into awful action. If Durgnot's Freudian connections are kept in mind, perhaps Norman, stuck in the anal stage of development, chooses to kill Marion at the very moment when she is furthest from the filth of excrement, cleansing herself with soap and water. Further, his decision to kill Marion when she is most relaxed and defenseless parallels Norman's lack of pity and remorse in disposing of her still naked corpse in the trunk of her car, and then burying both in the dark swamp. These choices do more than reveal Norman's cruel inhumanity; they point the way to the severity of his psychopathology.

At the risk of sounding like the psychiatrist at the end of Hitchcock's picture, reading *Psycho* psychoanalytically is crucial to making any sense of the film. For the mother-murderer figure that Norman constructs is not an accurate reflection of his actual mother's behavior. As oppressive a figure as we suspect her to have been, there is no evidence that she ever committed murder. It is Norman's *interpretation and reconstruction* of her fury filtered through his own unconscious desires—to possess and vanquish Marion sexually, to thwart the masculine authority figure that Arbogast represents, and Norman's own Oedipal guilt and rage toward self-destruction, all operating simultaneously—that constructs the deadly amalgamation Bates summons from the unfathomable swamp of his unconscious.

In discussing the issue of Norman's motherly identification, Durgnat believes that "Mrs. Bates' tirade is Norman haranguing himself" (99). Certainly this is literally true, as Marion and the audience hear Norman off camera appropriating Mrs. Bates's language and voice, but what is just as important is what Norman actually says, as the language he employs to re-animate his mother's presence goes beyond Durgnat's "crazy quilt of fantasy, memory and quotes from disorganized readings" (99). Employing his mother's voice, Norman scolds both Marion and himself for inviting "a strange woman" into the house to eat his mother's food and indulge his "cheap erotic fantasies." This is a much more specific rant than Durgnat acknowledges, as it attacks both women and sexuality. It is a sexually repressive rejoinder that has much more in common with the 1950s than it does with the decade in which *Psycho* was released. Moreover, Norman's sexually-charged diction prepares the viewer for the violent reaction he will soon summon as a consequence of seeing Marion in her black underwear and the naked wetness of her shower.

Norman's fragmented psyche is not only reflected in the various Gothic places featured in *Psycho*, but it is also evident in his response to Marion in the famous shower scene. At the same time that he desires Marion sexually (the shower murder is preceded by his voyeuristic spying through the peephole in his office and is, for Robin Wood, "a violent substitute for the rape that Norman dare not carry out" [*Hitchcock* 120], his perverse affiliation with his mother creates the need to punish himself and Marion for inciting this sexual urge. The murder itself, then, is sexual at the same time that it is punitive, as it immediately follows his obvious arousal in watching Marion undress. Norman's sexual frustration is evidenced in his phallic thrusts of the knife piercing Marion's naked torso; that part of Norman that identifies with his mother, though, punishes both the son's heterosexual desire and seeks to attack as well the object and inspiration of this desire. At the risk of complicating this swampy Freudian conundrum to the point of a migraine, that part of Norman still operative when dressed in Mother-drag may also wish to attack Marion because she is female and thus is linked to the mother for whom Norman harbors such strong ambivalent feelings. The shower murder also creates a split tension in the viewer as well. Marion's violation is both violent and pornographic; it is too erotic not to watch, but at the same time, too horrific to enjoy.

In his essay "The Uncanny," Freud defines the term "uncanny" as something that arouses dread, horror, or fear within an individual. Most of these fears appear to be baseless, yet they are things that nonetheless affect us. Examples of the uncanny include inanimate objects becoming animate, which is usually uncanny for adults but not for children; things that cannot be identified as dead or alive, such as robots or the undead; doppelgänger, dismemberment, disfigurement of any kind, but especially of the face; and the repetition of certain numbers or words, such as the association of "666" with the demonic. The uncanny is an idea that can take shape in many different ways in a horror film. It has become a popular paradigm for analyzing the genre because some of the most frightening ideas come from objects that are simultaneously known and familiar, yet when forced to assume a different shape and meaning are thereby transformed into something unfamiliar and strange. In *Psycho*, constructions of the uncanny center on the slippery identity of Norman Bates. His transvestism is uncanny in itself, as he assumes the role of the female when he should be operating within the boundaries of masculinity. What makes his feminization truly uncanny, however, is that he selects to dress as an older woman, a grandmother-type with frazzled gray hair and flowing dress. In the shower scene, when we are first introduced to this figure, the shape of the woman is overshadowed by her upraised butcher's knife. While the camera works to portray the utter terror of a beautiful woman interrupted in her shower, it is the presence of a mother-murderer that truly evokes Freud's conceptualization of the uncanny. The thrusting of the butcher's knife, Marion's screams, the violins, the blood running down the drain, and the mother-killer, who murders and then immediately exits, suddenly shatter the familiar portrait of a figure typically perceived as loving and nurturing. Analytically, the spectator's affiliations with the maternal—particularly the image of an older woman wearing a dress with her hair in a bun—are simultaneously undercut by her raised arm bearing the murderous blade. This moment will, of course, be made even more uncanny when the maternal figure will later reveal itself to be Norman, but the point is that *Psycho*'s shower scene illustrates

Freud's conceptualization of the uncanny while demonstrating how a horror film works to subvert the audience's perceptions and expectations.

Hitchcock's skill in direction is clearly evident in this famous murder sequence. Although the audience is pulled into the scene at the moment when Norman-mother pulls back the shower curtain to expose the naked Marion, we never actually see the knife puncture her body, nor are her breasts or genital area ever in view. The scene is all filmed through montage. Horror films that follow *Psycho*—the slasher genre in particular—will focus explicitly on the body, especially the female body, being ripped open. Hitchcock films the murder of Marion Crane, as Diana Fuss points out, to create the impression of "a knife slashing, as if tearing at the very screen, ripping the film" (*Identification Papers* 90). While *Psycho* is obviously more restrained in this exposition (highlighting the film's tension with industry Decency Codes, straining to conform to the demand for censorship even as it pushes against it), the picture nonetheless literally pulls back the curtain on the body's privacy. The editing terms used in cinematography—*cuts, splices, sutures*—suggest the parallel capacity horror filmmakers share with serial killers to investigate the human body, to dissect it and reassemble it in ways that reflect their immediate needs. From this point on in cinematic history, not only will the female body serve as a locus for terror, the bathroom itself, the place where Marion is so unceremoniously revealed and dissected, is likewise initiated as a baleful location in the horror film.

The bathroom represents the most "Gothic" space in most homes; water pipes and sewage lines form a direct conduit to the underworld. Further, activities are preformed within the room's space that is both idiosyncratic and not meant to be shared in public. At the moment when Marion's relaxing shower is so abruptly interrupted, in an event that again relies heavily upon Freud's identification of the uncanny, Hitchcock signals to the world that a location formerly as private and unthreatening as a bathtub could no longer be trusted. The fact that horror is capable of invading such sites means that no one is safe anywhere. From this point on, horror movies return again and again to the bathroom as a means for commenting on the way in which the horrific and the supernatural possess the ability to invade and displace the commonplace. For example, the most important moments in Stanley Kubrick's *The Shining* occur inside well-lit and sanitized bathrooms where the hotel "speaks" to and through characters in visual and verbal communications; the best sequence in Lawrence Kasden's otherwise regrettable movie, *Dreamcatcher*, takes place when the monster attempts to introduce itself by displacing a character seated on a toilet; while in Jonathan Demme's *The Silence of the Lambs*, Clarice Starling discovers a bathtub filled with the grisly remains of one of Jame Gumb's female victims just as the lights go out. The conveniently timed blackout saves both Starling and the audience from deeper examination into the tub's hideous contents, but nonetheless serves to whet the spectator's appetite for visceral horror in scenes still to come. *Psycho* not only provided the horror film with a new frontier in its unflinching exploration into the shadowy psychopathologies of the human mind, it also gave new license to explore forbidden places the camera had never before dared to expose.

Torturing the Women in Daylight: *The Birds*

In addition to their mutual desire to unnerve the spectator, *Psycho* and *The Birds* share analogous ground insofar as both films rely on abrupt plot shifts and unanticipated occurrences. *Psycho's* heroine is brutally dispatched a third of the way through the film, while in *The Birds*, the aggressiveness of multiple bird species is never wholly explained or justified. At least when Norman-Mrs. Bates attacks Marion in the shower, we understand eventually that it is provoked less by Marion herself than it is by what she represents; in *The Birds*, however, there is no apparent justification or logic associated with the sudden ornithological assaults—thereby rendering them as another example of Hitchcock's use of the uncanny—as innocent children are victimized as well as adults. Both pictures appear to operate in a God-abandoned universe where rational order and benevolence—human as well as natural—have been usurped and replaced by an absurd principle of cosmic chaos. Moreover, the action in both films is set in motion by two of Hitchcock's emboldened blonde females who draw our attention to themselves because of their willingness to violate the social order. Marion sleeps with her lover outside the sanctioned marriage bed, and she steals for him to lighten a financial burden that keeps him from marrying her. Melanie, in turn, is the catalyst for all the conflicts that are initiated when she descends on Bodega Bay in pursuit of a romantic relationship with Mitch Brenner. Melanie thus shares something in common with the aggressive seagull that attacks her for no apparent reason. Hitchcock's two films are linked further by birds of prey; while Norman's taxidermy may not include the gulls and sparrows that Hitchcock deliberately featured in *The Birds*, the more aggressive species featured in the Bateses' motel aviary certainly foreshadow the black crows that assemble ominously on the school exercise equipment prior to their attack on Melanie Daniels and the students fleeing Annie Hayworth's classroom. Indeed, Norman himself is a bird of prey when dressed in his mother's identity: His knife thrusts that kill Marion anticipate the sharp bird beaks that nearly slice Melanie to death in *The Birds*.

Although Mrs. Bates remains literally invisible throughout *Psycho*—as only her dress, hair, and rotting skeleton ever appear on camera—her anima is omnipresent throughout the film via Norman. In contrast, Mrs. Brenner in *The Birds* is very much a physical presence in this picture, but her influence over Mitch, her son, is always more subtle than the deathless scolding associated with the dead Mrs. Bates. Nonetheless, both mothers exert tremendous power over their respective sons, and several Hitchcock scholars have made much of the fact that the conflicts in both films hinge on the mutual problem of unresolved Oedipal fixations between sons and their mothers. In each of these movies, Paula Marantz Cohen points out, "The mother, or rather the idea of the mother in the imagination of the child, becomes central to the plot, a powerful obstacle to the union of the hero and heroine" (143). Margaret M. Horwitz concurs in her own psychoanalytic study, contending, "that in *The Birds*, as in *Psycho*, the heroine is punished by the hero's mother because of the heroine's desirability to him" (279). In *The Birds*, it appears that Mitch's case of arrested development centers as much on the extremely comfortable "nest" he has created in his mother's home—he visits her every weekend despite having an apartment in San Francisco—as it does on the level of attention he shows her, while Norman's mother-problem is, of course, much more ambiguously complex and volatile. Mitch's bond with Mrs. Brenner still manages to inhibit the development of his romantic connection with Melanie, who stalks him with the same relentless attention of the birds that descend on the town and its citizens.

If we acknowledge that there is no scientific explanation for the supernaturalism of the birds (and why only birds? Why not dogs and cats, or even the fish in the bay?), the film leaves the spectator with no other choice than to identify bad bird behavior with the sudden arrival of Melanie into the Bodega Bay community. She is the first to be attacked when a gull swoops down to nip her head after she has crossed the bay. Her arrival commences the full-scale violence from the birds, and the attacks grow in intensity and potency the longer she remains in town. She is usually the first person to notice the birds gathering or fluttering prior to an attack, as when they assemble outside the schoolyard or upstairs in the Brenner house. Additionally, the majority of the assaults that occur take place in her presence; she is either the principal victim (e.g., she is nearly pecked to death in a Brenner bedroom) or is an eyewitness to the airborne harassment against other humans, as in the scene where she is trapped inside a telephone booth when the gas pumps blow up and the town becomes unraveled.

Nearly everything about Melanie Daniels is affected. When the movie opens and we are introduced to her, she appears striding down a San Francisco street, the epitome of urban chic: long, black leather gloves over manicured fingernails, high stiletto heels that match a couture suit and elongated purse, platinum blonde hair swept up into an impeccable coiffure, perfect makeup. She is the prototype for Paris Hilton, a "Daddy's girl" patrician child of wealth and privilege whose newspaper-owner father sends her off to Rome to "find herself" by hanging out with "a wild crowd" and partying naked in public fountains. When Mitch meets her we learn that she has recently been forced to answer legal charges regarding the breaking of a window that resulted from one of her "practical jokes."

Camille Paglia tends to view Melanie's character as a protofeminist rebelling against the strictures of the 1950s, a "representative of modern female liberation" (29). A less generous and more critical judgment sees her as a woman who expects and is accustomed to the world conforming to her way of experiencing it. In the movie's second scene, Daniels hires a motorboat that she commands alone across the bay in perfect makeup and wearing a full-length fur coat, suede gloves, and her signature stiletto heels. After the gull attacks her in the boat, she lies to Mitch about attending school with Annie as well as the reason for her trip to Bogeda Bay. In summary, the introductory sequences featuring Melanie Daniels are not very positive. Although pictured as a regal beauty, they also reveal her to be a spoiled rich girl who does whatever she wants to get her way—in short, the epitome of an *unnatural*, highly cosmeticized woman out of place in rural nature who not only dresses inappropriately for where she is, but also behaves in a manner that draws immediate attention to herself (each time she enters the Bogeda Bay café, patrons freeze in mid-chew and are transfixed by her presence).

Daniels's arrival in Bogeda Bay might be termed as a kind of "attack" upon the community of the Brenner home and the town itself. While Mitch finds himself increasingly attracted to her, his widowed mother, Lydia, wishes to be rid of her as soon as possible. Melanie's intrusion severely disrupts Annie's world as well because the latter is still in love with Mitch. The unnatural disruptions caused by the birds, then, parallel the unnatural disruptions that attend Melanie's introduction into the microcosm of the small California town and its citizens. After the assault on the gas station, one of the residents claims that "when you got here, the whole thing started. I think you are the cause of all this. I think you're evil." Melanie is right to slap the hysterical woman in response to this suspicion because it is only partly true, as it fails to account for what happens to Daniels in the course of her visit.

We first sense that this is a woman with potential greater than that of mere fashion bimbo just before the bird attack at Cathy's birthday party. While touring the dunes sipping martinis with Mitch, Melanie surprises both her host and the viewer with her poignant and nearly tearful self-revelation that she is desperately searching for "meaning" in her life. This moment is different from any that precedes it; we know that this confession is no lie, that she has deliberately dropped her haughty bravada, and that her charity efforts to "send a little Korean boy through school" or to enroll in a semantics class at Berkeley have been well intentioned but ultimately superficial. Each of these efforts, however, bespeaks a woman searching for greater purpose to her life that extends beyond what Spoto aptly calls her "social and intellectual dilettantism" (334).

The "bird war" forces Melanie to confront change, to open herself to the possibility of needs that exist beyond her own immediate gratification and the practical jokes of a bored and narcissistic rich girl. This change is appropriately signaled in the slow deconstruction of Melanie's made up face and attire in the second half of the film. Although her wardrobe is restricted to the single green suit she brought with her on this trip, she is not afraid of looking disheveled (at least as much as Tippi Hedren could *ever* look disheveled) as she helps Mitch nail wooden boards over the windows and doorways in preparation for the next airborne assault. She grows less and less concerned with her makeup—indeed, she stops checking her face in her compact mirror and during the attack at the Brenner house she wears no lipstick—and her hair is often pictured coming loose from the tight chignon she maintained at the start of the film. After her attack in the Brenner bedroom, her manicured fingernails are chipped and broken. More importantly, by the end of the picture, Melanie has befriended Mitch's sister and mother (Melanie even comforts Cathy when she is sick and Mrs. Brenner is rendered helpless because of her own terror), and it is clear that Daniels has gained in both maturity and humility. Her relationship with Mitch progresses from adolescent flirting to sincere adult affection; indeed, the crisis with the birds brings them together in their shared struggle and suffering as a purifying ordeal that dismantles all their former artifice. Like the lovebirds in the cage who appear immune to the aggressiveness of the other birds, Hitchcock himself has noted that "love is going to survive the whole ordeal" and "that little couple of lovebirds lends an optimistic note to the theme" (Truffaut 218).

If the birds' violent interactions with humans are meant to underscore Melanie's aggressive behavior in the first half of the film, by the time the Brenner family makes its escape out of Bodega Bay at the picture's end, Melanie's character transformation is painfully and literally apparent. Horwitz offers a convincing explanation in linking the wild birds with a "maternal anxiety which seeks to punish any form of sexual expression" (282), but Hitchcock's gender conservatism would prefer the film's supernaturalism to extend further than Horwitz's assertion of "[f]emale hysteria connected with the wild birds" (284). Indeed, Horwitz's reading never does account for the fact that the birds attack *everyone*, including Lydia and Annie, who purportedly orchestrate and direct the assault against Melanie. Rather than an exclusively female collusion against Melanie, the "bird war" is an even larger indictment sent from nature itself that maintains a central attack locus upon Melanie, but extends to include anyone within her immediate proximity (which explains why the Brenner house appears to be singled out by so many birds at the end of the film).

Melanie's behavior has subverted Hitchcock's paradigm of the fundamental division separating masculine and feminine. As a consequence, the natural order rebels supernaturally until Melanie's transgression against the gender structure is corrected, and she reassumes her "rightful place" in the patriarchal order. Although still lovely, at the conclusion of the picture, she is no longer the prideful sorority queen who engaged in such aggressive verbal repartee with Mitch. Chastened, and even more importantly, silenced by the trauma she has undergone, Daniels has now become a marriageable female, and her place in the Brenner family is signaled in Mrs. Brenner's maternal embrace in the back seat of Melanie's sports car that Daniels is, significantly, no longer driving. Perhaps this is also why the assembled birds permit Daniels and the Brenners to escape at the end of the film: Melanie exits successfully declawed, the gender status quo reaffirmed. If the earlier *Rear Window* concludes with masculine and feminine role definitions left decidedly open and fluid, *The Birds* does not; the latter film insists upon rigid gender role modeling that is highlighted as early as Cathy Brenner's easily overlooked comment about identifying the two lovebirds as a "husband" and a "wife."

One aspect of *The Birds* that is of noteworthy commentary in the context of the horror genre is Hitchcock's desire to film the major ornithological attacks in broad daylight. Unlike the horror stories of Poe, which invariably take place at midnight, or the impenetrable veil of darkness that becomes the atmospheric backdrop for horror movies from *Frankenstein* to *Halloween*, the most terrifying events in *The Birds* break against genre tradition and occur in open spaces during bright daylight. This approach deserves critical attention for several reasons. First, and perhaps most obviously, providing such clarity to the assault only serves to deepen our own confusion about it. Unlike the single wayward bird that breaks its neck against Annie's front door early in the film, the other attacks cannot be explained away as possible examples of birds getting lost in rural darkness or bay fog. Furthermore, actually *seeing* masses of birds assemble on school exercise equipment or, as in the last sequence of the film, clustered, waiting atop telephone wires and poles, suggests that while their violence cannot be explained rationally, the birds nonetheless possess some capacity for interspecies communication, at least with one another. These occurrences, coupled with the fact that the birds are brazen enough to vent their fury in the middle of the afternoon and apparently against only human beings and their possessions—china teacups appear to be particularly vulnerable—serve only to deepen further the spectator's sense of unease. Like Marion's attack in the bathtub, if Melanie Daniels cannot feel safe enough even to smoke a cigarette outside a schoolyard at midday, then no one in this town, or anywhere else for that matter, has any right to feel safe anywhere. These are not, after all, pit bulls unleashed on a vulnerable human community; these are birds, arguably nature's most gentle creations, as the café ornithologist, Mrs. Bundy, points out.

The caged lovebirds frame the opening and closing sequences of the film. In between, it is the human world that finds itself trapped and intimidated inside caged spaces—telephone booths, automobiles, bedrooms, and barricaded homes—while the ornithological world acts with the kind of irrational violence and random cruelty that typically distinguishes human behavior from that of the animal kingdom. In other words, Hitchcock's film essentially challenges and reverses what we know to be true. Indeed, a film that begins as a 1960s romantic comedy—think of Rock Hudson and Doris Day—is undercut by the horror ordeal of its second half. Typically, the horror film preys upon our personal and collective insecurities. Perhaps reflecting the sea change that takes place in Melanie's character over the course of the movie, *The Birds* extends this maxim one better by preying upon what we *thought* was most secure, undermining the very reality we assume to be true.

Terrors from Beyond

The Day the Earth Stood Still,
Them!, The Alien Movies

The range of the horror genre is most evident in the resiliency of its themes and in its array of topical explorations. Just as the horror film has produced an entire subgenre of cinema devoted to the terrors inherent in claustrophobic examinations of the dysfunctional family and the tortured self, horror is likewise at home in probing fantastic worlds beyond our own. If films such as *Vertigo* and *Psycho* speak to us of the tragic flaws associated with being a monstrous human, *The Day the Earth Stood Still* and the *Alien* saga manage to discuss similar concerns from thousands of miles away. In other words, while the horror film is capable of telescoping itself into scenarios that are as radically disparate as an American suburban family battling evil forces inside their television and a spaceship commanded by aliens, the genre still typically circles back to core concerns: Defining humanity in the face of monstrosity and the monstrous as it is defined within humanity.

Horror art has revealed its adaptability in so many ways and over the course of so many years; in part because of its longevity, the horror film has influenced other cinematic genres to the point where immoderate injections of horror have produced unholy amalgamations, hybrid intricacies that bleed the lines of recognizable cinematic genres: the Gothic-thriller (*Taking Lives, Dressed to Kill, Sleeping with the Enemy, Single White Female*); the detective-noir-horror (*Seven, Chinatown, Blade Runner, The Bone Collector*); the comedic-horror (*Ghostbusters, Young Frankenstein, Scary Movie, Scooby-Do, Cursed*); Gothic-anime (*Legends of the*

Overfiend, Cowboy Beebop, Ghost in the Shell); the horror-musical (*The Rocky Horror Picture Show, Tanz der Vampire, Dracul: The Musical, Buffy the Vampire Slayer: Once More with Feeling*); dark fantasy (the *Batman* movies, *The Lord of the Rings, The Day After Tomorrow, The Nightmare Before Christmas*); juvenile-horror (the *Harry Potter* movies); the Gothic-Western (*The Unforgiven, The Quick and the Dead, From Dusk till Dawn*); and even the Gothic-gangster story (where the excessive and graphic levels of violence and the bifurcated persona of Tony Soprano, whose conflicted character constantly blurs the distinctions separating villain and victim, force *The Sopranos* to adhere as much to the paradigm of the gothic melodrama as to the prototypical gangster movie).

Of all the various hybrid genres that have been produced from horror's proliferate mergings, however, it is the techno-horror film that has arguably garnered the most titles and produced some of the worst and best adaptations of modern horror art. As the general history of the techno-horror film has evolved, it has tended to illustrate the impotence of science in the face of monumental problems it has tried to solve but only succeeded in exacerbating further. The most memorable of these movies pose some unsettling answers to the distinctly modern question of whether man is of nature or above it. In films such as *The Stand, The Terminator, Blade Runner, Minority Report*, and the *Alien* movies, corporate and governmental bureaucracies join with science to create an unholy tryst. The more sophisticated our scientific knowledge and machinery become, the greater our potential for losing control over them. In many of the first techno-horror films produced during the halcyon years of the 1950s, for example, technological advance was intended to aid in civilization's progress—as in the advent of nuclear energy or the exploration of space—but this technology inevitably turns out to be a curse, unleashing radioactive monsters from the earth's core and creatures from deep space. When mated with the technological hardware of science fiction, horror again serves to remind us of worst-case scenarios: the danger of tinkering with unnatural organisms, the dream of progress that must genuflect before reality, the potential burden of opening doors to knowledge we only partially understand, and the immorality of pursuing scientific research that is misused for corporate profit and military superiority.

It is important to note that the techno-horror film is a particular expression of just one culture—Western civilization (and Japan). The subgenre does not exist in India, Iran, China, Indonesia, or Egypt—all countries with flourishing and multigenre cinemas (Sardar 2). The techno-horror film reflects the particular anxieties of the developed world transformed through technological advances that have occurred—and continue to occur—with such speed that the implications of each new advance cannot be comprehended, much less assimilated, fully. Thus, techno-horror cinema highlights the darker aspects of Western material and scientific progress. The various oversized monsters that came stomping or oozing across the screen in the 1950s embody a range of Cold War anxieties including our collective fears about radiation; a paranoia about government, corporate, and military mismanagement of power; and the general collapse of a stable and comprehensible social matrix. It is no accident that the techno-horror film is the dominant expression of horror art in the 1950s immediately following the release of the atomic bomb, manned explorations of deep space, and the advent of Cold War politics. As Paul Wells suggests, "the United States had created its own monsters, and needed to understand them" (59). The films that attempt to do this may begin with a premise that originated in deep space or far under the earth's crust, but in nearly every case the resultant mutant or monster forces the consequences of its existence to be dealt with by humans living in communities immediately threatened by the alien intruder.

The place to begin this discussion is, unfortunately, with the acknowledgment that most of the techno-horror films produced in the 1950s, like the proliferation of Gothic novels in the 1790s, are failures as works of art by any aesthetic criterion and undeserving of much critical attention. Discussing the space-horror genre in a chapter of *Danse Macabre* entitled, "The Horror Movie as Junk Food," Stephen King asks the pertinent question: "Why have there been so many bad horror movies?" (206). King's answer is "exploitation," by which he means the tendency of filmmakers to exploit a concept until it is bereft of all artistic value and becomes a self-parody. Certainly King has seen his own work similarly exploited by Hollywood to a point at which the multiple celluloid sequels of *Children of the Corn* no longer resemble in the least the original short story of the same name. However, exploitations into space and radioactively inflating the insects that reside under the surface of the earth arguably have produced the most blatant and extensive "junk food" of any of horror's multiple subgenres.

While the giant bug and atomic creature features from the 1950s supplied the prototype for the provocative *Alien* series that would follow, the techno-horror genre also produced a series of regrettable movies such as *The Giant Spider Invasion*, *The Deadly Mantis*, *The Blob*, and *It Came from Outer Space*. Their primary audience consisted of male teenagers hoping to capitalize on general feminine squeamishness toward bugs at summer drive-ins. Less flippantly, these pictures speak to us of scientific intrusions and/or blunders that have resulted in the release of mutated insects and assorted space monsters. Although their general campiness tends to incite a contemporary audience more to laughter than fear, a few of these early films from the great beyond—*The Day the Earth Stood Still*, *Forbidden Planet*, and *Invasion of the Body Snatchers*, for example—manage to transcend the limitations of their generic brethren and anticipate and even influence later, more successful cinematic efforts such as *E.T.: The Extraterrestrial*, *The Terminator* series, and *28 Days Later*.

Invaded for Our Own Good:
The Day the Earth Stood Still

Midway through arguably the best techno-horror film to emerge from the 1950s, electrical fields all across the planet are suspended for thirty minutes in a planned show of force orchestrated by Klaatu, a space emissary from an advanced civilization who has landed on earth. His mission is to warn us of the impending doom that will accompany continuance of our aggressive forays into space and weapons proliferation: "Soon one of your nations will apply atomic energy to spaceships. That will create a threat to the peace and security of other planets. That, of course, we cannot tolerate. By threatening danger, your planet faces danger." Two things are of immediate relevance in Klaatu's message: First, that it is delivered in Washington, D.C., subtly indicting the United States as the most aggressive nation on the earth and thus in need of the most dire warning. Second, in demonstrating his own capacity to enforce his message, Klaatu chooses to highlight the world's reliance on electricity. By shutting down the power grid and making the earth stand still, the alien indicates that the most important feature that separates superpowers from developing nations, and thereby poses the greatest threat to the universe, is technology itself—without electricity, technology (and, by extension, the atomic threat) is essentially negated.

Throughout the film, Klaatu's criticism regarding the violent propensities of human interaction is justified in various acts of escalating human violence. It is noteworthy to point out that each act of violence directed at Klaatu is male generated. The film is highly critical of testosterone-driven aggression, and it is therefore appropriate that the only humans who provide Klaatu with any measure of comfort and support are Helen, her adolescent child, Bobby, and the "misunderstood" mathematician. Woman, child, and intellectual are able to bond with the alien because they, too, are aliens in this society of militaristic authority and cultural exclusivity. At the end of the film, Helen learns a painful truth about her fiancé that parallels her government's response to Klaatu: Compassion is reserved only for those we recognize as being exactly like us; any one else is exterminable. Klaatu's longest and most revealing dialogues take place with young Bobby because the alien is himself childlike. He maintains the same level of awe that a child feels about discovering new worlds; he cannot understand why his simple message is so difficult for earthlings to appreciate; he trades Bobby two priceless diamonds in exchange for two dollars; and his innocent and trusting nature leaves Klaatu open to experiencing repeated acts of violent abuse and betrayal.

Although released in 1951, *The Day the Earth Stood Still* has aged well as it still raises many disturbing truths. When the alien spacecraft lands in Washington, the government's exclusive and nearly automatic response is to send for the police and the army—heavily fortified with tanks, artillery, and machine guns—even before a clear threat to the nation is ascertained or a military show of force appears warranted. The potential violence inherent in this overreaction serves to underscore the reason why Klaatu has undertaken this mission in the first place. When he disembarks from the spaceship, the soldiers respond by raising their guns and aiming them at Klaatu. When he reaches inside his spacesuit to extract a token of friendship, an exotic gift for the president that will allow him to study other galaxies, one of the soldiers shoots him in the chest. Again, the significance of this scene is important to note. The unarmed alien's token of friendship is misconstrued by a nation accustomed to greeting strangers skeptically and with quick aggression. The symbolic opportunity to view life in alien galaxies is forfeited (the device is broken when Klaatu is shot) in favor of remaining self-enclosed and self-insulated (the army constructs a wooden fence that encircles the spacecraft and also encases Klaatu's robot in a thick block of plastic). Although easily overlooked in the larger design of the movie, the device that Klaatu wishes to present to the president is a priceless gift with unlimited potential to inspire and advance the celestial imagination. No one laments or apologizes for its destruction, indicating that no human in the film is capable of appreciating the opportunity that has been wasted; the same can be said about the general failure to appreciate the uniqueness of Klaatu's personality and long-distance message.

The massive extermination of human life so recently experienced in World War II and Korea appear to have taught Americans of the film's generation very little about the dangers inherent in an armed response to a differing ideology. It is interesting to note that in so many of the techno-horror films that emerged from the 1950s, the immediate response to an invasion of any kind is to trust in a military solution, rather than resort to any kind of political diplomacy. As Per Schelde argues, in the 1950s, "portraying the military in heroic terms was still the norm" (94), and in many techno-horror films, such as *Them!* and *The Thing*, the earth is saved only because of prompt military intervention. This shows just how radical and prophetic a film *The Day the Earth Stood Still* is, as it remains one of the few films from its era where all forms of patriarchal authority are suspect, particularly the military and the governmental officials who share in a collusion of ignorance. Indeed, much like the American soldiers who are so quick to raise their weapons against the spaceman, politicians from across the planet are unwilling even to sit down together and discuss whatever message the alien has come to impart. The president himself sends a courier to meet Klaatu in his place. All this impotent bureaucratic representative is capable of doing, however, is lamenting the general stubbornness among worldly leaders and the profound provincialism of the human race.

As the ultimate outsider from another planet, the American response to Klaatu is to capture or destroy the outsider, and eventually he is hunted down and murdered by overzealous soldiers serving a xenophobic society whose first impulse is to kill whatever is foreign or different. Half a century before September 11, 2001, the military has already assumed the position as the point guard for interacting with cultures Americans neither understand nor care to get to know; the film is an indictment of the way in which Americans interact with all strangers, human as well as extraterrestrial. The alien underscores the danger of allowing us to be so inadequately represented in his address to the scientists assembled at his spaceship where he is finally able to present his admonition: "The test of any such higher authority [i.e., civilization] is of course the police force that supports it." Little wonder that long ago the people of Klaatu's society decided to abandon all forms of armed aggression, self-policing themselves with robots such as Gort, who are programmed to react "at the first sign of violence automatically against the aggressor." Gort is the ultimate product of enlightened science, which is to be distinguished from the unenlightened science that produces the sophisticated but amoral military hardware on planet Earth that threatens interstellar space. In other films from this generation, science operates in a similarly bifurcated fashion. While it has produced, however unwittingly and indirectly, the monstrous bugs that attack humankind, the lone scientist is also the one figure sometimes capable, in the wake of military impotence, of finding a solution to the very monstrosities his science has unleashed from Pandora's box.

Not Everything Buried Remains Repressed: *Them!*

Them! begins promisingly with a high degree of mystery: Two state troopers find a little girl wandering through the New Mexico desert. Searching for the child's parents, the police come across the family trailer with an entire side torn away, as if something huge has clawed its way inside. The confusion is maintained through the first quarter of the film until its resident scientist, Dr. Medford, and his beautiful and brilliant daughter, who is also a Ph.D. in entomology, arrive to assemble the clues and recognize the association between atomic tests held in the desert and the mutated ants, "probably caused by lingering radiation from the atomic bomb."

As is often the case in techno-horror films from the 1950s, the scientist provides the explanation and offers potential solutions to the problem, while the military, or its surrogate representatives—in this case one of the state troopers and an FBI agent—is left to conduct the actual extermination. As Jonathan Lake Crane notes wryly, "In these films, only the scientists and their administrative colleagues kill, only scientists and pencil pushers can save, and only scientists and actuaries will determine our course of survival" (116). It is interesting that while Dr. Medford possesses the scientific insight necessary for reaching important conclusions to the problem at hand, he never passes judgment on the prostituted science that has resulted in these abominations of nature. At the end of the picture he vaguely acknowledges that "opening the door" to studies of the atom will produce consequences we cannot foresee. The job of the scientist in films from the 1950s was never to criticize overtly his country's explorations in space, the pollution of American streams and sewers, and active experiments into splitting the atom; his role was only to find a solution to the devastating results of these ill-advised actions.

One reason for the limits imposed on the academic seers is explained in the unworldly nature of the scientists themselves: They are men who appear never to shower, much less comb their hair, and their brilliance is more than compensated by their inability to function in everyday society. They represent the first generation of geeks, Hollywood's stereotype—confirmed by the general public itself—of the academic intellectual. During the era of American McCarthyism, the only scientist allowed to venture a direct political critique had to come from another planet. In *The Day the Earth Stood Still*, Klaatu's status as a citizen from another galaxy provides him with the freedom of expression glaringly absent in his American scientific colleagues from other techno-horror films of the 1950s; only an intergalactic foreigner is permitted to voice his outrage over the misappropriation of science for military purposes. Indeed, the American public, like the figure of the scientist himself, maintains a subordinate position to the military in these films that is reflected in *Them!*'s broadcast command declaring Marshall Law in Los Angeles: "Your personal safety, the entire safety of the city depends upon your full cooperation with the military authorities." Never mind that these authorities are the same people responsible for producing the threat to communal safety in the first place. This was the military that had, after all, saved the world from the specter of totalitarianism a mere decade earlier; it would take at least another decade for Americans to lose their unqualified faith in the Pentagon's ability to solve problems instead of exacerbating them.

The sole quest in the second half of *Them!* is to locate and destroy the female queens and their egg chambers. The issue at the heart of *Them!* anticipates the monstrous procreative energy that animates all the *Alien* sequels. *Them!* and the *Alien* series share a similar purpose and thematic design, as most of these films feature military personnel spending vast amounts of time and resources tracking down the nests of the monsters they seek to destroy. It is the responsibility of the humans under siege not only to survive their encounters with bug monsters, but also to find a way to thwart the insects' efforts at procreation. Thus, while a Faustian curiosity to experiment with things that are perhaps best left alone (e.g., atomic energy, the desire to domesticate monstrosity for corporate-military purposes) is often responsible for putting humans in jeopardy, somehow a combination of scientific knowledge and old-fashioned American courage in the face of slime and dismemberment allow the human protagonists to triumph over the insect mutants.

The films in the techno-horror genre—even those more silly than threatening—invite us to imagine a monstrous nature that is not merely indifferent to the plight of humankind but actively pursuing its destruction. I would suggest that we would need to go back to epochs of European plagues in order to find another time in history where nature appeared so distinct from—and antagonistic to—all things human. The difference, of course, is that in the Middle Ages, science did not know enough to understand where and why the pestilence originated; in the modern and postmodern techno-horror universe, it is scientific knowledge (and its quest to know even more) that has unleashed what it understands insufficiently to control.

The Ultimate Space Monster: *Alien*

The *Alien* movies owe much to the creature features we have been discussing; in fact, the various metallic insects that populate the *Alien* films are the next generation of space monsters that emerge as a result of advances in FX technology and cinematography, robotics, and makeup design. The first of these movies, *Alien*, was even loosely inspired by a low-budget 1958 picture entitled *It! The Terror from Beyond Space*, while the sequel, *Aliens*, closely resembles *Them!* in its insistence that the humans must focus their attention on destroying the queen monster. Similar to its grotesquely exaggerated creepy-crawly brethren from the 1950s, the Alien is a reptilian-like, parasitic beast that attacks with a relentless violence. It lurks in the shadows and preys on the men and women who must figure out a way to destroy it before it destroys them. So, in this sense, the *Alien* films are the ultimate examples of the creature invasion movie.

While *Alien* should be viewed in the evolutionary trajectory of the creature feature, especially insofar as it features a diabolical monster with a pronounced antipathy toward all humankind, it also bears some important distinctions in its development of the genre. In fact, the *Alien* movies signal a change in techno-horror focus as their plotlines turn away from the menace of what's out there in outer space coming down to pursue us (e.g., *It Came from Outer Space*) and toward the enemy within, what is already inside sharing space with us. In this way, then, the generation of *Alien* films also bears a common emphasis with other horror films about domestic hauntings and demonic familial possession from the 1970s, which will be the focus of the next chapter. While the sci-fi films of the 1950s warned filmgoers to watch the skies, the *Alien* saga suggests that we should watch the airshafts inside the buildings of our own creation. (Indeed, the real enemies in these films are corporate as much as they are extraterrestrial: The human crews stand in as much danger from infiltration by a Company cyborg, deceptive corporation men, or a pre-programmed space computer on board the ship as they do from the Alien itself.) Moreover, unlike the giant insects that infest many of the techno-horror films from the 1950s, there is very little about the physical presence of the Alien creature that is either unintentionally comic or easily dismissed; the Alien has, in contrast to most other techno-horror monsters, aged quite well. Much more than merely a set of pinchers attacking army soldiers and tanks, the Alien is a sleek and crafty killing machine. As Thomas Doherty concludes, the *Alien* series "closed the curtain on the classical era of pods and blobs, bug-eyed monsters and brain eaters, fifty-foot women and space bimbos" (182). After a generation of inflated reptiles and insects, the cinematic monster as true menace instead of rubber exaggeration had returned with a vengeance.

As a more advanced version of the techno-horror monster, the Alien is incredibly difficult to kill. Like the vampire, to which it is also kin, the Alien monster requires human hosts to perpetuate the Alien species; victims are often dispatched by a mouth-within-a-mouth of sharp incisors. Gallardo C. and Smith view the creature as a "hard-core porn version of the vampire whose double-jaws drip KY jelly"; like Dracula, the Alien is a deadly stowaway that kills the crew of the Nostromo one by one (45). The Alien again resembles the vampire in an Otherness that is defined by virtue of its gender blurring. Only the queen in the second picture is gendered female. In the sequence where the Alien embryo emerges from Kane's chest, the monster is a pulsating phallic form aggressively bursting out into the world, but as an adult its gender is harder to locate, as it is primarily identified by its salivating vagina dentata dual mouths that are perpetually thrusting forward and an elongated, svelte body shape. Vaginal and phallic when it assumes its crab-like face hugger incarnation with an intrusive tube, a queen mother in *Aliens*, and alternating phallus-head shaped hunter bearing a vagina dentata mouth in other sequels, the Alien is as elusive in its gender constructions as horror monsters ranging from the vampire to Leatherface. Most interestingly, the gender complications of the Alien parallel those of the human crew itself, especially the shifting dynamic found in *Aliens*.

Sharing yet another trait with the vampire, the Alien is a shape changer, maturing rapidly from egg sac, to fetal crab, to slithering infant, to adult. Despite its enormous size, the adult proves to be extremely agile, stealthlike in its stalkings. Above all else, the Alien readily adapts to its host's habitat, as Ash, the synthetic human in the first picture notes, "It's adapted remarkably well to our environment." In the first film, it hides throughout the ceiling and airshafts, folding its black body into darkened corners and small crannies onboard the ship. In *Aliens*, it manages to take over an entire section of a human life colony. Like the classical horror villains from earlier fiction and film, the Alien is at home in the Gothic subterranean passageways and claustrophobic airshafts of the ship or basement housing that it invades.

After the crew awakens in *Alien*, the film progresses slowly; its pacing requires a patience from the audience, as moments of horror are punctuated by long periods of mundane activity—e.g., eating, navigating the ship, fixing broken machinery onboard, descending to the planet's terrain. The moments of horror in this film literally spring out at the viewer and last for only a second or two before the camera cuts away. The Alien leaps from its egg sac, drops a tail down from an exhaust shaft, or explodes from Kane's stomach. The effect of all this is to make us experience a level of terror similar to that of Ripley and the rest of the human crew: We never obtain more than partial knowledge of the monster because we see only brief and fragmented images of its body throughout the film, and these are all designed to last only for an instant.

The opening of *Alien* presents a languid view of the spaceship as floating Gothic haunted castle. While the *Nostromo*'s crew continues its deep space sleep, we tour the ship's operational consoles and mazelike passageways that will soon become the hiding spots for the invading creature. In most horror films and Gothic novels, the haunted house/castle serves as a vehicle for mirroring the inner psychology of its inhabitants. The protagonist(s) appear trapped within its recesses especially as the house "awakens" to assume an infernal biology of its own. In *Alien*, the *Nostromo* is lost geographically, wandering in space. Soon after its crew awakens, they learn that "this is not our [solar] system," and the distress signal that is being emitted from a nearby planet is placed not to summon the crew, but as a warning to stay away.

An atmosphere of confusion and dislocation greets the crew of the ship shortly after they awaken and discover they are off course. Their geographical disorientation underscores the social fragmentation within the crew itself, as the individuals are clearly demarcated according to class: The machinists, Parker and Brett, work with their hands below and complain about their percentage of the purse (iron ore) that is being transported back to earth; Dallas, the chief officer, makes most of the decisions and confers with Mother, the computer that oversees all of the ship's operations; the two women on board, Ripley and Lambert, second in command and navigator, respectively, signal the gap in class status, as Ripley is a figure of intelligent authority and calm self-discipline, whereas Lambert appears more aligned with Parker and his blue-collar actions. William Paul suggests that *Alien* shares much in common with the World War II combat film insofar as the ship's crew represents a racial diversity and ethnic distribution to convey the sense of a democratic nation. However, the class conflict that emerges in *Alien* undermines the theme of diversity helping to create a cohesive fighting group that characterizes the combat war film; in *Alien*, we find, as Paul notes, "a social microcosm that is in constant danger of pulling apart" (393). The early sequences in the film highlight the gap that exists between the machinists and the executive crew, and this gap parallels the separation that is maintained between the officers in command and the corporation on earth that is financing the expedition of the *Nostromo*.

Naming the corporation's spaceship *Nostromo* is a deliberate allusion to Joseph Conrad's 1904 novel of the same name. The novel concerns the corrupting influence of money, particularly a cache of silver. Centered in the South American wilderness, *Nostromo* is a veiled critique of imperialism and the dangers inherent in sacrificing personal morality for selfish and greedy monetary adventures. Similarly, *Alien* is a science fiction model of corporate imperialism out of control. The film features an unholy alliance among the ship's central computer, Mother; the corporation financing this expedition; and Ash, the synthetic human. As Ripley discovers from Mother, the humans onboard are part of a caste system where the entire crew is deemed expendable; only the Alien is of importance to the corporation as a potential military weapon. Like the shipment of iron ore that was extracted from another planet, *Nostromo* is on an imperialist venture serving the ravenous design of a corporate entity back on earth many miles away.

As a vehicle for carrying out the nefarious will of the Company, Ash is effectively linked to the Alien itself, as both actively seek to undermine and violently dispose of the human crew. Ash admires the monster for its lack of conscience and amorality. He calls it "a perfect organism," which translates, in the lexicon of the cyborg, into the perfect machine, and in the techno-horror genre, machines made by corporations often put humans at risk. Ash tries to kill Ripley the same way that the Alien violates Kane: by sticking a rolled up pornography magazine (tube) down her throat. While the Alien is apparently an organic life form and Ash is a robot, the two would appear to share a similar metallic design and certain machine-like properties. Thus, Ash and the Alien are both linked to the Company by virtue of their mutual disregard for human life and their willingness to exploit humans in order to satisfy a parasitic need. When Ash is destroyed, white fluid spills out of his mouth. Like the Alien, Ash's mouth is the primary site of his abject humanity; it is the fluid secretions of Ash and the Alien that indicate their greatest separation from the flesh-and-blood humans that the monsters—reptilian and corporate—seek to exploit. Human gender is an irrelevant concern for both the creature and the Company that desires to possess it. All of humanity exists to serve the needs of the corporation and the monstrous mother, whether as "expendable" vehicles for bringing exotic life back to earth or as a womb/egg sac necessary for the birthing of baby Aliens.

As discussed in chapter 1, film critic Robin Wood believes that the subtexts of most horror films speak to us on a politically subversive level. If his theoretical paradigm is applied to *Alien*, a film released in 1979, then the monster and the parent corporation that desires to own it may be viewed as perfect metaphors for the age of Reagan capitalism: voracious appetites without conscience. Aligned together as they are in the course of the film, the Company and the Alien exploit human workers and ravage their environments. As we will see in *Aliens*, the second film in the series, the monster is a parasitic organism, resembling the Company itself: An entire colony of Aliens takes over the third level of a human installation on the planet LB426, setting up an elaborate system of cocoons where human victims are kept alive to serve as hosts for the Alien reproductive process. The Alien, then, is subtly aligned with the corporate entity that yearns to study it. How many times in the series do we hear a Company representative marvel over the beast as a "magnificent organism" or the chance to possess one as the scientific opportunity of a lifetime? Both monster and Company assume traits that Karl Marx affiliated with the capitalist-vampire. The Alien, like the Company, is similarly devoid of conscience, and its only concern is the perpetuation of a demonic tyranny through the exploitation of the humans that serve its needs.

In contrast to the selfish and exploitative design of the Alien and the Company, however, Ripley emerges as a woman who values life for its own sake and who strives to protect the collective whole. She suggests a feminine presence that counters the corporate paternalism and exploitation of living organisms identified with the Company and Alien. Ripley demands that Kane be quarantined until he can be medically examined in order to preserve the health of the ship's crew. In this film, individual men and women die when they act as individual action heroes: Kane goes exploring into the Alien's domain alone, Dallas does battle against the Alien by himself, Ash disobeys Ripley's order and allows the Alien fetus access to the ship, Parker is distracted by an overzealous need to do personal violence against the monster. That Ripley refuses to sacrifice the cat stands in direct opposition to Mother's command that the crew is expendable. In such a highly technological universe, the cat provides a certain element of normalcy and a connection with the distant earth. The cat also supplies Ripley with the opportunity to express a compassion and humanity that contrasts with the Alien's and the Company's mutual viciousness.

The Woman Warrior: *Aliens*

Many of the issues developed in the first film are revisited in the sequel. As in *Alien*, the spectator waits nearly an hour into the story line of *Aliens* before glimpsing any

Alien life. The weather on the planet is consistently chaotic, featuring strong winds, rain, and thick clouds. The complex where the "terraformers" live is completely abandoned when Ripley and the marines arrive, hinting at the dangerous nature of events. Upon descent to the planet, most of the time is spent following soldiers through abandoned corridors and spaces in search of an explanation for why the colonists of LB426 have abandoned their metallic installation. When the Aliens do attack for the first time, we see them primarily through closed-circuit monitors on the helmets of besieged marines. Thus, the grainy transmission makes it difficult to see exactly why or how humans are perishing, so once again the horror monster remains effectively unseen or highly obscured through nearly the first half of the movie.

Perhaps the most important issue that continues to connect *Alien* and *Aliens* is the pervasiveness of a betrayal theme. The corporation once again betrays Ripley and the soldiers who are sent out to protect its financial interests, prompting Ripley to remark "I don't know which species is worse. You don't see them [the Aliens] fucking each other for a percentage"; the commanding lieutenant, Gorman, fails to follow Ripley's insistence to pull his troops out when under attack the first time (he later redeems himself through a suicidal sacrifice); Burke, like Ash, is another unethical arm of the corporation, and he releases the Alien pods hoping one will gestate in Ripley or Newt and return to earth to serve the research interests of the corporation; even Ripley herself betrays an unspoken promise to the Queen Alien not to destroy her eggs.

Emerging in contrast to all these acts of betrayal is Ripley's unwavering loyalty to Newt and the promise that she will not leave her. Painfully aware of her failure to fulfill a pledge to attend a birthday party made to her biological daughter who died two years earlier, Ripley embraces Newt as a surrogate daughter (Newt spelled backward resembles "Twin."). This second promise to protect an orphaned daughter becomes the central motivator in Ripley's battle against the mother Alien. Curiously, Ripley shares a maternal bond with the Alien mother. The latter calls off the Alien drones, allowing Newt and Ripley to pass freely through the recently established egg bed for fear of having the pods disturbed. When Ripley burns them in her escape, the infuriated mother Alien pursues Newt and Ripley back to the spaceship.

The film begins in support of a variety of phallic images and masculine attitudes: the penile shape of the ship that transports the marines and Ripley into space, the corporation's uncompromising will to protect its interests, the huge guns that the marines carry, and even the fact that Ripley is treated as inferior to the soldiers onboard the ship and relegated to the periphery of the action (other than Ripley, the only other female onboard, Vasquez, is gendered extremely butch and holsters a flamethrower, the biggest weapon on the ship). Sergeant Apone further reveals that the marines view this mission in insolent and phallocentric terms when he declares, "There will be colonists' daughters we have to rescue from their virginity." As the film unfolds, however, all the men are destroyed or incapacitated, their phallic technology is futile in the face of the massive Alien assault, and Ripley emerges as the survivor-heroine. In short, the film is a kind of feminist techno-horror fable, where masculine values and weaponry prove ineffectual, especially against a matriarchal hive in which a queen-mother and her worker drones are solely dedicated to the perpetration of the species. It is interesting to note that by the conclusion of the movie, all masculine authority is essentially eliminated—men have been pushed to the periphery of the narrative—and the action is exclusively between Ripley and the Alien mother. In fact, the film's mise-en-scène gradually narrows to an ever-more circumscribed world where the human colony has been transformed into a giant incubator (the soldiers complain about the heat being generated in this womb-like installation) and the humans are cocooned in a state of suspended animation in order to serve as surrogate wombs for Alien babies. In a moment that resembles an old-fashioned Western showdown between two gunslingers, Ripley vanquishes the Alien queen not because of her ability to use phallic weapons (which have proved highly ineffectual), but by assuming a facsimile of the Alien shape in wearing a suit of robotic armor. In other words, Ripley inverts the biological design of the parasitic Aliens that require a host organism for gestation; she slips inside the body of the metallic lift and then fights the queen on her own terms, unintentionally anticipating the cloned hybrid that Ripley will become in the final sequel, *Alien Resurrection*. Additionally, Ripley fights with her head, remembering how she dispatched the original Alien in the first film, and once again maneuvers the queen into the spaceship's hatch where she is blasted into deep space. Tim Blackmore believes that the power loader ultimately inhibits Ripley, and that "only by abandoning the machine and relying on her own strength" (220) does she manage to vanquish the Alien queen.

Aliens shares several unique parallels with *The Wizard of Oz*. It features a dark queen that reigns over a fantastic realm surrounded by drones (the flying monkeys) that do her bidding. The Queen Alien, also black in color and clearly the leader of an oppressive regime, is afraid of fire, the inverse of the Wicked Witch of the West's fear of water. Ripley, of course, emerges as the Dorothy figure, who likewise has a pet, a desire to find her way home, and is directed on a dangerous quest by a duplicitous authority figure. Indeed, the Company is equivalent to the Wizard himself, as they are both highly incompetent patriarchal figures that control things from afar. In this scheme, Newt represents the Cowardly Lion as her hair forms a kind of mane around her face, and she is initially fearful of the marines. As the film progresses, however, she learns, like the Lion, to overcome her cowardly ways and becomes a courageous figure; she is, after all, the only colonist who survives.

Assuming the role of the Tin Man in the musical, Hicks, the last remaining survivor of the marines, wears a prominent red heart painted in the middle of his metallic armor; he grows to establish an intimate and respectful bond with Ripley and proves himself as a reliable soldier and friend. Lastly, Bishop, the synthetic human, emerges as the Scarecrow, after Dorothy and Ripley, perhaps the real hero of the movie and musical, respectively. At the conclusion of the film, Bishop's body is torn apart by the Alien queen, and he closely resembles the Scarecrow of Oz after the flying monkeys have pulled the straw out of his body. In many ways, Bishop proves himself to be the smartest of all the earth organisms as he represents the mechanical brains of the crew and directs the mother ship from a computer uplink. At one point, Bishop says to Ripley in language that might have been borrowed from Oz's Scarecrow himself: "I may be synthetic, but I'm not stupid."

Beyond Ripley: *Alien3* and *Alien Resurrection*

Thomas Doherty proposes that the *Alien* stories possess "a harmonious unity with a straight-through trajectory: growing organically, playing off one another, dependent on the previous episode for deep background and emotional wallop" (183). Doherty's summary is convincing insofar as each episode builds on the one before it, but it is important to note that while Ripley and some incarnation of the Alien monster survive in each of the sequels, none of the other characters from earlier films rejoin Ripley when she awakens from the hypersleep that begins each of the new episodes.

Critics who write about the series seem to be in general agreement that the *Alien* films diminish in quality after the original and its immediate sequel. The third and fourth movies extend the premise beyond even the suspended degree of disbelief necessary for most science fiction (how the Alien makes its way on board the ship at the end of *Aliens* and into Ripley herself, for example, is never convincingly explained). Much worse still, the last two films fail to advance the concept in any new or significant direction. Some of this is likely attributable to the fact that each of the four *Alien* movies was directed by a different director, and only the first three movies shared the writing team of David Giler and Walter Hill. Reanimating the incinerated Ripley and Alien queen through DNA splicing in the last installment is especially regrettable because it underscores the degree of exhaustion that typifies the conclusion of the story line; both Lieutenant Ripley and the saga itself deserved more dignified endings.

That said, the *Alien* movies served to advance the techno-horror film by making it relevant for a new generation. Science, the military, and corporate government interests in the *Alien* stories reflect the same misguided intentions that are critiqued in techno-horror prototypes such as *The Day the Earth Stood Still.* Reflecting the patriarchal chain of command, the role of women in the pictures produced in the 1950s was strictly limited to hysterical screaming and a timely rescue by the male hero. Ripley, on the other hand, is a heroine of her time; in fact, one might argue that she is one of the first of Clover's Final Girls, doing battle with a serial killer that is so much more intimidating than either Leatherface or Jason. I hardly think it an exaggeration to suggest that Lieutenant Ripley emerges as one of the great feminist prototypes of postmodern cinema. In each of the *Alien* films, Ripley's potential emerges when patriarchal authority breaks down; Ripley asserts herself when male commanders all fail in their duties, and no one is left in charge. She fills the male leadership vacuum by instructing others on how to fight the Alien, informing them about the monster's patterns of behavior and potential weaknesses, and encouraging those men who are left to continue fighting through the example set by her own impressive warrior skills. In all of these situations, it is a woman who does not panic, who emerges as a survivor, and who makes rational choices that save others from the monster. In short, Ripley's character embodies the sea change in gender roles that women experienced between 1950 and 1979.

What is interesting about the *Alien* series is the degree to which Ripley is increasingly beset by patriarchal threats as the saga advances. In the first film, that threat is specifically defined in Ash's efforts to assert the Company's will over her own and bring the Alien back to earth. In *Aliens*, the masculine threat appears in the form of the collective marine mentality and the duplicitous nature of Burke, who is merely an extension of the callous will of the Company. In *Alien3*, Ripley crash lands on a planet where she is the only female in a maximum-security correctional facility incarcerating an exclusively male population of murderers and rapists. The Alien creature remains a constant threat in all these films, but paralleling that issue is the monstrosity of a masculinity that grows ever more dangerous as Ripley makes her way through space. The Company itself, a patriarchal presence that is represented exclusively by men, seeks to subvert Ripley's authority in all of the films. In the midst of her battles against various Aliens of indiscriminate gender, Ripley must also battle a corporation that "knows everything" through their intrusive computers monitoring and sending back information "through the Network." Ripley is the sole character in the series that understands and tries to correct the problems that arise as a result of patriarchal science's meddling with nature. When the Company attempts to manipulate Ripley's chromosomes in *Alien Resurrection*, we have reached the ultimate degree of violation in her long association with corporate science. Because it is a woman who is put into this position, the films continue, as Cynthia Freeland posits, "Mary Shelley's thematic opposition between 'good' femininity and 'evil' masculinity" (67).

In *Alien3*, the monster refuses to kill Ripley because it knows she carries an

Alien embryo inside; when Dillon pretends to threaten Ripley, the monster instinctively seeks to protect her. Aside from Ripley herself, this level of concern for another organism is found nowhere else in the series. Ripley recognizes that the creature sees her as "a member of the [Alien] family," an ironic understatement of her position as an orphan lost in space. Ripley's closest ties are, finally, to the persistent parasite with which she becomes obsessed rather than to anyone within her own species. Indeed, each time she is attracted to a man sexually or shows her commitment to another human, their relationship ends in death. In the context of her cosmic isolation and constant gender struggles, it is difficult to concur altogether with Freeland's summary judgment that Ripley's genetic merger with the Alien queen in *Alien Resurrection* "was a mistaken step backward, pushing her into the inhuman . . . an excuse for her inhumanity as she simply becomes a big bug herself" (69). Ripley's suicide at the end of *Alien3* is as much a reflection of her own existential despair in the face of all things human—for a final time she refuses to believe any of the medical reassurances and the promises of maternity and a family that the Company proffers—as it is an effort to destroy the Alien queen gestating in her chest. Instead of entrusting herself to the Company that has proven itself capable of betrayal at every opportunity, Ripley retains control over her own body, at least for this moment, and chooses her own destiny. In the end, Ripley embodies the strengths as well as the problems that beset many feminists of her time: While she rises to every challenge and proves herself more capable than any man, she also learns that genuine warriors reside in very lonely places.

6.

Terrors from Within

The Tenant, Don't Look Now, The Fly, The Exorcist, Fatal Attraction, Panic Room

In his short stories written in the 1830s and 1840s, Edgar Allan Poe invested the Gothic form with a psychological, cerebral slant. According to scholar Benjamin Franklin Fisher, Poe's literary contribution to the Gothic entailed a "shift from physical fright, expressed through numerous outward miseries and villainous actions to psychological fear. The inward turn in fiction emphasized motivations, not their overt terrifying consequences" (177). The horror film takes a similar curve about the time Hitchcock released *Psycho*. After a generation of techno-horror films that focused on the terrors of deep space and the perversions of earth's insects as a consequence of atomic experimentation, Hitchcock, like Poe, began the decade of the 1960s by reminding us that it was not necessary to look to the skies or to mutant invertebrates in order to find abject terror; indeed, that the horror film could find plenty of terrible things inside the last house on the left, or within the demented psyche of a trusted lover or friend. In *Monsters and Mad Scientists*, Andrew Tutor argues that there exists a sharp distinction between the horror films released before 1960 and those which follow, and his main point of differentiation is that the contradictions inherent in post-1960 horror are a response to the crises of late capitalism. Citing two films from 1960, *Psycho* and *Peeping Tom*, as progenitors of what Tutor calls "paranoid horror" in contrast to "secure horror," the former features a "world in which the monstrous threat is increasing beyond control and order is therefore unlikely to be restored at narrative end" (108). What was explored in greater detail in chapter 4 is worth repeating again here. What Hitchcock did for the horror film parallels what Poe did for the Gothic tale: They brought the monster home, made him human, and forced viewers—however uncomfortable in doing so—to establish a level of intimacy with him.

Psycho inaugurated and inspired a subgenre of horror cinema that centered on the internal workings of American family life and the manner in which this instability contributed to highly conflicted and unstable configurations of gender. These concerns represent the subject of this chapter—the unraveling of the self's psychology in the midst of the nuclear family's crisis. Unlike the science-fiction film or the techno-horror genre more specifically, the terror associated with the pictures that follow from the 1970s and beyond is neither inhuman nor the product of human technology gone askew; it is, instead, man himself as monster and his most cherished institution, the family, as breeding ground for his gender anxieties and consequent monstrosity. Viewed traditionally as the repository of values and, to borrow from sociologist Christopher Lasch, a haven in a heartless world, the films considered in this chapter reflect a high level of domestic anxiety, often recognizing house and home as unstable and dangerous sites. However, while physical place may be under assault by protean forces of chaos (e.g., *The Exorcist* and *Fatal Attraction*), we will see that the films' truest points of attack are gender specific, as human minds and bodies are violated, challenged, and transformed.

Although I will have more to say about the role of the body under terror in a subsequent chapter dealing with the slasher film, the position the body occupies in horror art is always extremely noteworthy and oftentimes is employed to demarcate horror genre categories. For example, in certain films, evil is portrayed as working its way *inside* the body; it is seen as a force that comes from without and seeks to corrupt the psyche by penetration through the skin. Movies such as the traditional vampire picture, *Alien, 28 Days Later, The Shining*, and *Invasion of the Body Snatchers* feature monstrous energies that originate outside the self and work their way in. Conversely, *Dr. Jekyll and Mr. Hyde, Psycho, The Tenant, Don't Look Now*, and *The Fly* are films that invert this paradigm, suggesting that the monstrous can likewise be seen to emanate within the self, oftentimes discerned in severe psychological distortion and gender distress, and in the course of the narrative manifest itself by working its way out.

Another point worth noting about the films discussed in the first half of this chapter is that they reflect a post-Vietnam/Watergate sense of unease in their uncertainty about the safety of America and its citizens. Isabel Cristina Pinedo believes that what distinguishes "postmodern horror art" from films Pinedo refers to as "classical horror" is the possibility that "violence can burst upon us at any time, even when we least expect it, even when the sun is shining, even in the safety of our own beds, ravaging the life we take for granted, staging the spectacle of the ruined body" (93). More than any of the other horror categories constructed in this book, the films of this chapter, representing the renaissance decade of the horror film, anticipate our current, post-9/11 culture of paranoia. As Americans adjust to the latest set of limits and anxieties imposed in the age of terrorism, we have learned that while the threat of harm may originate from a distant source miles outside our national boundaries, the consequential impact is now most likely to be felt here—in our cities, to our fellow citizens, and to ourselves. What was once a recurring problem for some other government or culture to fret about, now affects us directly. The work analyzed in this chapter thus parallels and prefigures this sense of internal dread—of sudden danger erupting from within our families and within us—and I would speculate that at least for the foreseeable future horror art will continue to embody a similar thematic emphasis, even when it is disguised as a subtext.

It is no mere coincidence, then, that as I write this *The Village*, a contemporary nod to Henry David Thoreau's *Walden* in advocating a clean break from the "barbarism" of mainstream life, is currently the most successful film at multiplexes across America. Anxiety indulgence has become our new national pastime. What lingers in the mind after viewing this film is the sense that its real narrative concern is the subject of the self under assault by forces it cannot hope to control or recognize. Thus, the insulated community the elders found is out of an effort to protect its citizens from the unspecified and random—and therefore all the more terrifying—violence that threatens from without. The film is well considered as a possible response to a post-9/11 world, and perhaps will be emblematic of a specific trend in future cinema. While President Bush and the American military adhere to a strategy of active confrontation with shadowy enemies they neither understand nor can completely contain, *The Village* posits that another approach to such a nebulous situation is to take our loved ones and simply withdraw. However, even as *The Village* offers a respite from the paranoia—both personal and collective—its inhabitants were made to feel while living in postmodern America, the solution of radical isolationism that the town's elders offer is as muddy and miasmatic as the forest that forms a barrier between their compound and the modern world. While its leaders purport to provide an answer to the baser evil that exists beyond the secluded village, the community's security is ultimately sustained upon a lie, and this duplicity makes it impossible for the group to continue to view itself either as "innocent" or as morally superior to the postmodern condition it has forsaken. Failing to provide a viable alternative to the terror of contemporary life, *The Village* only succeeds in finally reminding us of the futility of trying to improve—or escape—human nature.

"There's Something Odd in My Building": *The Tenant*

Roman Polanski is arguably the horror genre's most accomplished student of abnormal psychology; he would appear to be quite at home directing the inhabitants of an insane asylum. *Chinatown, Macbeth, Rosemary's Baby*, and *Tess*, his most mainstream work, all touch on issues of encroaching mental illness. When we consider films such as *Repulsion* and *The Tenant*, however, psychic disintegration is no longer the unfortunate consequence of external evil or sociological forces affecting the individual, as is most definitively stated in *Tess* and *Chinatown*. In *Repulsion* and *The Tenant*, the audience is virtually trapped *inside* the narrowing point of view of psychologically unstable protagonists huddled in apartments that contain, respectively, a rotting rabbit carcass and the feminine undergarments of a recent suicide. The inhabitants of these dwellings suffer from delusions that are not entirely explained by either film, but both protagonists have warped into highly emotive self-destructive states. Polanski's films are about vulnerable psyches turned painfully inward, but whose repression must then unleash itself in acts of horrific violence. In *Repulsion*, that violence occurs against the men Carol secretly desires, while in *The Tenant*, the violence that takes place is self-inflicted and self-contained. Cynthia Freeland's remarks about *Repulsion* could apply equally to *The Tenant*: These pictures present "the condition of horror as one of hopeless disruption and fragmentation rather than resolution; of suffering and reacting rather than acting" (197). The two movies are thus representative of the horror genre's fascination with the doubled or fragmented self that connects back to Poe and *Jekyll and Hyde* while also anticipating films such as *The Dark Half, Fatal Attraction*, and *Secret Window*.

The Tenant concerns the fate of Trelkovsky, a timid little man who is alone in Paris searching for a place to live. He finds an apartment whose former tenant, Simone, "was in good spirits two nights before" plunging to her death in a suicidal fall. Initially, Trelkovsky's reaction to Simone's demise is as indifferent as the coldhearted neighbors who live in the building's other apartments. He tells Simone's friend, Stella, "I'll never understand suicide; it's beyond my comprehension." Once he moves into her flat and begins to discover the last remaining vestiges of her life, however, Trelkovsky begins to obsess over Simone. He attends her funeral, reads a book on Egyptology that once belonged to her, has sex with Stella, is continually drawn to the broken glass that marks Simone's fall in the courtyard, and becomes ever more fascinated with various personal items the suicide victim has left behind—her bra and stockings, a black floral dress, red lipstick and nail polish, a tooth. In addition, Trelkovsky gains a special insight into Simone's life and a possible explanation for her suicide in the neighbors with whom he must interact. The inhabitants in the surrounding apartments appear in training for occupations as Parisian waiters, as they are the least friendly people in town (even the concierge's dog, a miniature Cerberus, snaps viciously at Trelkovsky's fingers when he tries to pet it). The neighbors who share his building object to the noise he makes on a Saturday night, pound on the ceiling when he attempts to rearrange furniture, sign petitions against one another, scowl as they pass Trelkovsky on the stairs, and stare blankly into his windows from across the courtyard.

As his neighbors push Trelkovsky deeper within himself and into the tiny apartment in which he appears ever more constrained, his identification with Simone crosses over into the pathological. He wonders, "At what precise moment does an individual stop being who he thinks he is?" As if in answer to this question, Trelkovsky decides to transform himself into the dead girl—dressing in Simone's clothes, wearing her makeup, so fully identifying with the alienation and loneliness she felt as a single woman that he likewise tries to kill himself the same way. His decision to "become" Simone is both a protest against her victimization and a surrendering of his own identity to a similar doom. Trelkovsky reaches a point where he finds it impossible to maintain separation between his (and apparently Simone's as well) paranoid delusions of persecution and any degree of objective reality.

The film remains unclear as to whether Trelkovsky's mental unraveling is shaped by living in the shadow of Simone's tragic persona, his own inexorable deterioration, the neighbors who fuel his sense of paranoia, or a combination of them all. What is certain, however, is that regardless of whatever served as the catalyst for Trelkovsky's own suicide, his psychosis is centered and emanates from within. Polanski reveals in the last half of the film that his protagonist's vision of the world is highly skewed, and that it is entirely subjective. We witness his hallucinations precisely as hallucinations—the monstrous faces that he sees are actually people often trying to help him, as with the couple that accidentally hits him with their car. At one point early in the film, the manager of the apartment house asks Trelkovsky if he is a Russian. Although he answers that he is Polish, Trelkovsky's situation in this film closely resembles that of a protagonist from a nineteenth-century Russian novel; like one of Dostoevski's or Gogol's alienated men, Trelkovsky prowls the Paris streets with nowhere to go and no one to visit. Even before becoming personally involved in Simone's tragic life, Polanski's antihero is a man searching for something to provide the void of his existence with meaning. His sexual encounters with Stella are desperately superficial; his fellow workers, who call themselves his friends, actually mock him and revel in his humiliation; it becomes clear why Simone's suicide becomes the most encompassing moment in his own sterile life.

The camera follows Trelkovsky and the haunting billboard that often appears behind him as he wanders through the city streets. It features an expressionistic picture of three bald and garishly painted male heads with their hands outstretched in an ambiguous gesture of supplication (or perhaps frustration, as it is hard to be sure). These exaggerated faces that appear almost to be following the protagonist across town mirror the severe torment in Trelkovsky's soul, a torment that he is too timid to express himself, and so he appropriates Simone's persona to articulate it. His close identification with Simone probably has little, if anything, to do with a desire for cross-gendered sexual realignment. Rather, it centers on the common condition of personal—and spiritual—alienation that the two clearly share in common. Her wrecked body, her internal anguish, and her self-destruction parallel the condition of Trelkovsky's own inner self. Trelkovsky forms such an intimate bond with Simone because his own identity is so unstable and tortured, and he perceives the girl's suicide as an expression of his own deepest—but until now, repressed—sentiments. Trelkovsky's self-alienation exists to such a degree that he experiences his own suicidal annihilation as an aesthetic pleasure. His elation explains why he orchestrates and details so meticulously his efforts to recreate himself in the image of a woman he has never actually met, and why at the end of the movie, he envisions his own death in operatic terms, featuring the film's cast of characters assembled together on balconies and rooftops excitedly anticipating his death plunge. Simone's Edvard Munch-like scream of internal anguish, the only sound she utters from beneath her bandages before dying, parallels Trelkovsky's own scream—the last sound he makes as the picture ends—as a final echo of their mutual isolation and despair.

There is more to say about why Polanski's protagonist is compelled to identify with Simone so completely that he chooses to "become" her, to transform himself into a woman. Why isn't it sufficient enough for Trelkovsky to empathize with Simone's suicidal plight, and even to emulate it, while remaining a gendered male? What does becoming a woman permit him to do? How is his literal desire to switch genders related to his expressions of despair and alienation? *The Tenant* makes no effort to offer specific answers to these questions, but we might surmise that turning himself into a female, we presume for the first time in his life, puts Trelkovsky into a gendered disaffection that parallels his feelings of alienation as a foreigner living in Paris. More explicitly, the change in gender allows the protagonist to express most completely his sense of self-estrangement and personal instability, that he has lost himself on nearly every level possible—as a social being, for sure, but now, also in defining himself in the most fundamental terms: as a gendered male. As Kafka's Gregor Samsa in *The Metamorphosis* willed himself into a cockroach to reflect his own self-condemnation as a human being, Trelkovsky's choice to transform into a female indicts his failures as a man. Moreover, his masculine abandonment may well underscore Trelkovsky's understanding that he has surrendered the survival traits most typically associated with being a gendered male—

endurance in the face of suffering, the capacity for self-discipline, and the ability to assert control over threatening forces—in giving himself over to emotional trauma stereotypically gendered feminine.

Psychic Fragmentation: *Don't Look Now*

One item that remains quite remarkable about *The Tenant* and *Don't Look Now* is how both films have been underappreciated in film scholarship history. I do not really have an explanation for why this is the case, especially in light of the fact that these films are generally recognized as superb, visually stunning productions of disquieting beauty and dreamlike dislocation that defy their reductive dismissal as dated works of cinema. Nevertheless, critical surveys of horror films, essay collections dealing with representative movies, and issue-analysis volumes specializing in genre studies provide seldom more than a nodding acquaintance with either picture. It is instructive to note the amount of serious criticism *The Exorcist*, released the same year as *Don't Look Now*, has garnered in contrast. Stephen King, for example, includes *Don't Look Now* on his list of one hundred horror films notable for their "excellence," but he has nothing substantive to say about the movie anywhere in *Danse Macabre*. *The Tenant* and *Don't Look Now* have attained near-cult status among fans of the genre; *Don't Look Now* even managed to attain the number five position in a 1995 survey conducted by *The London Times* of the Top 100 Cult Films of all time (Sanderson 8). However, because they are highly cerebral horror films—and thus present a difficulty in categorizing—mainstream film critics, and even those working specifically in the horror field, still largely underappreciate both. The fact that these pictures have not received the critical attention they justly deserve may be a further indication of how the horror genre, and especially *cult* horror films, remains marginalized in the world of film scholarship. *The Tenant* and *Don't Look Now* do not establish their terror via demonic intrusion or from the visceral assault of a serial killer fixated on butchering young students (horror film topics that originated in and dominated the decade that also produced *The Tenant* and *Don't Look Now*). Rather, there is a subtler—and thus all the more unsettling—brand of terror at work in these two movies: It is the numbing fear of an individual mind challenged and systematically unraveling, the appreciation of what Emily Dickinson referred to in poem 670 as "a superior spectre . . . Ourself behind ourself, concealed" (333).

Laura and John Baxter lost their daughter, Christine, when she drowned in a small pond in the back of their property. Following the opening sequence, the rest of *Don't Look Now* is set several months after the tragedy, following the Baxters' move to Venice. Although he had a premonition of Christine's death, John appears fully recovered from his grief as he goes about the daily business of restoring an ancient Venetian church. Laura, on the other hand, still suffers deeply. Her sadness surrounds her like the thick winter fog in Venice, and she has sought professional counseling and prescription medication to ameliorate her misery. When Laura establishes a bond with Heather, a psychic who tells her, "your daughter wants you to know that she is happy," John dismisses the revelation as "mumbo jumbo," even though such knowledge brings his wife a measure of relief that is signaled in the healthy sexual appetite she shares with her husband immediately afterwards: "I'm happier than I've been in weeks, maybe months."

What the film is careful not to reveal until its conclusion is that John Baxter (and the audience) have misconstrued definitions of psychic balance. It is really Laura who is the healthiest member of this marriage, expressing her grief naturally and seeking a spiritual peace with the lost daughter she is reluctant to give up. (Laura has packed in her suitcase the ball Christine was chasing on the day of her drowning, an indication that this mother refuses to repress or to be intimidated by *anything* associated with her dead daughter, even the object she pursued that resulted in her tragedy.) Nicolas Roeg, the British director of *Don't Look Now*, describes the final scene of the film this way: "Laura has lost her husband and her child but she knows the two are together and happy. It is the others who are crying. Laura is in a state of grace, that's why she smiles" (Sanderson 79). The reason for this "state of grace" is Laura's secure faith in the existence of a world beyond this one, which puts her and the marriage at odds with the rationalism of her husband. As in *The Tenant*, the film likewise underscores stereotyped gender roles, but this time at the expense of the male: Laura does not work in Venice and dwells on her emotional condition, while her husband loses himself in his restoration work in order to avoid confronting his own emotions centering on his recent loss. Baxter assures his wife he is "going to take some time off," but he never does, even when their son Johnny is injured in a boarding school accident that causes Bishop Barbarrigo to chide the art historian for neglecting his son.

John Baxter, in contrast to his wife, is in total denial of everything he cannot physically see or touch—reflected in his dismissive attitude toward both Heather and Christine. It turns out that it is really John who is fragmented psychically, and his eventual effort to admit emotion, spirituality, and wholeness into his life is too little and comes too late. In the course of the film, John pursues the fragmented image of what appears to be a small child wearing a bright red coat with attached hood. What he sees reminds him, at least subconsciously, of Christine, who wore a red mackintosh on the afternoon of her death. It is also the sight of someone wearing a red hood that is pictured off to the side oozing blood in one of his art slides that stimulates Baxter's premonition of his child's plight the day she drowns. The ubiquitous red terror in this film harkens back to the fairy tale "Little Red Riding

Hood" and to Poe's "Masque of the Red Death" at the same time as it looks forward to a chilling cinematic bloodline still to come: the little girl's red coat in *Schindler's List*, Stanley Kubrick's inversion of *murder* as *redrum* in *The Shining*, and the ambiguous scarlet terror that lurks in the woods of *The Village* (Lane 91). The Venetian setting—with its reflective surfaces of water, narrow canals and stone passageways, multiple bridges that John and Laura cross and recross, and pervasive silence—is emblematic of the complex and layered levels of confusion in John's mind. Indeed, the first time Baxter notices the red-hooded figure is at night when Laura and he are lost deep in the bowels of this secreted city. The picture's enigmatic and mysterious winter Venetian imagery is meant to suggest that John's degree of self-understanding remains dangerously frozen. Christine's link to the cold, still waters found in Venice, the red dwarf's association with death (she is later revealed to be the serial killer currently stalking the city) and Christine, and John's repressed urge to avoid thinking about his drowned child all come together in a tragic confluence.

Because Baxter refuses to open himself to the possibility of worlds beyond the visible, he is ignorant to the mysteries of death and the spiritual realm. His job as a restorer of religious artifacts underscores his plight as well as his forfeited potential. He gains great satisfaction in repairing broken and weathered artwork. On the one hand, his occupation is recreating visual beauty (the painstaking work of piecing together new mosaic tiles on the face of an ancient Christ brings him obvious delight and is an attempt to restore meaning to a past that is in constant danger of being eroded), but his vocation should also take him, on the other, into the religious sphere of the unseen and the mysteries of faith. Because John is a rationalist, he is blunted to the spiritual side of his work and his own psychic "gift"—"a curse as well as a gift," Heather reminds us. As Mark Sanderson points out, "John is ruled by the head, [Laura] is ruled by the heart" (44). His failure to recognize and operate in recognition of dimensions that exist beyond the temporal is the main source of conflict in an otherwise loving marriage, and it ends up costing Baxter his life. His dead daughter employs Heather as a medium for warning her father that "his life is in danger while he is in Venice." However, Baxter maintains "my daughter is *dead*; she does not come peeping with messages from beyond the fucking grave," and, therefore, he leaves himself open to being overwhelmed by all the things the hooded dwarf comes to represent for him. Steady pursuit of this enigmatic figure finally forces Baxter to make a sudden—and fatal—connection with the dead Christine. He cannot escape his inner psyche; attempts at repression lead to emotion, and then to a place that is out of his ability to negotiate.

Although Baxter spends most of the movie operating from a position of spiritual doubt, there is a point where he begins to question his complacent belief system. *Don't Look Now* hinges on the moment when fate intersects with choice. Two revelations help to convince him that Heather is a true psychic and that he has been denying his own access to psychic phenomena and Christine's efforts to contact him. When Baxter envisions Laura on a funeral barge (prefiguring his own death) just after he is nearly decapitated by a falling board in the church where he works, the rational skeptic begins to doubt his own skepticism. Unfortunately, he is wholly unprepared to manage the insight that is dawning and the responsibilities that attend it.

In the film's penultimate sequence, when Baxter follows the hooded dwarf into a darkened building, everything about his actions suggests his projecting onto the dwarf the figure of his lost child and the compulsion to seek absolution, as his wife has earlier accused him, "for letting her play next to the pond . . . she's trying to get in touch with us, maybe to forgive." When the dwarf leads him into the building, John locks a gate behind them to make sure that neither one will escape. In a reversal of the film's lyrical opening sequence, Laura runs along the dark water trying to save her husband from what she knows is about to happen to him. When she reaches the locked gate Laura extends her hands through its grating and utters the last word she will say in the film—"Darlings!"—the tender plural indicates her own premonition that John is leaving her behind in an effort to join their daughter. (see Figure 3, p. 192).

In the chase scene that follows, the building again appears analogous to the corridors of the haunted mind, as John passes through a misty and shrouded dreamscape in relentless pursuit of something he only vaguely understands. Baxter hopes this figure will allow him the opportunity to become like Laura: to grieve openly and act upon his deepest impulses that have up until this point been repressed. His dark quest also encompasses the full array of contradictory sensations that are often associated with the human grieving process, as this father seeks both forgiveness and punishment at the same time. His determined effort to contact the mysterious red dwarf is simultaneously indicative of a father's urge to help a lost child, of a desperate longing to reconnect with Christine, and of his own "half in love with easeful death" desire for self-destruction. When he first approaches the red-hooded murderer with its back facing him in a corner of the structure, the dwarf is sobbing, making sounds like a small child in pain. John approaches the figure as a father, gently offering it comfort and aid. However, when the dwarf is revealed to be a grotesque gnome (paralleling an earlier scene when Baxter removes the sack covering off the figure of a gnarled stone carving on the outside of the church) instead of finding the daughter his subconscious mind has pursued through the dark, John is punished for his excursion into a realm where he is still an apprentice. Opening himself to the non-rational world—where his daughter and his own repressed psychic energies reside—occurs too late to provide direction. The dwarf monster seems to acknowledge this when she responds to Baxter's confused "wait," by shaking her head negatively and then slashing his throat. He ends up following his true daughter into the realm of death—the blood he saw earlier oozing from the art slide becomes his own—as a result of his failure to integrate the various aspects of his psychic personality and acknowledge the intersection of multiple worlds.

Transforming the Body: *The Fly*

Over the past three decades, director David Cronenberg has developed virtually his own kind of cinema of pathology in which the ultimate horror is the horror of the diseased psyche that finds its appropriate correspondence in a mutated body (Verniere 55). In *The Brood*, an experimentally malformed woman gives birth to murderous demon-children; in *Crash*, the body's destruction in violent automobile crashes becomes an inspiration for firing the libido, featuring characters who injure themselves emotionally and physically in car wrecks and abnormal sexual liaisons. Cronenberg understands that the human body will ultimately betray us—that we will not be able to control the processes of aging, and dying, and that eventually we must lose command over our body parts, our internal organs, even our mental facilities.

In spite of this immutable law, Cronenberg's protagonists—who are typically white, middle-class males—all seek to impose their imaginative vision on reality. Thus, we recognize the hubris inherent in Seth Brundle's introduction to Veronica at the cocktail party early in *The Fly*. His first words to her are that the three other scientists she has come to interview as a journalist for *Particle Magazine* are not as worthy of her attention as is Seth, because they are not working on something that "will change the world, and human life as we know it." In the course of this film, however, *he* is the one who will change—not the world. His transformation is perhaps the most viscerally terrible of all the many mutations that occur to human flesh in Cronenberg's horror canon. It begins with an initial feeling of euphoric liberation as he moves outside the realm of the merely human and toward the abject, his body systematically degenerating due to the corruption of his DNA. While the transformation is occurring, Brundle experiences the excitement of becoming a human sex machine, gymnast acrobat, and superhero strongman. These physical attributes serve to inflate what was an already alarmingly gargantuan ego, as he insists that Ronnie must join him in exploring the realm of the flesh, and transcending the limits of the known through immersion in "the plasma pool": "To be destroyed and re-created. Drink deep or taste not the plasma spring. I'm not just talking about sex and penetration. I'm talking about penetration beyond the veil of the flesh: the deep, penetrating dive into the plasma pool."

As Brundle turns into Brundlefly, the sensual body he has indulged betrays him—his fingernails dissolve, his ears fall off, his teeth drop out—and the process is even referred to as "a bizarre form of cancer." When flesh meets machine in Cronenberg, a horrible transformation takes place. If not resulting in a cyborg variant, as in *Videodrome* or *eXistenZ*, where a machine becomes a physical part of human flesh, then some kind of hybrid monstrosity is born, "where we absorb technology into our bodies and our brains and our concept of things. It's a real fusion and no separate thing" (Cronenberg 16). In this literal merging of technology and human flesh, the latter is immutably altered into a hideous variant of its former self. At the end of *The Fly*, the already hideous Brundlefly melds with his telepod and becomes a man-insect-machine hybrid that is barely capable of being described. Cables stretch out from exposed organs as the creature stumbles across the room on spindle legs revealing itself to be a wholly new being—a transgression of categories and structures that makes the Frankenstein monster appear positively wholesome.

Most of Cronenberg's films are interested in exploring the nightmare that occurs to male sexuality—and masculinity—when it is put into dangerous situations; opening the door to sexuality ushers in love and, in turn, the monstrous. His *oeuvre* is a weird conflation of science, sexuality, love, and ego, resulting in strange births that do not produce grander, more beautiful selves, but a horror of the body out of control and engaged actively in the process of self-disintegration. At the conclusion of each of his movies, Cronenberg's males comprehend the very limits of their own physicality—the body's deconstruction once the barrier of sexuality is broached in *The Brood*, *The Fly*, *The Dead Zone*, *Dead Ringers*, *Crash*, and *M. Butterfly*—and these tragic realizations help to thwart the visionary potential to which his protagonists aspire. William Beard, one of the most insightful critics writing about Cronenberg's canon, views the protagonists in each of these films as artist figures: "Primarily they are compulsive imaginers whose 'talent' arises from their personal dysfunctionality and who are devastated by their own visions" (367). I can think of no Cronenberg protagonist who is ever saved from his hideous destiny by virtue of intimate contact with another person or through the redemptive grace of a close-knit family bond. Indeed, their personal quests push them to the edge of society and civilized life. In the course of the director's narratives, his characters are pressed deeper within themselves and their highly suspect understanding of reality.

Cronenberg's work forms a complex matrix of various intellectual and scientific explorations that ultimately resort to a starkly simple and bleak formulation of existential loneliness and despair. His characters, despite their highly idiosyncratic kinks and grotesque supernatural excursions, arrive at the same awareness of an abject otherness that is inherent in being human—the plot of the respective film narrative merely unleashes the latent monster that lurks within. All of his males are postmodern versions of Dr. Jekyll—aware of their growing separation from meaningful correspondences in mainstream life, yet compelled to pursue whatever lethal vision was first conjured in their dark imaginations and has now metastasized into an obsession.

In *The Dead Zone*, John Smith is tortured by his desire to live a "normal" life, but he is ultimately warped by the psychic burden that keeps pulling him away from domestic pursuits and toward isolation and death. In *M. Butterfly*, the main protagonist is drawn into a romantic relationship with a woman who is actually a transvestite; when the ruse is finally uncovered, the protagonist transforms himself into a suicidal version of his lost lover, the "woman" who has betrayed him. In *The Fly*, Seth recognizes that he possesses little knowledge about whatever is producing his transformation: "It wants to turn me into something else. Something that never existed before—Brundlefly." His earlier dream of changing the world through a technology it has never seen comes back to mock him in the ever-changing face of the monstrous other that stares back at him from his bathroom mirror. From the onset of the movie, even before his genes are spliced with those of fly, there is a strong suggestion that Seth is already at war with himself. He admits to Ronnie, "I don't have a life, so there's nothing for you to interfere with." He even experiences motion sickness while a passenger for a short car ride with her, an odd debilitation in a man whose greatest desire is to perfect a transportation machine. Cronenberg's males are often forced into confronting a kind of Hemingway awareness of an authentic self unsentimentally revealed: So many of his movies end in suicide because his protagonists cannot cope with whatever truth they have uncovered about themselves.

Cronenberg thus offers a unique treatment of gender in the horror tale; not only do male—rather than the usual female—bodies appear under siege, women in his films serve primarily as muses and temptations, as catalysts for action, but seldom as the focus of the director's obsession with change and decay. Beard summarizes best the typical Cronenberg scenario: "An encapsulated protagonist is drawn from his shell by some form of relationship with a woman, momentarily flourishes, and then is destroyed by something that has been loosed in that breaking down of the barrier of solitude" (203). For Seth, Ronnie is first temptress (she initiates their sexual relationship), then inspiration, then betrayer, and then destroyer. Although Ronnie helps to break Brundle out of a world that is so sterile and predictable that he wears the same clothes day after day, she cannot save him from himself or the hideous process that is taking place within his metabolism. Her presence in his life inspires him to push beyond the limits of the human; in doing so, she puts him in touch with his own animalistic urges, and he follows the imploded baboon into the realm of the nonhuman. At the end of the movie, Brundlefly is the fallen angel, crippled by his own machine and the consequences of distorting nature. Like the baboon experiment that results in a bloody mess at the beginning of the picture, his body is turned inside out in a grotesque manifestation of Lovecraftian "wrong geometry."

In his role as a scientist, Brundle is obsessed with crossing boundaries. Ronnie's personal attention and intense sexuality help to unleash an emotional torrent in Brundle that makes him behave recklessly, his ego intoxicated to the point where he is willing to push the envelope to an unsafe level (as Seth's decision to test a human—himself—in his transporter machine is the result of drunkenness and emotional anguish over Ronnie's perceived sexual betrayal). Once Brundle begins his metamorphosis, however, the narrative shifts its emphasis to Ronnie because the audience can no longer identify with Brundle's transformation into the nonhuman. She becomes the unwitting historian of record—employing tape and video machines while serving as Brundlefly's symbolic gaze/mirror. When he is first trying to attract her attention and yet keep her from revealing the secret of his transporter, Brundle promises Ronnie access to his scientific work, "the complete record of the most earth-shattering invention ever. The one that ended all concepts of transport, of borders and frontiers, of time and space." After Ronnie has witnessed the horrific results of the scientific achievement that originally excited her as a journalist, she acknowledges her implicit role in the experiment when she defines herself ironically as "the only recorder of the event from the inside out," a remark with lots of overtones inherent in it. Consequently, when he looks at her or shows her his collection of obsolete Brundle body parts, he measures her facial reaction to each new boundary crossed. Like Jekyll standing transfixed in front of his laboratory mirror watching Hyde work his way out, there is a part of Brundlefly that remains the Faustian scientist to the end—interested in seeing what will be the final result of this grotesque experiment. Ronnie serves to mediate the changes wrecked upon Seth; like Brundlefly himself, the audience views and gauges her reaction.

In the end, she must be the one to release him from the horror of what he has become. This insight parallels her own decision to abort her pregnancy. She does not want whatever Brundle-thing is growing inside her body. Her desire for an abortion echoes the body-at-war-with-itself theme of Brundle-Brundlefly, but she has none of his scientific fascination to see where this experiment will ultimately lead. Although repulsed by what Brundlefly has become, she continues to visit him in his lair and loves him until it is no longer humanly possible for her to do so. While Brundle transforms into the monstrous, Ronnie remains vigilant and balanced: capable of pitying the horrible thing that was once her lover, but at the same time rational enough to avoid following him into the transporter or serving as the abject mother for his deformed progeny. Ronnie must be the one who re-establishes the status quo—the norm control in the experiment that Brundle was once so excited to show off—by righting the disruption she has unwittingly inspired. She brings Brundlefly his release from a monstrous life just as she earlier provided him a release from another, also monstrous life of scientific monotony and human loneliness.

Familial Disruptions: *The Exorcist*

In his book *Hearths of Darkness: The Family in the American Horror Film*, Tony Williams argues that in horror films released during the 1970s, the institution of marriage underwent severe assault. The antagonist was no inhuman monster from space or classic monster-beast hybrid; instead the threat came from within. Certainly Polanski's *Repulsion, Rosemary's Baby, The Tenant*, and Roeg's *Don't Look Now* either anticipate or are themselves appropriate examples of Williams's thesis. The depiction of family distress in the horror film culminates in *Fatal Attraction* (1987), but leading up to that picture are several important illustrations of familial crises that disrupt the ideological norms of American family life portrayed in the era's television sitcoms (e.g., *Good Times* and *All in the Family*) and mainstream films. Mutated babies and the dissolution of the American nuclear family are central to movies as disparate as *It's Alive* (1973), *The Texas Chainsaw Massacre* (1974), *Demon Seed* (1977), and *The Hills Have Eyes* (1977). Even so, it is really *The Exorcist* (1973) that emerges as the most important horror film of the 1970s and the most dramatic illustration of an individual psyche and family under assault.

While resting on a stairwell after their attempt to exorcise the demon residing in Regan MacNeil, Father Karris asks Father Merrin, "Why this girl? It doesn't make sense." By way of offering some kind of attempt at an explanation, the exhausted Merrin replies: "I think the point is to make us despair. To see ourselves as animal and ugly, to reject the possibility that God could love us." After watching Regan vomit green bile and masturbate with a bloodied crucifix, Merrin's answer is plausible enough, but the audience is left, like Father Karris himself, only partially satisfied with the older priest's explanation, for it is ultimately too generalized for the context supplied by this film. So, we come back to the issue of what *does* "make sense" about the Devil's deliberate selection of this particular girl. Although the demon's presence is first discerned by Chris MacNeil, Regan's mother, as originating in the attic of the Georgetown house they are renting, it is equally certain that the demon is interested in Regan exclusively; except in their interactions with the possessed girl, all the other inhabitants of this house are left alone. The possession, then, has less to do with the house or its tenants *per se* than it does with the female child residing in it.

What do we know about Regan that would make her an appropriate host for the Devil? Why is this girl selected from all the other girls who live in Washington? Perhaps the most important information the film supplies about this daughter concerns her familial situation: She is the only child of a divorced couple; her father, now living in Europe, is so unconnected to her life that he totally overlooks her birthday; and her mother, while definitely fond of her offspring, is also distracted by her career as a movie actress and her status as a single woman. Add to this the facts that Regan and Chris are newly arrived in Washington and Regan's thirteenth birthday signals the advent of her emergence into puberty and womanhood. From all this the audience intuits that Regan may harbor a secret self beneath the pretty and precocious girl we meet early in the film. This part of Regan not only views itself as "animal and ugly" (a self-definition that most female teenagers share at frequent points in their lives), but also despairs of her current loneliness (To help fill the void she invents an imaginary playmate, "Captain Howdy," whose name is strongly reminiscent of her missing father, Howard.). Regan is also the name of Lear's daughter in Shakespeare's play about an Oedipal struggle that results in the terrible estrangement of a father from his daughter. Issues of unresolved Oedipal conflicts between parents and children hover continually on the perimeters of *The Exorcist*. When Chris attempts to contact Howard to castigate him for ignoring his daughter's birthday, Regan is shown in the foreground eavesdropping on the obscene language barrage her mother employs with a pensive look on her young face. No critic writing about this film has yet noted that Howard MacNeil never does return his wife's call nor is he summoned back to America at any point during his child's traumatic ordeal.

In place of the missing biological father, the film offers two Catholic priests as potential father substitutes. If Father Merrin is right in his assertion that the point of the possession is to capitalize on our feelings of despair and "to reject the possibility that God could love us," then Regan—especially at this junction in her life— appears as a vulnerable host ideally sympathetic to such sentiments. Perhaps an unconscious connection is underscored in Regan's crayon drawing of a winged animal that Karris and Chris discover in the basement anticipating the arrival of the winged demon Pazuzu: Devil and abandoned child share a profound correspondence before the actual possession even manifests itself.

After early evidence of an absent and/or debilitated patriarchy—familial as well as medical scientific—the movie gradually re-establishes its faith in male authority. The picture is less a study in religious exorcism than in the re-instatement of patriarchal power. In the course of the film, male physical aggression deepens in frequency and intensity, especially over the battle for Regan's body. Father Merrin engages Pazuzu in a shouting match, while Father Karris resorts to pummeling the possessed Regan with his bare fists. Issues of metaphysics and the religious struggle between good and evil are finally less paramount, particularly in the last third of the film, than physical exhibitions of masculine force. *The Exorcist* is a film that restates the importance of the father to the family. It ends with the father, albeit as a surrogate figure, imposing his authority and legitimacy once again over the feminine, which—in the wake of Regan's dispossessed body and Chris's psychological collapse—has become abject because it is out of control.

In addition to the collapse of her relationship with the patriarchy, a break so severe that it requires the addition of new and more potent father figures, Regan's bond with the demon is meant to highlight the fact that mother and daughter are likewise growing ever more estranged from one another. The Devil's ability to turn offspring against parent in this movie serves to highlight the growing gap in their association that typifies a child's emergence into adolescence and puberty. Even before the Devil takes up residency in Regan, it is clear that the girl feels a definite level of awkwardness in relation to her mother's potential male suitors and rumors of her impending marriage to Burke Dennings. Although Chris does her best to deny such gossip and reassure her daughter with promises that they will mark her upcoming birthday together in private, it is worth noting that Chris feels the need to make this a topic of conversation, indicating that it is an emerging problem that concerns both females. Later events in the film, especially Dennings's gruesome murder, add another layer to this conversation, suggesting Regan's own unconscious aggression toward outsiders who threaten the tenuous bond she maintains with her mother. This theme of generational discord is evident in the movie Chris is in town to make on the Georgetown University campus. The scene we witness in *The Exorcist* is a student protest rally held against the school administration, and Chris affiliates herself completely with adult hegemony, reminding the wayward students that they must work for change "within the system." Chris's efforts at communication with the student protesters prove as ineffective as her attempts to communicate with the alien being inside her daughter.

The topic of parent-child discord is initiated early in the film when Chris finds a copy of *Photoplay* magazine hidden in Regan's bed. On the cover is a photograph of mother and daughter accompanied with the headline: "Big Trouble in the MacNeil Marriage! The Night Howard Walked Out on His Wife." Although Chris dismisses the publication, director Friedkin does not mean that the audience should do likewise. The magazine's cover story highlights perfectly the level of familial dissonance that still haunts Regan, as the cover photograph itself—featuring head shots of Chris behind large sunglasses and Regan looking in a different direction from her mother in front of a black backdrop—further separates mother from daughter. Chris comments on her daughter's image that "It's not even a good picture of you. You look so mature," a subtle indication that mother is having difficulty recognizing her child (which will attain a level of extreme exacerbation as the film progresses) and reconciling with Regan's impending maturation. Lastly, that Regan has secreted the magazine under her bed covers (in the same bed that will become the central site in her battle with evil) is evidence of just how deeply her parents' breakup continues to obsess her: Regan takes the disturbing information to bed with her, but tries to hide its impact from her mother. In the end, Regan's bonding with Pazuzu can be at least partially explained as the consequence of parental abandonment that results in "mak[ing] us despair."

The mother-child tension that creates a void and invites the intrusion of demonic possession in *The Exorcist* is paralleled in the relationship that Father Karris maintains with his aging mother. When he visits her for the last time before her death in the hospital, he finds his mother strapped down in bed in a position that is a remarkable reminder of Regan's prone and bound posture throughout much of the time during her possession. This deliberate juxtaposition of lost children separated from mothers is designed to set up the self-sacrifice Karris eventually makes in extracting the demon from Regan and internalizing it within himself. During his conversations with Pazuzu as the Devil speaks through Regan, Karris is chastised continually for his failings as a son. The Devil informs him that Karris's recently deceased mother "is in here with us" and that she blames her son for not taking better care of her during her life. Karris's earlier dream of his mother beseeching him on a New York City street anticipates these demonic accusations. In this dream Karris sees himself running toward but being ultimately unable to reach his mother as she wails his name and then walks down into a subway entrance that is meant to symbolize her own sense of abandonment by her son and descent into hell. The fact that this scene appears to Karris via a dreamscape just after his mother dies alone in the hospital signifies his own level of guilt even before Pazuzu preys upon it through Regan. The repressed self-loathing this activates is seen in the severity of Karris's reaction when Pazuzu later speaks in Mrs. Karris's voice, prompting the priest to cry out, "You're not my mother!" Thus, Karris's choice of self-destruction at the end of the film—which parallels closely Baxter's compulsion to pursue the red dwarf in *Don't Look Now*—is as much about his own efforts to seek exculpation for his perceived failure as a son as it is about trying to save Regan from the Devil.

The issue of the film's eventual conception of the Devil as inhuman evil or as an expression of the distorted psyche is worth some further exploration. On the one hand, it is significant that the film's most powerful scenes of horror center on Regan's maturing body as a sort of "no man's land," the uncharted territory of the female abject. As Barbara Creed has argued, "The abject is placed on the side of the feminine: it exists in opposition to the paternal symbolic, which is governed by rules and laws . . . Regan's body is represented as a body in revolt" (37, 40). The bloody misuse of the crucifix and its accompanying invocation of menstrual blood, the projectile vomit, and the exhibitionistic urination on the floor during her mother's party all point to a conception of the demonic as emerging from the female body, which is connected to the conviction that evil comes from within, invading the domestic world from the inside out. Although we never know for certain, the Devil that takes control over Regan's body may well be gendered feminine. The voice of the demon, after all, is that of Mercedes McCambridge, a female actor. Certainly one of the most disquieting elements of the film is in witnessing the transformation of a pretty and feminine teenage girl into a vile and repulsive thing; had the filmmakers chosen to return to the male subject who was the original inspiration for Blatty's novel about female possession, *The Exorcist* would have been a very different picture.

The opening of the film, where Pazuzu appears to be unearthed in Iraq from the natural world, suggests the possibility that evil has cycles of dormancy followed by periods of wakefulness (the two dogs fighting in front of Pazuzu's statue) as well as from the domestic sphere. The film seems content to allow these two realms of transgression to co-exist, in fact, to imply that they are not necessarily mutually exclusive. The Devil finds his power in the weaknesses and failings of the human animal during moments of despair that neither the structures of the family nor the strength of the individual can altogether forego.

Transgressing Marital Boundaries: *Fatal Attraction*

Although maintaining differing narrative configurations and presentation strategies, *The Exorcist* and *Fatal Attraction* both project the monstrous in similar terms and view it both as linked symbolically to the feminine and as physical extensions of an assault upon the hearth and home. The fragmentation of her personal world leaves Regan susceptible to the intrusive satanic assault; the absence of her biological father and her mother's career distractions, her sense of isolation in a new home, and her emerging puberty are psychic openings that evil exploits. Moreover, it is interesting that the Devil manifests his control over Regan through explicitly sexual acts of aggression, at one point forcing the child to attack her mother by thrusting Chris's face toward her bleeding crotch and growling "lick me" in a guttural voice. Dan Gallagher's intemperate libido isolates him in a similar fashion, leaving his family and him vulnerable to monstrous intervention, and Alex Forest herself should be read paradoxically as an embodiment of both the unrestrained id and, conversely, the repressive energy of the superego. As in *The Exorcist*, *Fatal Attraction* posits that evil manifests itself primarily through physicality, in bodies— and especially the body's sexuality—out of control. Both films are also, each in its own respective way, explorations of individual psychic breakdowns in gender stability that produce, in turn, disruptions to familial norms and order. The monstrous in both films is closely aligned with the collapse of traditional gender roles assigned to women.

But it is perhaps *The Fly* that bears the more immediate parallel to *Fatal Attraction* insofar as both films consider the consequences of what occurs when the male forsakes self-repression and gives himself over (through impure contact with the female) to the domain of sexuality and fleshly indulgence. The sex that Brundle and Dan engaged in these films breaks down a necessary barrier that releases the monstrous. In *The Fly*, it is an innate monstrosity—the monstrous self; in *Fatal Attraction*, the female object of desire is more than just the catalyst for this masculine release, as sexual contact also unleashes something terrible in Alex herself. Neither Dan nor Alex remains inviolable once they have entered the domain of Brundlefly's "plasma pool."

In Dan Gallagher we find the epitome of a postmodern successful American male. He is a lawyer in a firm that values his contributions; he possesses good friends and inhabits a comfortable apartment in Manhattan. He is husband to a beautiful woman and father to a sweet daughter. He is, in short, a man who has the best of everything, even the city itself appears as his playground; the first half hour of the film is something of a whirlwind tour of Dan's affluent urban lifestyle. Thus, it is not very surprising when Dan sleeps with a beautiful woman one weekend when his wife is out of town. Alex is merely another object for Dan to possess, enjoy, and then discard—the culmination of a lifestyle that centers on pleasure, play, and significant disposable income. Had Alex decided to "play by the rules," their illicit liaison might have had consequences no more severe than a broken bottle of wine or a torn party dress. However, she refuses to allow Dan "to treat me like some slut you can just bang and then throw in the garbage." As such, *Fatal Attraction* establishes itself as a cautionary tale about the dangers of various kinds of reckless consumption. This theme may best be identified in the downtown parking garage scene, where Dan strides confidently through levels of concrete and expensive cars, carrying the rabbit that he knows will delight his family, only to discover acid spilled on the hood of his Volvo. This is the threat that Alex poses: She has no qualms about disrupting and inverting Dan's status in his comfortable bourgeois world; in fact, this disruption emerges as a paradoxical blend of her desire to share a romantic life with him and simultaneously to punish him for his refusal to facilitate her fantasy.

The film thereby poses a neat inversion of Gothic gender archetypes: In the course of the film, Alex emerges as the monstrous, typically male figure, forcing Dan into the role of the persecuted, typically female, victim. (His wife ultimately rescues Dan, after all, as he fails utterly in his own attempts to protect himself and his family from Alex's violations.) As her attack deepens to intrude upon and terrorize the safety of his protected domestic sphere—the ringing telephone in his home comes to symbolize Alex's ability to enter and interrupt his life at will—she pushes him back toward the security that his family represents. It is no mere plot coincidence that midway through this film its central locale moves from the city to the country. Alex embodies the random terror of the urban world. Once Dan becomes privy to the unwanted aspects of urban life (i.e., Alex), he changes his mind about a home in the country and flees the city with the purpose of avoiding further entanglements with Alex and likewise guarding his family from her. The ironic message of this film, however, which is also reflected in other movies examined in this chapter, is that it is impossible to hide from the monster, especially once the monster has established an intimate connection with the protagonist. As in the Frankenstein myth, the monster finds its way into the home and demands to be confronted and destroyed.

In one of the most disturbing scenes in this movie, Alex announces to Dan at an underground subway station that she is pregnant with his baby. The news is certainly unsettling enough to the married man, but after he indicates his willingness to pay for an abortion, he learns that Forest intends to keep the child and offers Dan a role in raising it: "You play fair with me, I'll play fair with you." It is at this point in the film that the full terror and complexity of Gallagher's situation becomes clear for both the lawyer and the audience. As Alex reminds him behind a nearly beatific grin, "If your life is so damn complete, what were you doing with me?" While the two former lovers engage in this tense conversation, on the subway wall directly behind Dan is an advertisement for liquor: An enlarged color photograph of an attractive, well-dressed young couple, a dark-haired man and a blonde woman, who toast one another above a caption that reads, "A Glorious Beginning." The irony of this sign is, of course, difficult to ignore given the context of the news Alex imparts. The sign mirrors and mocks their recent sexual courtship at the same time that it signals the advent of Alex's pregnancy. Perhaps more ominously, it also serves to announce the "beginning" of a new stage in their relationship, the horrific ordeal she intends to pursue in an effort to make absolutely certain she and her child "won't be ignored" and that Dan "faces up to [his] responsibilities."

Behind Alex's attractive and feminine façade, lurks a determined and emotionally unstable personality. Alex is a creature of the night. Her knowledge of the pulsating and sensuous nightlife of New York (the Latin dance club) complements her lack of fear as she floats, witchlike, across the darkened open fields surrounding the Gallaghers' new home in the country (her first name is masculine, while her last name, *Forest*, suggests the untamed mysteriousness of her inner nature). An heir to both the traditions of the vampire and the witch, Alex has no qualms about invading and disrupting the domestic sphere of the Gallagher family. She continually violates the security of their world in a way that indicates Alex has little respect for social barriers of any nature—familial or those typically associated with female behavior. In addition to living independently as a single working woman,

Alex is openly sexual. In her early scenes with Dan, she not only enjoys sex, but she is the sexual aggressor, initiating and demanding his compliance to her urges. Despite the fact that she lives in a chic apartment that is decorated completely in white, it is located in the meatpacking district, where open fires burn in metal containers, and the neighborhood streets appear dingy and ominous. To reach her flat, she must enter through a steel door, ride an ancient lift with iron gates and grinding gears, and enter through a series of locks on her apartment door.

Alex's white apartment tucked inside a dark neighborhood parallels the dualism in her personality and dress code. Unlike Beth, Dan's demure and ultrafeminine wife, the undefined gender signaled in Alex's name suggests that this is a supremely ambiguous being, one moment weeping and groveling for forgiveness after an attempted suicide or an aggressive verbal confrontation, only to then insult Dan with obscenities or murder the Gallagher pet rabbit in a boiling cauldron. In keeping with the ambiguous nature of her persona, Alex is always dressed either entirely in white (in the first half of the film before their relationship becomes sexual) or entirely in black (symbolizing the emergence of her personality's dark side when she begins to stalk the Gallaghers). While associated with either white or black clothing throughout the film, her lips and nails are always painted red, she drinks red wine, and frequently wears high heels. Alex is the ultimate femme fatale, a vampiric woman who blends the attractiveness of a lethal femininity with violent propensities that are more typically associated with the male Gothic monster.

Alex is the "perfect" Gothic female villain because of her gender complexity and willingness to violate barriers. Her dualistic nature—continually restated in her black or white attire choices, radical mood swings, an obsession with the beautiful music of self-destruction in the opera *Madame Butterfly*, and the paradoxical quest to destroy what she also aches to possess—represents the ultimate threat to the rational and staid nature of the Gallagher marriage. Alex is beautiful and sexy, yet her expectations of a future with Dan, which are really inconsistent with her character elsewhere in the film, make her behave as a monster, willing to annihilate Beth and Ellen without even a moment of conscience so that she may satisfy her own needs and desires, regardless of how unrealistic these dreams are or their effect on others. In the end, Alex's behavior is a perverse extension of, and mirror to, Dan's own initial selfishness in his willingness to risk his own security and the fates of those he loves for gratification of immediate sexual release. Alex represents that part of Dan—his hunger for intense passion, illicit sex outside the marriage bed, and sensual gratification—that he has repressed and ignored to sustain roles that emphasize stability: husband, father, and attorney. It is important to note that their daughter's sleeplessness and the ringing of the telephone interrupt the only two moments in the film when Dan and his wife appear on the verge of having sex.

Alex merely forces Dan to acknowledge and act on urges that exist in spite of his apparently happy marriage and lifestyle. That these urges manifest themselves through such a violent and persistent force is an indication of just how difficult it has been for Dan to repress them.

Domestic Assault: *Panic Room*

The narrative milieus of director David Fincher's movies—dark and perpetually damp, situated in claustrophobic places filmed in a thick, underwater green light— always create a distinctive atmosphere that sustains the revelation of unsavory and frequently grotesque subject matter. His journey in *Se7en* takes us beneath the surface of a large American city and down into the inferno-like recesses of criminality; accordingly, much of the film is a literal vertical descent into the secreted worlds of distorted violence and religious perversity. The Manhattan of *Panic Room*, similar to the atmosphere of *Se7en*, is dark, rainy, and desolate. The opening credits provide a view of New York City as defined by sterile skyscrapers that are devoid of any human presence. This image suggests that even in a place that contains a dense urban population, it is easy to feel alone and unsafe. Moreover, because this picture has at its center an urban building as character, and specifically, a room inside that building as indomitable, the opening sequence is designed to impart the measure of concrete and steel as monolithic presences. Although the rest of the film will focus on the struggle between two groups—newly separated Meg and her daughter Sarah, and three criminals who wish to steal the contents of a safe located in a room just off the master bedroom that is equipped with food, a surveillance system, and an impenetrable steel door—this human struggle is played out as an assault on the house Sarah has recently purchased and the steel panic room contained within it.

Fincher manages to sustain a delicate sense of balance in the stalemate that ensues. The efforts of the opposing groups are countered just as they appear to be successful: The safety of the panic room is initially threatened when the burglars pump gas into the air vent, but in exploding the gas before it can fill up the room, Meg turns the effort against the criminals; when Meg appears to gain access to a telephone within the room, her attempt to summon outside assistance is thwarted by the robbers who cut the telephone lines from the house. In an excellent turn of events, the robbers eventually work their way inside the panic room only to find themselves then trapped by Meg outside the room and in control of their gun; after they obtain the bonds, she manages to complicate their efforts to escape from the house itself. However, in spite of the gun, Meg is helpless because her daughter, seriously incapacitated because of insulin shock, remains in the panic room with the criminals.

Similar to *The Exorcist* and *Fatal Attraction*, *Panic Room* achieves its terror through the penetration of familial space by disruptive forces. On their first night in their new home, Meg and Sarah realize three burglars have invaded their new dwelling, and the women are forced to seek refuge. When the intruders elect to pursue the robbery in spite of the fact that the two women inhabit what was supposed to be an empty building, they do so because they are confident that Meg and her daughter will be unable to put up any serious resistance: "We can do it. It's just a woman and a kid. Daddy isn't coming home. It's just her and the kid." Meg and Sarah, however, prove to be more formidable opponents than the intruders initially anticipate. Because of the desperate bond they share as two females alone against the world, the situation is reminiscent of *Fatal Attraction* and *The Shining*, wherein mothers risk their lives to protect their children without the help of men. When Meg's estranged husband shows up at the house, he is rendered impotent, beaten savagely by the burglars; underscoring the vacuum his absence has created in this family, the man who supposedly should be able to right the domestic violation that is occurring is rendered useless as he sits bleeding in a chair with a broken arm, mumbling, "Why are you doing this?"

Because Meg and Sarah are new to the mansion and therefore do not yet feel comfortable with all the various places in the house, they are embattled by the male intruders as well as by the forces contained within the house itself. Fincher even employs camera shots that creep through walls, move along pipelines and ducts, and seem to glide from behind the furniture in order to convey the mystery of the old house. Further isolated by a world where wind and rain storm incessantly against the night, separated in a house that is so large and self-contained that no one is able to hear their cries, the women appear on the edge of hysterical panic even before they are forced into a room that resembles a death chamber. This dislocation symbolizes the condition Stephen Altman has unwittingly placed upon his child and estranged wife when he deserted them both for a new life with a younger woman. Abandoned by the patriarchal figure in their lives, the women are left to fend for themselves. The panic room, then, becomes a metaphor for the transformed familial situation to which the two women must adapt.

During a tour of the mansion before purchasing the property, Meg claims that the panic room makes her nervous. When the real estate agent wonders why, she responds by asking, "Ever read any Poe?" The panic room as a potential burial site is again referenced by Sarah later in the film when she tries to calm her mother by informing her that "You know people never get buried alive anymore. I guess it used to happen all the time." In spite of Sarah's assurances, the panic room as steel sarcophagus certainly has its symbolic appeal insofar as mother and daughter emerge reborn from their nearly lethal experiences. Sarah suffers a severe diabetic seizure, and Meg barely escapes being murdered by one of the thugs at the end of the picture. From these traumatic events, however, mother and daughter emerge stronger and more self-reliant, a sharp contrast to the initial images of Sarah fretting about her new bedroom being "too dark" while Meg gets drunk and weeps in self-pity for the loss of her former life. The film ends appropriately with the two women out on their own, looking for a new place to live, and capable of doing so without the assistance of the impotent and displaced husband-father.

In many of the films examined within this chapter, families are often placed in situations that inspire terror. It is interesting to note, however, that despite their precariousness it is typically the family—or at least what remains of it—that manages to survive in horror films, in contrast to the individual who operates independently enough to explore a forbidden realm (*The Fly* and *The Shining*) or is left isolated from the bond of endurance proffered through familial alliance (*Repulsion, The Tenant*, and *Fatal Attraction*). When the family encounters an assault from outside forces, as we have witnessed in *The Exorcist, Fatal Attraction*, and *Panic Room* (and the list might also extend to include *Poltergeist, E.T.: The Extraterrestrial, Cujo,* and *Dolores Claiborne*, among others), the embattled members of the group manage somehow to pull together to create a scenario for survival. The horror tale is compelled to return to themes of the terrorized family because it establishes a condition with which the audience can readily identify: We want a mother and her endangered child to overcome the enormity of evil operating against them.

There is something else at work here as well. In the horror film, the family is frequently the place where human monstrosity is conceived. *Psycho, Carrie*, and *The Texas Chainsaw Massacre* are examples of the many available illustrations that indict the dysfunctional family as a repository of brutal negativity, oppression, and conformity. Nevertheless, although family terror must be viewed an integral component of the horror genre, parent-children bonds also create the opportunity for selfless acts of heroism that are rewarded in terror film narratives, even if this does not always turn out to be the case in real life. This tendency tends to underscore the conservative nature inherent in horror art—stray from the group and you'll be punished—at the same time as it suggests that Hollywood horror is no less susceptible to the happy ending than other film genres.

Whenever the stability of the family is threatened or rendered dysfunctional in horror art, individual members of the family unit itself frequently display a gender ambiguity that is reflective of and generated by disruptions to the unit. In *The Powers of Horror*, Julia Kristeva associates this kind of ambiguity with what she terms "abjection" because traditional familial boundaries and borders are not respected by whatever source "disturbs identity, system, order" (4). The degree to which such gender destabilization becomes monstrous is dependent on the corresponding degree in the breakdown in the family structure itself. The films considered in this chapter offer interesting evidence of gender abjection as a means for signaling the dysfunctional condition of the family and/or immediate community: *The Tenant* and *The Exorcist*, for example, define monstrosity in terms of an abject feminine that asserts itself in the void of a viable patriarchal presence. *Fatal Attraction* likewise situates the threat of familial rupture in the destabilization of traditional gender coding.

The multiple gender disruptions in *Fatal Attraction* culminate in Beth Gallagher's transformation from long-suffering housewife-mother—to whom all major actions in this film are performed against—and into an assertive agent who takes final control over events. Her appropriation of the phallic gun at the end of the film reverses her feminized object role with which she is affiliated throughout the movie and links her ironically to the very target of her aggression: the knife wielding phallic-woman whose monstrous femininity is responsible for the disruption to Beth's family. In a picture where gender subversion increases in direct correspondence to the degree of familial danger, Beth usurps the traditional masculine role in defending her family and self against a masculinized femme fatale who has entered the Gallagher home in order to destroy it. The film's range of gender abjections even includes Dan Gallagher's character, which, as noted elsewhere in this chapter, is feminized because of his inability to control Alex. Dan is rendered nearly impotent by the assault on his family; he assumes the role of the Gothic female forced to await ultimate rescue from a source outside him/herself.

The disruptive and contradictory nature of horror film, in suggesting the instability of gender roles when the family is placed under stress, offers an ideological challenge to the status quo at the same time as it conversely reaffirms traditional masculine and feminine constructions by aligning the monster with gender upheaval. Because Kristeva locates the abject at "the place where meaning collapses" (2), sometimes family reconfigurations embodied in the horror genre present new possibilities toward redefining what values the institution should represent and how it might be reconstructed. In *The Exorcist*, *Fatal Attraction*, and *Panic Room*, the family is reshaped into single mother-daughter relationships that exist outside the purview of a traditional patriarchal figure, the latter either absent or rendered impotent. In this context, it is instructive to consider that what distinguishes *The Exorcist* from *Panic Room* is that the mother and daughter in the latter are beneficiaries of a postfeminist sensibility while those in the former are not. Although the women in each of these pictures find themselves nearly overwhelmed by their respective encounters with evil, the thirty years separating these two films allow for very different solutions to similar problems.

The Exorcist was based on the history of a real exorcism performed on an adolescent male. Screenwriter William Peter Blatty and director William Friedkin altered the gender of the protagonist in the film in part to embrace the thesis that unbridled female sexuality is a dangerous thing. As Barbara Creed notes, it is the "refusal of the mother and child to recognize the paternal order [that] produces the monstrous" in this film (38). (Note the symbolism of paralleling the desecrated statue of Mary with Regan, as their respective virginities are transformed into grotesque parodies of transgressive sexuality.) The film implies that the demonic is aligned with the abdication of patriarchal authority (bad fathers beget bad happenings), and evil is counterbalanced only by the re-imposition of a patriarchal presence in the two good Catholic "fathers" who sacrifice themselves in order to rescue mother and daughter. Both fathers in *Panic Room*, Stephen Altman and his misguided alter ego, Burnham, in contrast, are unable to help either of their endangered families; in fact, to varying degrees these two fathers are to blame for setting in motion the events that cause the situation that imperils Meg and her daughter. *Panic Room* offers quite a different solution to *The Exorcist* in its recognition of abandoned women in position to take control over their own destinies. Thus, while the horror film features elements of fragmentation, inversion, and distress, it likewise subtly notes that problem-solving techniques and human adaptability exist to counterbalance forces aligned with the monstrous. The genre more often than not associates these survivalist traits with familial endurance—most notably when the family is reconstituted into a relationship minus the traditional patriarchal figure—than with the preservation of an individual going at it alone.

7.

Kubrickian Terrors

*2001: A Space Odyssey, A Clockwork Orange,
The Shining, Eyes Wide Shut*

In film noir, the viewer expects to see an urban landscape, a duplicitous femme fatale wearing too much makeup and too few clothes, and some level of criminal activity played out under the umbrella of a convoluted plot. Similarly, most Westerns speak to us of masculine bravado, a steady undercurrent of violence, and the inevitable clash between civilized values and the wilderness. Horror film is a more difficult genre to categorize. There are pictures featuring monstrous dolls, voracious leprechauns, and extraterrestrial creatures culled from a hallucinogenic nightmare; one of horror's more recent subgenres takes us into the tortured psy-ches of psychopathic cannibals and urbane serial killers; while another generation of horror movies hinges on an infernal biology of place that animates inanimate spaces: houses, hotels, automobiles, television sets and computers, cyborg machin-ery, dark wooded forests, even deepest space.

The broad range of horror topics notwithstanding, one of the common threads that unifies Gothic cinema, besides, of course, the requisite element of terror itself, is the theme of human isolation. Modern and postmodern horror films are about alienation—from oneself, from other people, from the social mainstream, from God Himself. An ironic aspect of horror art is its reliance on the existence of an afterlife—e.g., ghosts and supernatural visitors of various persuasions—with-out the counterbalancing presence of a divinity favorably disposed toward human-ity and our earthly affairs. The supernatural agencies that animate the horror film are almost exclusively evil, and humankind's cosmic loneliness is confirmed insofar as we must struggle against these evils on our own and without the active support of an equally powerful benevolent deity. In films made from Stephen King's fiction, for example, supernatural evil is thwarted only by humans helping other humans; no divine intermediary is present as a proactive force to offset the malefic spirits in permanent residency at the Overlook Hotel in *The Shining*, the revenant energies that animate the soured burial ground in *Pet Sematary*, the car in *Christine*, or the infernal machinery of *Maximum Overdrive* and *The Mangler*.

All horror films are, on some level, about some kind of loneliness and isolation. Indeed, in many of these films the horror occurs at the inescapable conjunction of past and present, the nexus point where individuals are trapped by a tragic inheritance they neither understand nor are capable of exorcising completely. The loneliness of a girl's distant murder continues to haunt those in the present who are unfortunate enough to uncover evidence of the child's depravity and doom in *The Ring*; it occurs in the spatial isolation of Edward Scissorhands, the boy-man resident of a Gothic amusement park who finds himself suddenly out of place in a stifling bourgeois neighborhood; it resides in the psychological loneliness of Norman Bates, rendered sexually dysfunctional because of an Oedipal obsession with his mother; it is the rejection that Carrie White experiences from her tortured and torturing peers because of the combination of her terrible telekinetic power and her equally terrible naïveté; and it is also evinced in the breakdown in communication and friendship that exacerbates the severe geographical displacement of *The Blair Witch Project*. Horror art is a confirmation of humanity's terrible existential fate: We are born into the world alone, we exit the same way, and most of our time in between is a desperate struggle to find someone to trust, much less to love. The themes of isolation and displacement that permeate the horror film are as essential to our understanding of the human condition in modern and postmodern times as Michelangelo's statue of *David* is to our grasp of the Italian Renaissance. Perhaps this is a major reason why horror art has emerged as such a dominant aspect of contemporary Western culture: It not only identifies the central fact of our existence—that we are isolated bodies plugged into an array of electronic toys and gadgetry but essentially cut off from the continuity and community of what it means to be human—it also reveals this fact without artifice or sentimental efforts to dilute its pervasiveness.

The films of Stanley Kubrick are all about human isolation and loneliness. Their terror is located in the inability of human beings to communicate (and thereby to lessen their isolation)—man to woman (*Lolita*, *The Shining* and *Eyes Wide Shut*), man to man (*Barry Lyndon*), man to technology (*2001*, *Clockwork Orange*, and *A.I.*), and man to his institutional bureaucracies (*Paths of Glory*, *Dr. Strangelove*, and *Full Metal Jacket*). In the play *No Exit*, Jean-Paul Sartre defined hell as "other people." One could argue that the same definition holds true in Kubrick's cinematic universe, except that it would be necessary to expand the concept to include myriad forms of technology and bureaucracy in addition to one's own self.

On the subject of cosmic isolation, Kubrick has noted, "If man merely sat back and thought about his impending termination, and his terrifying insignificance and aloneness in the cosmos, he would surely go mad, or succumb to a numbing sense of futility. Why bother . . . when he is no more than a momentary microbe on a dust mote whirling through the unimaginable immensity of space?" (Norden 85).

Throughout his career, Stanley Kubrick has directed technically brilliant masterpieces of postmodern terror and despair. His genius is evident in scenes that underscore humanity's puniness in the face of forces—natural and social—that strip away all veneers to reveal the essential cruelty and emptiness at the core of human nature and the societies we invent to hide this fact. This is why there are so few moments of genuine tenderness or warmth in Kubrick's oeuvre. In *The Shining* and *Eyes Wide Shut*, married couples are more apt to engage in acts of deception and hostility than acts of love; Kubrick's last film *A. I.* may have received some optimistic revising in Steven Spielberg's final editing efforts, but Kubrick's own artistic vision nevertheless concluded in the obliteration of the human race; even man's relationship to technological science in *Doctor Strangelove*, *A Clockwork Orange*, and *2001* is less about freeing humanity to pursue its full potential than it is about demonstrating how susceptible we are to being enslaved by the very machinery and pharmaceuticals that once promised a window to liberation.

Technologies of Terror: *2001* to *A Clockwork Orange*

Released in 1968, *2001: A Space Odyssey* prophesizes the future of techno-horror. While occasional moments in the film are a psychedelic carnival ride bordering on vertigo, of primary fascination only to those tripping on acid and in search of a kaleidoscope, most of the picture is a visual feast. *2001* really commences Kubrick's directorial fascination with vivid color, particularly the color red, that becomes a defining trait of the auteur's subsequent cinema. Although the director "discovered" color only after the release of his first nine films, relatively late in his career, Kubrick's major work shows its strong influence. In part a response to the psychedelia of the 1960s, *2001* and *Clockwork* present color in manner that is nearly overwhelming. There are moments in both films where Kubrick's choice of classical music is inextricably related to the colors of a setting, reaffirming the association that links music and color to the evocation of mood. Moreover, the particular use of red as the keynote color in Kubrick's cinematic palette speaks directly to cinematic meaning: The color red underscores varying levels of physical and psychological violence present in *Clockwork*, *The Shining*, and *Barry Lyndon*; forces the viewer to make a connection between HAL and demonic energies in *2001*; and is associated with the carnal sexuality present in nearly every sequence of *Eyes Wide Shut*.

2001's grand vistas of deep space and planetary bodies, of spacecraft floating in the dark immensity of the universe, especially when set in the context of George Lucas and the *Star Wars* (1977) saga on the cusp of the horizon, anticipate Hollywood's fascination with space travel in the future and become the prototype for a myriad of subsequent films. Moreover, it is not just the movie industry that would emulate Kubrick's vision, but history as well; *2001* provided us with the first credible view of life in space and man exploring extraterrestrial landscapes just as the Americans were anticipating landing on the moon. That the film also reveals itself as a cautionary tale about human overreliance upon a fragile technology, especially in light of the Challenger and Columbia shuttle disasters, is perhaps its ultimate legacy.

2001 opens with three minutes of black screen accompanied by the dramatic chords of *Thus Spake Zarathustra* before the audience is brought into the dazzling display of moon, earth, and sun as viewed from space. The effect of both—the black void followed immediately by heavenly bodies—is to provide the viewer with an appreciation of the immensity and grandeur of space, but also its vastness, its emptiness, its utter lack of anything human. This same sentiment continues when Kubrick lowers us down through the earth's atmosphere and into "The Dawn of Man." As with the prior view from the space, the viewer is once again entranced with the vistas of earth's landscape: long horizon shots of pristine sunsets still untainted by hydrocarbons, mountains and broad plains, the sound of wind blowing deathlessly across a landscape featuring only shrubs and rocks. Again, though, in spite of its raw aesthetics, nothing human is present in a universe untouched by man. The opening sequences of *2001* anticipate the initial overhead views of the Rocky Mountains in *The Shining*. In both films we are profoundly aware of nature's enormity, of its fierce beauty, and of its utter indifference to man's place in its composition. The unmistakable sense here is that these landscapes existed before man left his imprint, and that they will exist long after whatever imprint he has left fades. Whether cruising above the majestic peaks of the Rockies or peering into the hearts of galaxies still forming at the dawn of cosmic time, Kubrick's range of vision reveals the stark and cold beauty of a world where humans are the ultimate aliens.

When "men" finally appear in *2001*, it is in their most rudimentary evolutionary incarnation—as apes—and they restate the impression of loneliness and isolation mirrored in the landscape they inhabit. One ape willingly cooperates with another only until the other is a threat to the food or water supply. What is perhaps most notable about Kubrick's ape-human nexus is the degree to which individuals and groups fail to interact harmoniously: When one ape learns that a dried animal bone may be employed as a weapon, its use begins the process of individual and group domination of a species. When the film then fast-forwards millennia into the future, where man is fully evolved, having escaped the bonds of earth and now engaged in the process of conquering the rest of the galaxy, the viewer is once again impressed with the loneliness of his condition. Centuries of scientific and technological advancement have done nothing to ease this burden. In fact, the story of the HAL 9000 computer suggests that man may have originally built this incredible machine, but he may have built it too much in his own image as it is unclear whether he is still in control of it. Man may now be in the position to walk upright—indeed, the extremely disorienting camera angles used to film the Jupiter Mission sequence indicate that he has mastered the art of walking upside-down and sideways in a gravity-free environment—but this may represent the real extent of his evolutionary progress. Kubrick's astronauts appear as mere extensions of the spaceship and especially of HAL itself; their jobs are to listen to HAL's instructions and to carry out the computer's orders. As such, machines have replaced humans; HAL's quest for ultimate dominance merely takes the unequal relationship to its logical extreme.

HAL is the "brain and central nervous system" of the spaceship. As the computer describes itself in a television interview, HAL is the most advanced computer ever created; it is "foolproof and incapable of error." The self-conceit of the machine is, of course, merely a reflection of the hubris of its human creator. In fact, it is this hubris, the machine's most direct link to humanity, that propels HAL toward its self-designed rebellion against its own crew under the premise that "this mission is too important" to be jeopardized by less than perfect participants. Walker et al. believe that HAL's behavior is the direct result of its inability to admit to its own fallibility, that it has "made a mistake and begins to suffer a paranoid breakdown, exhibiting overanxiety about [its] own infallible reputation and then trying to cover up [its] error by a murderous attack on the human witnesses" (187). This is an interesting argument especially in light of HAL's hubris, but it all but eliminates or at minimum, excuses the sinister design of the computer's will to dominate. Beneath the surface of HAL's manipulative obsequiousness and its falsely nurturing monotone, lurks the classic horror monster: the red eye of a technological *id* biding its time before warping out of its programmed orbit. HAL has perverted its own logic, and in doing so morphs into a mechanized version of Francis Dolarhyde or even Dracula himself, viewing humans as necessary but disposable impediments to the realization of the monster's mad dream of conquest.

Like the humans who built it, HAL reveals its ultimate connection to the warring apes in its primitive desire for domination. Very little dialogue takes place onboard the Jupiter Mission (less than forty minutes of total spoken dialogue occurs in the entire film). In addition, most of the language that we hear onboard the ship is the mechanical drone uttered by HAL, whether in general conversation with Frank and Dave, the only two conscious astronauts onboard, or as part of the computer's clever duplicity that aids it in its quest to take over the mission. Murdering all the hibernating humans on board the Discovery, HAL uses language to manipulate and deceive Dave and Frank in trying to trap them into leaving the ship and thereby surrendering it over entirely to HAL. Amid the stark beauty of space, 2001 thereby offers a terrifying reality: That man has no one in the universe to trust; even the machines spawned by his own mind and hands are capable of betraying him. When HAL murders the crew while Dave is outside the ship trying to rescue Frank, and then refuses the order to allow Dave to re-enter, it is the ultimate betrayal and rebellion of machine technology. HAL's actions anticipate future generations of renegade cinematic cyborgs—from the replicants in *Blade Runner*, to the rampaging machines in *Maximum Overdrive*, to the *Terminator* generation of robots. As they drift in between planetary worlds with only their machinery separating them from the airless void that ends up consuming Frank, Kubrick's astronauts, despite the aid of their advanced technology, are no closer to unlocking the mysteries of life and the universe—aptly symbolized by the forever cryptic black monolith—than were their simian ancestors featured in the beginning of the film who were likewise baffled by the rectangular life force.

At one point in mid-flight before HAL's "malfunctioning," two parents appear on a video screen with a prerecorded birthday greeting for their astronaut son. The astronaut's robotic reaction to the gesture is so unaffected and detached that the viewer comes away feeling that HAL may be the single life form onboard the ship in possession of the deepest emotions. At one point this question is even asked: Is it possible that a computer as sophisticated as HAL could eventually develop human emotions? Indeed, both Frank and Dave barely speak to one another, choosing to eat their meals in silence while watching video news on their console monitors teleported from earth. The human world has seldom been portrayed with a greater level of sterility than what we find in 2001. It is as if the loneliness of space, the mysterious "dark energy" that is wrenching the cosmos apart, likewise defines the human community itself. This lack of communication is particularly ironic in light of the fact that the Jupiter Mission's goal is the pursuit of extraterrestrial life on planets at the furthest ends of the galaxy.

Underscoring his misanthropic view of existence, a recurring definition of madness and monstrosity in Kubrick's oeuvre is found in the self's total absorption with itself to the exclusion of meaningful interpersonal connections with others. Consider, for example, the fate that both HAL and Alex Burgess in *A Clockwork Orange* share in common. Although HAL is a computer, it is also a monster, viewing humans as expendable to its will, objects to be jettisoned into space once they are no longer useful to it. Alex is another version of HAL, insofar as he is a being without conscience or humanity. His gratuitous love of violence and sexual degradation is a symptom of his cynicism toward society; his sense of self-superiority, similar to HAL's, allows him to operate without remorse or an accurate appreciation of his shared place in a world of others.

Clockwork is a film drunk on extreme levels of terror and violence. More than three decades after its initial theatrical release and the countless movies that have tried in vain to emulate the complicated set of implications associated with the brutality in which it appears to revel, Clockwork embodies the quintessential horror aesthetic in its capacity to captivate at the same time that it severely disturbs. The movie portrays relentlessly one scene of mayhem after another; the nocturnal battle with Billy Boy is followed by an even more visceral and grisly beating and rape in the country home of a writer, Mr. Alexander, and his wife. The extreme dislocations that occur to Alex's personality are restated in Kubrick's employment of various classical music scores to choreograph episodes of violence that occur throughout the film. Thus, the beauty of Beethoven's Ninth Symphony, "a bird of rarest spun heavenly metal," or The William Tell Overture accompanies Alex's acts of wanton and random carnage, as if the audience is being made to juxtapose directly the extreme polarities of humanity itself—its glorious potential for creating and being inspired by high art and its opposite descent into barbaric bestiality. The film actually uses, as Vincent Canby recognized when it was first released, its violent feast as a means for protesting violence itself: "It is a horror show, but cool, so removed from reality that it would take someone who really cherished his perversions to get any vicarious pleasure from it. To isolate its violence is to ignore everything else that is at work in the movie" (1).

A Clockwork Orange opens with Alex and his gang of three droogs in a drug-induced stupor sitting inside the bizarre, mildly futuristic, and surreal Korova milk bar. The droogs as well as the other patrons in the bar sit on couches along the perimeter walls of a rectangular room. Throughout this initial scene, which lasts a total of 73 seconds, no one in the bar speaks a word, and no one in the bar appears conscious of anyone else, indicating the relative degree of their common alienation and drug-induced condition. Indeed, the degree of interpersonal social alienation shared among the customers at the milk bar is highlighted in their need to attain a near comatose condition through the ingestion of powerful pharmaceuticals. Alex's words are issued in a voice-over that informs us the droogs have been drinking a "milk-plus" libation designed to "sharpen you up and make you ready for a bit of the old ultra violence." Ironically, instead of appearing "sharp" and hyped "up," all the patrons in this bar look listless and morose, as if they would be more likely to be fighting naps than one another.

This is the first of several contradictory elements embedded in the film's opening sequence, as the scene opens out to provide a variety of insights into the themes central to the rest of the picture. It was not until late in the filming that Kubrick shot this opening, but as Walker et al. point out, "one would swear it was the first thing he did. It is less a 'scene' than an overture" (196). First, there is the matter of the "milk bar" itself. That Alex and his droogs consume a spiked *milk* concoction immediately offers a cue to their ages; not quite adults, nor are they still children, the droogs appear to be lost in an in-between state of identity formulation. Dressed in identical white uniforms and similar derby hats (at the same time blending the kind of jumpsuits perhaps best associated with childhood and the type of hat worn by bourgeois English businessmen), Alex and the droogs represent the worst legacy of the 1960s: They are emblematic of the era's overindulged children who abuse psychedelic drugs; are devoid of conscience, morality and responsibility for their actions; and seek their own hedonistic pleasure at the expense of others. High school students who have absolutely no commitment to their studies—Alex has been absent from school for the past week—the droogs "live for the evening" when they escape the garbage-strewn, lower middle-class housing projects they live in with their parents. Alex's parents are only dimly aware of their son's behavior, as his father skeptically "wonder[s] where exactly is it he goes to work at evenings." His mother is deluded enough to believe Alex's fabrication that he is engaged in some kind of "helping" activity for the less fortunate, rather than preying on them. In fact, the parents are not particularly pleased when their "cured" son is unexpectedly released from the Ludovico clinic, having conveniently replaced him with a substitute son/lodger who possesses many of the same aggressive traits that once characterized Alex.

Alex is very much a postmodern psychopath who is obsessed with images of violence and brutal sexuality; he exists beyond the domains of parents, school authorities, and the police. "If you need a motor car, you pluck it from the trees. If you need pretty Polly, you take it." Neither the product of poverty nor of domestic violence, Alex and the droogs (their very name suggests a synthesis of drugs and rock band nomenclature) would rather plunder and pillage than work for what they want, although it is never clear what it is they want, other than to plunder and pillage. Their criminality has its origins in boredom and rebellion from bourgeois values, even as Alex's bedroom is equipped with an expensive stereo system, his nightstand drawer filled with stolen watches and cash, and he dresses at the height of elegant mod fashion when he seduces two teenyboppers in the music store. As Thomas Allen Nelson assesses correctly, Alex is "the Star-Child of the Id, who explores and acts out the dark secrets of interior space as an alternative to 'growing up' in a clockwork society" (141).

Let us return once more to the Korova milk bar (see Figure 5, p. 193). Its inte-

rior features several naked, extremely lifelike, alabaster-white ceramic female bodies, unsettling in their physical beauty because the women statues exist not only
as erotic art but also as functional furniture used as tables and chairs by the bar's
patrons. The degrading of the feminine in the film's opening interior scene extends
to include the attitude Alex and the droogs manifest toward flesh and blood
females throughout the movie. Neither maternal nor particularly erotic except in
the most sadomasochistic way, women are reduced to mere furniture objects to be
used, tossed around, violated, and then discarded. Their presence in the milk
bar—as silent and stationary dispensers of tainted milk and fetishized body parts—
merely prefigures the manner in which they are perceived by Alex and his droogs
in real life. (Note how often images of women bound and silenced appear in the
course of this film: Several of the alabaster milk ladies are wearing silver chains
around their white hands which are bound behind their backs; Mrs. Alexander has
her hands and mouth taped and gagged prior to her rape in the country home scene;
and there is an elaborate, framed pornographic painting of a woman wearing a cloth
gag over her mouth in the home of the cat lady.)

The breasts of the bar's ceramic women distribute milk, but it is not *pure*
milk, nor does this liquid nurture so much as it perverts all those who suckle from
these artificial teats. Additionally, the opening confirms the cynical assessment of
the drunken homeless man that the droogs pummel in the subsequent scene:
Society has reached its nadir, a point where it largely tolerates, and even sanctions
in the (apparently legal) juice that is served up in the milk bar, daily acts of violence against its most vulnerable citizenry. Lastly, the chemically treated milk
that the droogs consume in the bar on two separate occasions initiates the techno-
horror theme that is developed more extensively later in the film.

Alex's psyche is the subject of various paramedical experiments throughout
Clockwork, beginning with the spiked milk potent he willingly ingests and leading
up to the government-sponsored behavior-modification program that is imposed
upon him with the goal of eradicating his violent urges and making him a compli-
ant citizen. The perverse range of psycho-transformational drugs featured in this
film produce extreme reactions in Alex—from the ultraviolent street punk in the
first half of the picture to the ultrapassive doormat in the second half. Kubrick suggests that both these extreme conditions are grotesquely artificial, that neither state
is optimal or desirable, and that the reality of human nature appears to fall somewhere in between. The core terror of *Clockwork* is the inability of Alex to find this
middle ground; in his role as either victim or monster he lacks balance and purpose.

His situation as a lost man in a lost world is severely complicated by the hyp-
ocritical machinations of politicians that seek to protect themselves at all costs,
even when their technological experiment produces a disastrous failure. In the end,
government remains indifferent to Alex as an individual—his physical and psycho-

logical welfare as well as his moral reformation. As the Minister of the Interior reveals in the final scene of the film, all that the ruling party values is its image in the media and how that image might improve its chances for being re-elected. When Alex performs like a trained dog in front of an audience of bureaucrats that applauds his aversion to violence and sex, his reactions are strictly monitored by the minister for the duration of the exhibition. However, once returned to the real world, Alex is left completely on his own and is as helpless as a declawed cat; in the violence of postmodern society, the "true Christian, willing to turn the other cheek, ready to be crucified than to crucify" becomes an easy target. All that the state-sponsored behavior modification program reveals is that the government is willing to go to any length—including manipulating the advances of medical technology—to make "the problem of criminal violence a thing of the past." In response to the prison chaplain's charge that the state has stripped Alex of his free will, the minister counters, "We are not concerned with the motives or the higher ethics. We are concerned only with cutting down crime."

Just before Alex is selected to undergo the Ludovico procedure, to "kill the criminal reflex," the minister speculates "soon we may be needing all our prisons for political offenders." This disturbing threat to democratic principles reflects the attitude of the film's government and prison authorities as well. Indeed, Mr. Alexander, the handicapped writer who seeks to revenge himself upon Alex, is "put away" at the end of the movie, taken to a place where his diatribes against the state will be censored. The Ludovico procedure is informed by a belief that man's free will leads him into trouble and that the right combination of environment and drugs will lead him into "socially acceptable" behavioral patterns. Just as Dostoevsky railed against such rational reductions in *Notes from the Underground* a hundred years earlier, Kubrick argues likewise in *Clockwork*; man's free will may result in the horrors of self-destructive and antisocial behavior, but this is forever preferable to the mindless zombies of governmental manipulation. In the end, the unholy alliance forged between science and the state is even more odious and horrific than the nihilism of Alex and the droogs. The state apparatus portrayed in *Clockwork* proves itself just as aggressive and prone to violence as the criminals it seeks to reform, yet the government codes its work under the veneer of social advancement and the pursuit of law. It is thus no mere coincidence that Kubrick features documentary film footage from the Nazi era to stimulate Alex's drug-induced aversion to violence. In addition to its idealization of brutality, the Nazi footage also poses a direct, albeit ironic, comment on a nascent English totalitarianism that visits its own brand of experimental violence on its citizens.

In its contradictory function as a tool meant to aid in man's evolutionary design, the science in this film ends up stripping him of his very humanity. Instead of "enhancing human life, technology annihilates it, as in *Dr. Strangelove*; depletes it, as in *2001*; or perverts it, as in *Clockwork Orange*" (Walker et al. 215). Beneath the attractive social panacea promised by technological innovation (contrast the state-of-the-art facilities and progressive doublespeak of the Ludovico clinic with the dreary Christian fundamentalist cant Alex finds in prison), Kubrick warns, lurks a darkly disturbing reality. The new creature that postmodern science unleashes in *Clockwork* proves to be just as undesirable as the monster that emerged from Dr. Frankenstein's laboratory.

The Marriage Group: *The Shining* to *Eyes Wide Shut*

The early work of Stanley Kubrick is to a certain degree characterized by a fascination with space and futuristic scenarios. As the director's work matured, his focus returned to earth, specifically the arena of domestic relationships. Kubrick traded, in other words, the eeriness of space and the threat of machine technology for the eeriness and equally viable threat of matrimony. In both cases, his human protagonists appear equally as dislocated and lost. Marriage, in Kubrick's world, brings little comfort and even less security; his marital couples are no less grounded or whole than the alien loners in *Clockwork* or the space drifters in *Dr. Strangelove* and *2001*.

Kubrick's interest in exploring the terrain of gender warfare can be traced as far back as *Lolita*, and *Barry Lyndon* is likewise a film that suggests the ultimate incompatibility of men and women despite their moments of profound sexual attraction. However, *The Shining* is unequivocally his darkest exploration into the horrors of masculine behavior and its impact on the marital union. Midway through the movie, Wendy visits her husband while the latter is seated in front of his typewriter. She is cheerful and genuinely soliticitous about his writing progress; she tries to help by asking if later on he might like to show her something that he's written. For the first time in the film, Jack's reaction is an overreaction. He dismisses his wife's concern by informing her that each time she interrupts him she breaks his creative concentration. Most importantly, he banishes her from the Colorado Lounge with the patronizing command: "We're going to make a new rule. When I'm in here, and you hear me typing, or whether you don't hear me typing, or whatever the fuck you hear me doing in here, that means don't come in."

This scene is important for several reasons. First, it is the initial moment in the picture when the audience sees for itself that Jack's temper and frustration levels do not fall within an acceptable range, that he is not just being "grouchy"; that he is more than capable of exploding violently; and that Wendy is not only terrified of her own husband, she is also unwilling to confront his boorish behavior. For these reasons, the audience is now prepared for the escalating violence and deepening loss of respect for Wendy that will characterize Jack's personality for the remainder of the picture. The scene's violence embedded in Jack's tone and diction alerts us to the reality that this is a writer suffering more than a mere case of writer's block.

Additionally, the confrontation centers on Jack's writing—his talent at communicating through the medium of language. Wendy clearly understands the importance of his work both as a means for Jack to find self-worth and for the family to regain its financial independence; indeed, she actually submits to his imperious cruelty as if it were an element in the composing process. In light of these literary impressions, later on in the film when Wendy and the audience discover simultaneously the contents of Jack's manuscript—the repeated phrase "All work and no play makes Jack a dull boy"—the revelation is all the more shocking. Kubrick senses the importance of this literary revelation, how it signals the ultimate demise of Jack's rational faculties, and he films it with methodical care. We view Wendy's discovery of the manuscript, the text for which she has willingly undergone such humiliation in order for her husband to produce, from underneath the desk. Her face reflects a slow unfolding of terror as she rifles disbelievingly through page after page of the same typed phrase. When Jack startles her reading by sneaking up from behind and asking sardonically, "How do you like it?" Wendy's fear is encapsulated in her response immediately after her scream, "Stay away from me," and her willingness now to employ the baseball bat as a weapon against her husband.

It is not only his writing *work* that makes Jack a dull boy who refuses to *play* with his wife unless the game is of his design and played on his terms. The cryptic phrase also opens out in all sorts of interesting directions, starting with but certainly not limited to the work that the Torrance marriage appears to require in order for it to survive. Prior to their arrival at the Overlook, Jack has labored hard in undertaking some of this requisite work, but it has come at the expense of too many opportunities for selfish play: indulging his alcoholism and volatile temper, his desire to be a famous writer (and all the delicious fruits that would attend such success), his attraction to other women (as clearly indicated in Jack's response to the naked female in room 237), and his not-so-repressed urge to be alone—like one of the free spirits in residence at the Overlook, liberated from the dual burdens of family and monetary responsibilities.

While *The Shining* employs more of the standard paraphernalia associated with the horror film—e.g., a haunted house, ghosts, shocking murders—its truest connection is to Kubrick's own oeuvre, particularly *2001* and *Clockwork Orange*, rather than to other more traditional haunted-house movies. For, like its predecessors in Kubrick's cinematic canon, *The Shining* is less about fear of unexplained supernatural phenomena (note how insignificant the actual ghosts at the Overlook are as corporeal entities and the fact that they do not emerge en masse until late in the picture) than it is about the terror of human silence and miscommunication.

What scares us in this film is that a man can become so isolated within himself that he prefers the ghosts that haunt his imagination to the potential life-affirming relationship he shares with his family. Like Alex, Jack is petrified of becoming a "clockwork" man, fearful of being further reduced in stature to "shoveling driveways [and] work in a car wash." Ironically, the ghosts at the Overlook transform him into the ultimate "clockwork" nightmare: By the end of the film his will is no longer his own and he is nothing more than an extension of the evil machinery (HAL?) that runs the Overlook. What better illustration of this "clockwork" condition is there than the reduction of Torrance's language talents to the single mindless mantra, *All Work and No Play*, retyped endlessly? Torrance's writing project is equivalent to HAL's diminished consciousness after Dave enters its brain and begins dismantling the computer's thinking processes, leaving the machine unable to do more than slur the words to "Daisy."

In the essay, "What About Jack? Another Perspective on Family Relationships in Stanley Kubrick's *The Shining*," Frank Manchel insists that Torrance is as much a victim in this film as Wendy and Danny. According to Manchel, the real monster in *The Shining* is the spirit of patriarchal capitalism firmly entrenched at the Overlook and the undue influence it exerts over Torrance as an American male: "Jack is spiritually alone. His patriarchal conditioning tells him to work hard, provide for his family, and repress 'feminine' characteristics" (91). In his failure to live up to these expectations and "deluded myths of success and a second chance, Jack Torrance is a sad figure more deserving of our pity than our contempt" (92). Manchel's position notwithstanding, Jack Torrance is, simultaneously, both the victim of an evil design and an active participant in his own self-destruction. Like one of Shakespeare's tragic protagonists, Torrance is both responsible for his own doom and a pawn, as Manchel notes, under the sway of forces that he neither understands nor is fully cognizant of their influence over him.

In the scene to which I have already alluded, where Wendy interrupts Jack's writing in the Colorado Lounge, it is easy to overlook the scrapbook that rests face open on the table to the right of Jack's typewriter and that becomes a kind of symbolic barrier measuring the divide that exists between husband and wife. Throughout Kubrick's film, the scrapbook is barely present; none of the characters even reference it. Even so, Kubrick means the observant filmgoer to identify the book with Torrance's writing. In King's novel, the scrapbook is of critical importance; it occupies its own entire chapter (18) and serves as a microcosm of the hotel's nefarious history that sparks—and then overwhelms—Jack's creative imagination. The one aspect of the scrapbook's relevance that King and Kubrick appear to share in common is the fact that in both novel and film Jack refuses to share information about the scrapbook's existence with his wife. Clearly, Kubrick means for us to see the scrapbook as connected to—perhaps even inspiring—Jack's *All*

Work and No Play writing project. Why else would it be included in the mise-en-scènes, lying open and juxtaposed to Jack's typewriter, on two separate occasions?

As a history of the Overlook, the scrapbook contains its darkest secrets, just as the *All Work and No Play* typing exercise is one of the secrets Jack has been keeping from Wendy throughout their tenure at the hotel. The events chronicled in the hotel's scrapbook are aligned to Torrance's own private, uneasily buried past and unconscious fantasies. The hotel's eras of prestige and opulence impress Jack because he is a man who is in a desperate search for something to believe in personally—a success story of his own. Conversely, the hotel's penchant for depravity attracts him for the same reason: Torrance recognizes, however dimly, his own history of self-destructive behavior in the hotel's most iniquitous moments. So, just as the secret history of the Overlook—and the America it "overlooks" from a mountaintop at the middle of the continent—is one of violence and corruption under the veneer of affluence and sophisticated elegance, Jack is reluctant to acknowledge that just beneath the surface of his occupation as a teacher and a serious man of letters lurks Mr. Hyde, the beast who is capable of breaking his son's arm and murdering his wife with an axe.

Manchel concludes his essay by asking: "What could Wendy and Danny have done to offset [Jack's] feelings of inadequacy? Why couldn't the family have shown more love and understanding to each other instead of so much suspicion and disdain?" (93). Both these questions underscore the helplessness of the situation Kubrick poses in this film, but perhaps more important is that such sentiments are always undermined in Jack's concealed behavior: his choice to keep secret the hotel's scrapbook as well as the disturbing writing project that occupies so much of his attention. Jack's tendency is always to reject Wendy's offers of support and concern—ignoring her invitations, as he does in the Colorado Lounge scene—by avoiding revelation of his deepest vulnerabilities. He thereby misses the opportunity to lighten his psychological burden. He believes he must repress the shadow of his past rather than employ Wendy or Danny to help him grow beyond the mistakes he has made. As King himself has speculated, "the tragedy of *The Shining* might have been averted if somewhere along the line Jack had taken Wendy by the hand and said, 'Dear, I think I need counseling'" (Magistrale 19). It is no small thing that Jack chooses to reveal his version of Danny's broken arm "accident" to Lloyd the bartender, a strange ghoul he has either conjured in his own head or met recently, rather than to discuss it further with his immediate family. Jack's refusal to admit Wendy and Danny into the darkest corner of his psyche is closely connected to his unwillingness to share both the existence of the hotel's scrapbook and his unsettling one-line manuscript: This is a man whose habit of secret-keeping is finally more important to him than his marriage.

Forbidden knowledge is a common link that connects *The Shining* to *Eyes Wide Shut*. Whether in the maintaining of secrets, such as the Overlook's scrapbook, or in their spiteful revelation, such as a wife's confession of her adulterous fantasies, Kubrick's protagonists are pushed toward isolation and into a state that undermines the trust necessary to sustaining any marital union. The secrets men and women keep in these films do not merely highlight the differences that divide men and women, husbands and wives along gender lines; the tragic consequences associated with forbidden knowledge also strikes a cautionary note that generally pervades horror cinema—a sobering reminder that secrets protect the existence of certain places we have no business going, certain knowledge that will ultimately cost us our happiness and sanity.

Both *The Shining* and *Eyes* feature husbands who are drawn into secreted worlds that closely resemble one another in terms of their mutual decadence and dark seclusion. As Torrance's association with the spectral energies that reside at the Overlook deepens, his relationship to Wendy and Danny (and, for that matter, his literary career) diminishes reciprocally. By the end of the picture, Torrance is literally frozen inside himself, no longer able to communicate with, much less protect, his embattled family. This is also why *The Shining* ends with a framed photograph of Torrance at the center of the hotel's July 4, 1921, gala. He is pictured in the exact role he has long desired, perhaps even before his arrival at the Overlook: as the entertaining, freewheeling Master of Ceremonies, finally extricated from the dual burdens of wife and child, and immersed in the perpetual party that serves as an embodiment of the Roaring Twenties.

Similarly, it is the secret knowledge of a wife's sexual fantasy indulgence that alienates her husband in *Eyes Wide Shut*. Like Torrance, *Eyes*' William Harford spends most of the movie estranged from his spouse and in pursuit of a highly internalized agenda that threatens the marital bond. While Harford never turns sociopathic, he is equally as trapped within his own psyche as Jack Torrance is in his. The problem with both the marriages in these two pictures is that they feature individuals who have almost no ability to communicate effectively with one another.

In the transition toward Romanticism that took place in the last two decades of the eighteenth century, as the reasoned balance of the Enlightenment gave way to the emotional disruptions that characterized the Gothic, perhaps the clearest way of describing this antithetical shift in values is as a movement away from rational objectivity and toward the subjective, interior world of highly stressed emotions. Kubrick's own brand of horror reflects something of this dualism. His filmmaking owes something to the rational aesthetics of the Enlightenment; it is technically brilliant, even to the extreme of creating a mise-en-scène—as in *2001* or in *Dr. Strangelove*—that is stripped of human emotion bordering on technological fetishism. Moreover, his portrayal of subject themes reflects the unsentimental sentiments of eighteenth-century history and sensibility. In the movie 2001, for example, human beings are subordinate to the positioning and operation of machinery, the latter of far more interest to both the director and the audience.

In *The Shining* and *Eyes Wide Shut*, however, Kubrick descends into a less-sanitized Gothic realm where the unconscious, subjective psyche of the protagonist entirely dominates the camera's vision as well as the direction of the movie's plot. The audience is essentially "lost" in the distorted and tortured psyches of the two male protagonists in *The Shining* and *Eyes*; neither one of these men retains a balanced or rational worldview as both reside exclusively in their own imaginary realms. The ordered and detached survival guide of the Enlightenment gives way to messy and personalized quests that are prototypically Romantic. Helpless in the face of escalating madness and emotional disruption, Kubrick's husbands rebel against the confinement of the marriage bed and head into the uncharted and dangerous territory of the unconscious. Francisco Goya's painting, "The Sleep of Reason Breeds Monsters," is an apt commentary on what occurs in these two films.

Literally, as well as psychologically, *Eyes* begins where *The Shining* ends. Even Kubrick's attraction to the dominant color scheme found at the Overlook—gold, ochre, and red—reappears in the glittering Christmas party dance hall décor of *Eyes*. Indeed, throughout *Eyes* the careful viewer of Kubrick cannot help but feel reintroduced into a psychosexual landscape that closely resembles the one in place at the Overlook when the ghouls have fully morphed into human form and commenced to participate in the "great party," as it is judged by the ghost-man whose head is bleeding but whose whiskey drink takes precedence over his wound. In both movies, the adult combinations of sex, alcohol, and temptation reach a point where flirtation leads to betrayal; pleasure leads to decadence; and play leads to violence.

In his discussion of the many variables that may contribute to the relatively simple act of inspiring terror, James Twitchell generalizes that "The art of horror is the art of generating breakdown, where signifier and signified no longer can be kept separate, where distinctions can no longer be made, where old masks fall and new masks are not yet made" (16). Perhaps no better single statement could be made about what makes *Eyes* such a disturbing work of horror. In a picture that relies so heavily upon masks—literal as well as metaphorical—we find ourselves in the comfortable life of Dr. William Harford, a well-respected physician in New York City, who lives in elegant quarters with a beautiful wife and daughter, and whose cozy world has abruptly been turned upside down. His wife, Alice Harford, after partaking in some powerful mind-altering marijuana, discloses an elaborate sexual fantasy to her husband involving a dashing stranger she encountered months earlier in a hotel lobby. Although her sexual projection is merely that, no actual act of infidelity has taken place except in the highly explicit imagination of Mrs. Harford, her husband is so unnerved by his wife's disclosure that for the remainder of the film he undergoes a "breakdown" similar in extent and intensity to what Twitchell describes above. Moreover, as Twitchell notes, Harford finds it impossible to maintain distinctions among separate worlds of signifiers, as fantasy blurs into reality and an interiorized psychology usurps the condition of everyday normality. The audience is never certain, anymore than is Bill Harford, what parts of the film represent objective reality and what parts are a visual projections of the doctor's unleashed unconscious.

At the Christmas party early in the film, before we know much of anything about the Harfords, the spectator learns perhaps the most important thing she needs to know: Both husband and wife, like the rest of us, flirt with, and are highly susceptible to, the temptation to stray sexually from their nine-year-old marriage. Although tipsy on champagne, Alice is sober enough to recognize that she is highly vulnerable to the charms of the slick Hungarian flaneur, and that she had better relocate her husband before his seduction progresses any further. Dr. Harford, however, is equally distracted by two female models who appear on the verge of initiating him into a ménage a trois before their design is interrupted by a summons to attend Victor Ziegler's girlfriend, who has overdosed on drugs. These parallel near seductions set a context for the film's examination of issues of adultery and sexual experimentation. The Christmas party opens the door to the topic of marital infidelity, prompting Alice, when she and her husband are alone the following night, to reveal her sexual fantasy about the naval officer in the hotel. The disclosure of this urge is merely a continuation of the flirtation/seduction scenes that commence the film at the Ziegler Christmas party.

The level of his wife's candor and unbridled passion produces in the good doctor a jealous reaction that unleashes the monster within himself. It is as if Alice's *willingness* to risk everything in their marriage in order to sleep with a strange man is worse than actually performing the act itself. Moreover, the fact that his wife has not physically betrayed him provides little comfort to the formerly self-disciplined Dr. Harford as it only fuels the full range of his own imaginary explorations (filmed in black and white) into what his wife might have done had the opportunity presented itself. In a matter of minutes William Harford undergoes a jarring dislocation; he discovers the frail bonds that hold together the existence he has created for himself and his family. While technically not betrayed by his spouse, his naïve conception of her character and the marriage upon which he put his faith—"I know *you* would never be unfaithful to me," he tells Alice before her revelation—are severely rocked; his innocence is shaken. It is as if there are suddenly two Alices: The woman he thought he knew—his loyal wife and mother of their child (note how often in the film Alice is shown to be a loving and doting parent)—and another woman who exists behind her domesticated *mask*, who is willing and capable of betraying and wrecking the complacent universe the Harfords have constructed. The language and lascivious tone Alice employs in making her confession contains all the destructive sexual energy of the id that Freud recognized and cautioned against: "If he wanted me, even if it was only for one night, I was ready to give up everything—you, Helena, my whole fucking future. Everything." The emergence of Alice's sexual alter ego, in turn, forces her husband likewise to confront his own secreted self that exists beneath his identity as respected doctor and monogamous husband-father. No longer capable of making clear distinctions in his life—of maintaining the balance necessary for sustaining order in his marriage and his personal microcosm—Dr. Harford follows his wife's experience and undertakes a psychological journey of his own where he encounters a self-imposed nightmare and becomes as spiritually lost as Jack Torrance, wandering aimlessly inside the frozen hedge maze, or Barry Lyndon after the latter assaults his stepson, Bullingdon, and shames both Mrs. Lyndon and Barry's status as a gentleman through the loss of his temper.

For two days after his wife's disclosure, Dr. Harford inhabits a place where Twitchell speculates, "distinctions can no longer be made," as the distraught husband cannot keep himself from envisioning Alice in passionate embraces with the handsome stranger she has described. No sooner does his wife reveal her sexual urge than Harford finds himself kissing the grieving daughter of a recently deceased patient. Although it is Harford who pulls away and appears to be confused by her kiss and proclamation of love, "we barely know each other" he protests, the awkward scene is actually a subjective projection of the doctor's own need to re-establish control over women. After his humiliating experience with his wife, in this fantasy sequence that immediately follows it Harford returns to the role of the omniscient and paternalistic physician whose sensible yet sensitive rationality reasserts control over a desperate woman's impulsive sexuality (while safely avoiding taking it seriously). The fact that he is incapable of managing the threatening libidinous urges of his wife is underscored in his need to re-establish dominance over feminine sexuality with the very next woman he encounters.

Similarly, the audience then follows the doctor into the highly unrealistic worlds of a kind and beautiful urban prostitute (who remains only remotely interested in his money) and an equally surreal suburban cult party where the party revelers, except for their elaborate masks and stark nudity, are as unnaturally affected as the social parlor play of *Barry Lyndon*'s aristocrats. Instead of simply accepting his wife's proclamation that good women are also capable of "doing a bad, bad thing," Dr. Harford's patriarchal orientation toward female marital purity and his own superficial understanding of his wife force him to confront a world that he can no longer comfortably identify or control. The highly professional exterior of his daytime Dr. Jekyll persona contrasts with the Mr. Hyde who emerges to prowl the nocturnal streets of New York in a desperate search of his own fantasy fulfillment, an exploration that, ironically, remains as much relegated to the imagination as Alice's sexual liaison with the naval officer. Like Dr. Jekyll, Dr. Harford opens himself to the darkest recesses of his own repressed psyche. The suburban masquerade party he crashes is merely a projection of Harford's quest into his unconscious, and perhaps this sheds some light on the unexplained appearance of a displaced party mask on the doctor's own bedroom pillow at the conclusion of the film. The "eyes wide shut" oxymoron is an apt description of both the doctor's severely limited understanding of women, especially his own wife ("If you men only knew," Alice chastises), as well as the condition of a waking dream, the state of a suspended reality that Harford inhabits for most of the film. Indeed, the dreamlike scene where he is confronted and exposed as an interloper in front of the assembled party revelers indicates the doctor's own subconscious awareness of the fact that he possesses neither the courage nor the true desire to undergo a full immersion into the decadent world of sin and illicit sex. While he acknowledges a willingness to "go to someplace more private" with one of the masked beauties, as in the early sequence with the two seductive models at the Christmas party, he never actually does so. Instead, he immediately punishes himself for articulating this desire when he is publicly humiliated in front of the orgy participants and commanded to take off his clothes.

In further confirmation of this, all of Harford's excursions around the perimeters of illicit sex bring no real satisfaction or even much sustained eroticism as each of his titillating encounters ends up focusing on only the most terrifying aspects of sexuality: the lovely prostitute he meets on the street turns out to be HIV-positive; the secret sex cult in the suburbs proves to be more about acts of masochistic humiliation and retribution than it is about sexual liberation or fun; Alice's own dream of multiple lovers exists solely to debase her husband, "to make fun of you, to laugh in your face"; even the sex proffered from the young girl in the theatrical costume shop is perversely unappealing. Afraid of fulfilling his own unconscious projections, even as he is compelled to pursue them, Harford's dreams of coitus are always interrupted—suggesting a frustrating debilitation, intercourse with neither orgasm nor emotional relief—by a telephone call from his wife, an officious sex priest in scarlet, a summons to resuscitate Ziegler's drugged party girl, a sobering revelation of an AIDS diagnosis that deflates an erotic liaison with the street prostitute's roommate, or the awkward intrusion of a fiancé to interrupt a passionate kiss. Like his wife's submission to the erotic stranger, Bill Harford's fantasy life is less about sex than it is about self-debasement and punishment for libidinous urges he never gets to consummate.

In their final conversation at the end of the film, husband and wife appear to acknowledge that the experiences they have undergone were more imaginary than real: "We should be grateful that we managed to survive all of our adventures, whether they were real or only a dream," Alice Harford posits, more unsettled than she is relieved by everything that the couple has undergone. Kubrick's Dr. Harford flirts with the same level of sensual dissipation that dooms Dr. Jekyll, but he pulls back in time before the Hydes that lurk both within and without irrevocably ruin his life. Although husband and wife are allowed to escape their collective nightmare, to retreat back into the safe and exclusive union of their bourgeois marriage, Kubrick's message in this film is that neither does so unscathed. As a sobered Dr. Harford concludes, "No dream is ever just a dream"; the dark places that exist within the human psyche, even a relatively normal and well-adjusted psyche, informs us that nothing touched by the human is ever again wholly innocent or managable.

8.

The Body Terrified

The Texas Chainsaw Massacre, Halloween, Friday the 13th, A Nightmare on Elm Street

With its emphases on random serial killings of teenagers (often in some state of undress and/or copulation), violent displays of young bodies ripped open by phallic weaponry (razor-fingers, chainsaws, drills, knives), and its fascination with psychotic male murderers who stalk the night in search of human prey, slasher— also known as splatter—films, despite the limitations of their identical plots and other resemblances to one another, have proven to be both resilient and bankable commodities. The slasher movie is a subgenre of the horror film that originated in pictures released during the 1970s (*The Texas Chainsaw Massacre* and *Halloween*) and reached its bloody apex in the mid-1980s. Like its principal character psychopaths, however, the splatter genre has stubbornly refused to die and is resuscitated periodically as evinced in *Halloween H20: Twenty Years Later* (1998), *Halloween Resurrection* (2002), and the *Freddy vs. Jason* standoff of 2003.

Because many of the plot mechanics associated with the slasher film keep coming back to issues of gender—the monster is invariably a single male (*Friday the 13th* is the notable exception, where the spirit of Jason works through his mother, although the murderous son inhabits his own male form in the sequels), and his favorite prey is female—the genre has also attracted more than its share of attention from feminist scholars. Many argue that despite its reductive plotline and the superhuman ability of the killer to survive somehow in order to be reborn in the invariable sequels, the slasher film has much to say to us about the proliferation of male aggression in postmodern society and the emerging survival skills of post-feminist women (e.g., Clover's Final Girl). Recent feminist social theorists, such as Jane Caputi and Robin Morgan, have linked serial sex murderers to the issue of patriarchal abuse. They argue that both the criminals who perpetrate these crimes, as well as those of us who remain fascinated with them either in real life or in their artistic representations, are motivated by some of the more sinister aspects of phallocentrism and the fear or hatred of women.

Barbara Creed and Linda Williams have both traced in certain strains of horror art a reliance on monstrous maternal figures. In her essay "Film Bodies: Gender, Genre, and Excess," commenting on the differences between horror and melodrama, Williams says this about the former: "Horror is the genre that seems to endlessly repeat the trauma of castration, as if to 'explain' by repetitive mastery, the original problem of sexual difference" (154). No subgenre in the horror field has felt the need to emphasize these observations—especially the trauma of castration and the compulsion to reenact symbolically its violence—more than the slasher film. The castrating mother is seen to humiliate and then punish the sexuality of her son, and this, in turn, gives rise to the son's violent antipathy toward all women who are reduced to mother substitutes. Films such as *The Texas Chainsaw Massacre* and *Friday the 13th* follow *Psycho*—the archetypical example for what Williams has in mind, and arguably the first of the slasher films—in duplicating this pattern. The male monster vents continually his internalized-castrating mother's rage against the sexual arousal inspired by attractive females in addition to his own encompassing and personalized revenge against the gender that has oppressed him.

Consequently, the male monster in the slasher film is never interested in his own sexuality per se—as arousal serves only to stimulate his compulsion to assault the object of his lust rather than bond with her. Although he wishes passionately to penetrate female flesh, his efforts are not about procuring pleasure or release for either himself or his victim. The slasher film emphasizes the open wound of the broken body, the resplendently appointed corpse that is penetrated in order to open it out, like one of Francis Bacon's paintings, to display itself as a visual feast (Crane 141). Since punishment is the compulsive motivator that stimulates the libido for the serial killer in these films, it is not surprising that Leatherface, Michael, Jason, and Freddy, among their plethora of imitators, rely on mechanized or metallic phallic surrogates to do violence against the bodies of women. Their own sexual energies are sublimated into their phallic weapons of choice, and even if any of these killers possessed the remote desire for normal sex, it is unlikely that they would be able to function on their own. When a distraught Sally beseeches the males in *Texas Chainsaw Massacre* with the pledge "I'll do anything you want," it is a clear attempt to trade sex for her life. However, the members of the cannibal family barely react to her invitation; their interest in Sally is on a level far more perverse than mere rape. Most the male killers who appear in slasher films are impotent in some fashion. They are either sexually dysfunctional or have sublimated their libidos into compulsive acts of mayhem.

So, where does this white male anger against women—specifically, young, assertive, and sexually desirable women—come from? As this violent pattern is repeated throughout the genre, it seems impossible not to view it, at least in part, as a reaction against the emerging independent female of a fledgling women's liberation movement and the corresponding erosion of power and gender identity associated with the traditional patriarchy. Women characters in these films drink, smoke dope, swear, fuck. They have appropriated male desires and privileges and confront men for the things they want, especially sex. The killer seeks to reestablish masculine dominance over a world that women have turned upside down. This is why the slasher male obtains such obvious pleasure in watching his female victims cower and scream: In his mind, and in the collective subconscious of many members of the audience, women need to reassume their place as subordinates to the will of men. In the slasher genre, it ultimately requires the death of women to affirm male dominance, but part of this process is also in stalking the female—making her aware of her physical vulnerability, threatening her self-confidence, and imposing psychological control over her world.

I will have more to say about the disturbing absence of language evinced by the killers in the slasher genre elsewhere in this chapter, but for now let it suffice that their silences highlight the depth of rage in their beings. As such, they are dark extensions of Western culture's masculine opprobrium against revealing deep emotion (thus, the killers' ubiquitous facial masks) and the feminization of language. At the same time, it can be noted that the killers' utter refusal to explain themselves or provide motivation for their behavior reasserts the masculine prerogative to act toward women in ways that are both reprehensible and unaccountable.

The male murderers in this genre, emerging as they do in the late 1970s and throughout the 1980s, embody the range of rage and frustration that attended the challenges occurring to patriarchal hegemony during this historical period. The election of Ronald Reagan as president during this time with his emphasis on a return to traditional patriarchal values corresponds perfectly to the rise of the American slasher film in mainstream cinema, as both Reagan and the serial killers in these movies sought a return to white male authority. One advocated this revision by extolling traditional family values, Christian piety, and the supremacy of the Caucasian male over minorities and women; the other attacked the most blatant source for the erosion of these principles: the liberated female.

Although murder and visceral carnage are the end results the slasher killers pursue, again recalling *Psycho*, it is impossible not to think of the violence of their actions in a sexual context. First, there is the emotional frenzy that attends their assault; these serial killers go about their business with a recklessness and passion that resembles sexual arousal. Clover suggests that the killers' "fury is unmistakable sexual in both roots and expression" (28). Second, their attacks frequently coincide with or immediately follow acts of sexual activity by their victims; the killer's violence appears motivated as much by jealous identification with the teenage lovers he often watches surreptitiously off camera as it is by the compulsion to punish the lovers for their expressions of sexuality. Lastly, the audience views the carnage from the killer's point of view where women become scrutinized sexual "objects of aggression" (Dika 90).

In the best example, the opening sequence of Carpenter's *Halloween*, the audience is forced to view its violent conclusion through the eyeholes of a Halloween mask. We see what the stalker sees: his nearly naked sister sensuously brushing her hair just after having sex with her boyfriend. That the female victim recognizes the intruder as her brother provides little comfort for the audience especially after the camera stops in the kitchen to procure a butcher's knife. What is important to note here is that in the slasher film, the mise-en-scène most often reflects the killer's point of view and forces the viewer to identify with his actions. That is why the camera lingers long and hard on the female body before and after her victimization. The sexuality of her corpus is just as appreciated by the killer (and his audience) when postcoital glow is displaced by the bloody spectacle of death. In fact, the camera/killer's perspective lavishes the kind of close and lengthy attention to death's entry points that one might expect a lover to bestow on the anatomy of his beloved. In *Halloween*, Michael's eye lingers on the messy bed where his sister has recently copulated with the same prurient interest that he employs while looking at her bloodied corpse. This association is meant to highlight the incestuous desire Michael maintains for his sister and the consequent jealous anger he feels when she betrays him with someone else. That she dares to do this in his home while their parents are out makes her transgression all the more egregious and explains why Michael will spend the rest of the film attempting to punish sister surrogates who are so easily distracted from their baby-sitting jobs.

Far more deliberate than a random choice of costume in which to celebrate the holiday, the young boy's appearance at the end of the opening sequence wearing a clown suit and holding a knife streaked with his sister's blood conflates concepts of adult and child, violence and play, buffoon and agent of revenge that Michael will never resolve satisfactorily. In essence, the serial killers in the slasher film are necrophiles, sexually charged by the proximity of death and its association with feminine sexuality. As Clover demonstrates convincingly, in the slasher film male deaths are quicker and more likely to occur offscreen, whereas female deaths are extended, take place at close range, and are more erotically charged than those of their male counterparts (35).

All this raises the crucial issue of why such graphic levels of cinematic violence and perversity have achieved such levels of popularity. What does it reveal about a culture that makes nine sequels of *Friday the 13ᵗʰ* economically viable, for the motion picture industry would not produce these pictures if the demand were not there to consume them. For Jonathan Lake Crane, the slasher genre is more reflective of philosophical unease than of bodily terrors. It speaks to us of a future resigned "to the rarefied pleasures of horror without hope" (140). The fact that the victims are all young people suggests "our fascination with extinction and the extermination of the future" (140). The violated body becomes a metaphor for the destruction of our belief system and a faith that goodness will triumph over madness: "Not only does the center no longer hold, nor do inviolate beliefs survive in this world, but even the body, the form with which we are presumably most familiar, cannot hold itself together" (141). The slasher's primary audience has always consisted of teenagers, a noteworthy phenomenon as the subject matter would appear to suggest a bifurcation in its audience's loyalties by first encouraging it to identify with the libidinous rage of the psychotic monster, only to then provide a symbolic vision of self-cannibalism in watching fellow teenagers graphically ripped apart. The association forged between sexual expression and violent punishment as a consequence in these films reinforces typical teenager angst about their hormonally charged bodies and the mysteries of sexuality. So, even on a subconscious level, the slasher film underscores the dangers inherent in adolescent transgression and reconfirms lingering taboos linked to premarital sex. Once more, there is evidence to suggest that the genre supported the backlash against liberal values that transformed American society during the 1960s and early 1970s.

Carol Clover's work on the fluid loyalties of the slasher's audience during the course of the movie is especially instructive in helping to explain the enormous popularity of the genre as well as providing a rich complexity to films that are frequently dismissed even by horror aficionados. Her insistence that the audience's alliances shift when the Final Girl demonstrates her ability to incorporate gendered masculine survivalist skills would appear to contradict Crane's view that the splatter film parallels the nihilism of young people depressed by their own helplessness in the face of an uncertain future. Clover views the genre much more optimistically, almost as a fairy-tale paradigm, where survival—even if it is only one girl at the end of the picture—is emphasized as a potent counter to the chaos of a killer's madness. Even taking a stance somewhere in between Crane and Clover opens the genre to a seriousness of purpose that again belies easy dismissal. The splatter film, similar to most other kinds of horror art, is most viably engaged on a subtextual level, for it is most adept at revealing our general impotence at the same time as it speaks to our hope for endurance.

Of all the various categories of horror that we have considered thus far, the slasher film represents the genre from which many people, and especially women, derive the least pleasure, and it reflects what is most objectionable about horror film as a genre. The violent spectacle of the body under assault is so graphically displayed that all other aspects of the filmic experience—psychological content, cinematography, character acting—are wholly subordinate to the reductive life-and-death focus on pursuit and escape.

In the slasher film, the abject terror generated by the male monster is single-minded and testosterone driven, while females on the screen, on the other hand, are given several options in their choice of reaction to the psychopathic killer pursuing them. They may accept passively their fate in being in the wrong place at the wrong time and submit to instant death; they may run from the killer and seek help from outside agents (ultimately to no avail in both attempts); they may stop running and turn to face the danger. This last choice requires a heroine who is willing to employ extreme violence in her decision to fight back. In her employment of deadly force, however, she encroaches upon the male domain, and it is here that the slasher film reaches its greatest expression of male anxiety about feminism and gender control. How ironic that a film genre so scorned by the general public past the age of twenty—and women advocates in particular—has provided some of the most liberated female characters in cinematic history. Sarah Michelle Geller, who, for many years has played a variety of roles in horror celluloid—from Buffy the intrepid vampire slayer with whom we were acquainted in chapter 3 to the more traditional Gothic female in the haunted house story *The Grudge*—is in a unique position to comment on the possibilities available to actresses in horror cinema: "A lot of times, you're relegated to the girlfriend, the sister. But horror is where women can take the lead—Naomi Watts in *The Ring*. Women can really shine" (Jensen 34). The slasher film, as Pinedo points out, "stages a fantasy in which humiliation is transformed into unbridled female rage . . . providing a cathartic outlet, and in some cases even an expression of feminist feeling" (86). It is in the slasher genre that the horror heroine actually fights back and, when she does, emerges victorious more often than not. Little wonder, then, that the genre's most trenchant critics over the past two decades have all been feminist scholars.

Sally Gets a Dinner Invitation: *The Texas Chainsaw Massacre*

The Texas Chainsaw Massacre truly pushed the horror film in new directions and not just in terms of cinematic blood or gore, because the movie really exhibits very little of either. The $125,000 investment it cost to make the original picture in 1974 has blossomed into a return now estimated to be over $300 million; more importantly, for our purposes, it took the horror film in an entirely new direction. *Texas* forced filmmakers out of the confines of the Victorian Gothic novel and opened the possibilities for viewing horror as a vehicle for articulating twentieth-century pessimism. This is a film where everything has gone to hell; attractive young people are being randomly butchered and, more to the point, their killers are getting away with it. Without *Chainsaw Massacre*, we would not have the work of David Cronenberg, John Carpenter, or most of the postmodern cinematic horror that is worth viewing. Additionally, we would not have most of the postmodern horror that is not worth watching, but that is not necessarily *Chainsaw*'s fault.

Sally is the titular leader of a group of five young people, including her handicapped brother, Franklin, who journey across a stretch of Texas on one of the hottest days of the summer. The teenagers are seeking the former home of Sally and Franklin's grandparents, a deserted and dilapidated house that just happens to be located next door to a family of cannibals. The two houses underscore the film's message that nothing is as it seems, that what appears as normal often contains the abnormal, as the grandparents' house resembles the typical Gothic dwelling while the white house belonging to the cannibals appears, at least from the outside, to be well kept and unassuming. One by one, the young adults wander off and are captured by Leatherface, the odd gender-challenged brother/mother/son of the all-male cannibal family. Finally, only Sally remains after her sibling and friends are massacred in various unsavory ways. The second half of the film is dedicated exclusively to Sally's grisly ordeal through the night as she is captured and manages to escape on two separate occasions from Leatherface and his family of former slaughterhouse workers. Screaming hysterically through all her interactions with the cannibal family, Sally finally jumps through the front window, climbs in the back of a pickup truck and rides away, a bloody but triumphant mess, into the morning light.

The film is typified by countless moments of "creeping" horror, of fast cuts and sudden jumps in camera angle and proximity, scenes that are deliberately filmed by a handheld camera to highlight the relationship between female victim running away from deranged male killer. This cinematography gives the narrative its raw "documentary" feel, but it also skews the viewer's relationship to the filmic text. Just as Sally finds herself perpetually under assault and in a state of utter bewilderment, so, too, does the frenetic eye of the camera manipulate the audience. This state of shared confusion between female protagonist and audience, where the viewer witnesses her violently escalating hysteria and her bare escape, reaches its apogee in the infamous sequence where the captured Sally is treated to a horrific dinner hosted by the cannibalistic family. This moment epitomizes the energy of the entire film, typified by the invasive nature of the camera. Similar to the individual men that surround their female guest, forcing their threatening faces toward her as they eat various unsavory pieces of flesh, the camera delves deeper into Sally's personal space, recording her terrified screams and facial expressions, employing extreme close-ups that at one point nearly attempt to enter into the frightened woman's bloodstream.

The dinner scene opens with an exhausted Sally bound and gagged in a chair at the head of the dining room table, abducted by the cannibals after a long, futile effort to escape. The opening shot is centered tightly on her, and thus the viewer has no initial sense of the rest of the room. As we watch her drift back into consciousness, the camera switches to a point of view shot for Sally. She awakens to a Halloween nightmare: the family eating "barbecue," a butchered chicken head and bird claws staring directly at her, a human skeleton hanging in the corner, a skull as a table centerpiece, and finally the emaciated features of Grandpa cannibal slouched directly across the table from her (see Figure 1, p. 191). Above Sally hangs a ceiling lamp covered with the hide of an earlier victim. All of these cannibalized images and totems might be linked by way of historical implication to the infamous atrocities that took place in Vietnam shortly before the film was made— from the My Lai massacre to soldiers collecting unsavory fetish objects from their dead victims—for some reason, particularly ears—as souvenirs of their conquest.

The audience identifies with Sally from her position at the end of the table, but the camera's rapid jump cuts also force us to share the perspective of her tormentors seated around the rest of the table. This rapid switching of perspectives is further complicated by a third, omniscient "gaze" which invades Sally's terror from high-angled shots originating close to the ceiling. The camera eye is never more carnivorous than throughout this sequence as it ravishes Sally's features, establishing extreme levels of intimacy, even attempting to invade the surface of her bloodshot eyeball. The terrifying curiosity of the camera as it sweeps along to include various objects on the table, the distorted faces of Sally's tormentors, and Sally's own abject state of fear and loathing forces the audience to partake in the unstable flow of a constantly shifting misé-en-scene, even as it is invited to probe the female victim voyeuristically. We are meant to experience vicariously Sally's abject state, but we also exploit it by joining with the slaughter family and their distinct point of view in savoring her suffering. Thus, we are made to probe various elements of the scene only to then telescope back as the camera erratically switches points of view, angles of filming, and contrasting degrees of focus. We are Sally, then we are not her; we are afraid for her and shutter at her pain, and yet we are simultaneously absorbed perversely in the details of her torment.

As considered in chapter 6, the postmodern horror film has tended to center on the family and the home, and both of these elements are in evidence throughout the dinner sequence. Director Tobe Hooper has been cited as saying that *Chainsaw Massacre* is "about the disintegration of the American family" (Jaworzyn

96) because in the slaughter clan we see evidence of a family that is devoid of moral direction and on the verge of self-destructing. The dysfunctional family theme is never more apparent than in this particular scene. Leatherface changes faces, appropriating the "pretty woman" mask replete with garish makeup and wig. He shuffles around the table daintily wearing an apron and serving others food that he brings in from the kitchen. The absence of a real woman to guide and moderate this all-male family is grotesquely in evidence in the dinner scene, and perhaps this helps to explain why Sally, as the only "real" woman in the house, is treated as a bizarre "guest of honor," seated in a literal "arm chair" at the head of the table. Leatherface's feeble effort to appropriate femininity highlights the barren dysfunctional nature of the patriarchy as it appears in this movie. There is no maternal presence, and the cannibal family longs for it—why else would Leatherface serve supper in drag—to mediate the random cruelty of the men around the table. Indeed, all through the scene, the hitchhiker and the older male (father?) figure, who is referred to as "just a cook" because of his apparent distaste for human butchery, engage a constant level of bickering that is disturbingly reminiscent of typical family squabbles that take place at the dinner table at the same time that it dramatizes the inability of this family to communicate on any kind of rational level.

The collapse of patriarchal potency in this family is best illustrated in the character of Grandpa, a man so feeble that he can barely lift the sledgehammer to strike Sally; his sons even seek to revivify him when Sally is first tied to the chair by having him suck blood, vampirelike, from her cut finger. Although the other males defer to Grandpa in giving him the honor of the sacrificial killing, the fact that he cannot lift the hammer suggests his impotence—and by extension the rest of the patriarchy in this gender-restricted family—and likewise contributes to Sally's ultimate escape. Grandpa's impotence extends to include all the males in his family. The men have no wives or children, nor are they interested in sex with Sally or the other female victim. Leatherface's generalized anger toward all the young people he encounters may well be seen as his attempt to punish them for a thriving sexuality at the same time that he wishes to eliminate whatever potential threat their sexual energy holds for the impotent male. Thus, some critics are inspired to see a close parallel between Franklin, the handicapped brother of Sally who is physically and socially impotent, and the slaughter family boys, Leatherface and Hitchhiker. The obvious fury that Franklin unleashes when the others leave him downstairs in his grandparents' house is connected to the sexual frustration he feels when his sister and friends abandon him to go upstairs to "play" in the bedrooms. His unspecified rage matches that of Leatherface, who likewise directs his own personal frustration upon sexually active young people.

The absence of women and the impotent patriarchy in *Chainsaw* symbolize the political and social anxieties that were especially present in feminist and post-Vietnam America. Having just lost the first major war in his history, and passing through the troubled waters of civil rights violence that threatened both the tranquility of his cities and, as in Vietnam, his sense of racial superiority, the American white male found himself in a position that roughly paralleled the aimless confusion present in the men of the slaughter family. Add the total absence of sobering maternal and wifely figures, and the slaughter family dynamics suggest some of the radical changes that were occurring to males in the American domestic sphere during the 1970s. Through divorce or by returning to the workplace, many women abandoned the traditional role of stay-at-home wife and mother, forcing families into the kind of domestic confusion that the slaughter family embodies in the extreme.

The soundtrack also adds to the impending terror unleashed in this scene and, for that matter, throughout the entire film. The extreme close-up zooms of Sally are accompanied by sounds that are seldom associated with dinner: the grunting of a pig, the screech of machinery that is operating off camera, jarring music that enters and then dissipates. These diegetical sounds appear to come from nowhere; indeed, they are not sounds associated with anything immediately recognizable, perhaps not even human. It is the cacophony attendant to a world turned upside down and inside out where humans have descended into madness and savagery, remorselessly participating in the ultimate taboos of Western civilization: murder and cannibalism.

While the cacophonous soundtrack serves to underscore the hysteria of Sally's torment in the dinner scene, the discordant sounds of machinery operating unattended or with malefic design can be found throughout the film: the opening sequence in which photographs of disinterred corpses in a desecrated graveyard are accompanied by the sound of flashbulbs popping; the news report on the van radio that describes oil spills, buildings collapsing, and other instances of technological failure; the defective soda machine that Sally and Pam attempt to use at the gas station, along with the fact that there is no gas available for the teenagers to purchase; the barbequed meat of questionable origin that Sally observes simmering behind a red-tinted window in the gas station; the incessant whine of the generator running without apparent purpose outside of Leatherface's house; and certainly the signature roar of the chainsaw itself. Moments of both abject terror and general unease are heightened throughout the film by sounds of operating machinery. These mechanized sounds set loose in midsummer in rural Texas help to fuel various Marxist readings of the film. Robin Wood, for example, argues in "An Introduction to the American Horror Film," that Leatherface and his family are products of industrial capitalist oppression: unemployed slaughterhouse employees whose skills are rendered obsolete by technological automation (20). Their total reduction of human life to nothing more than "meat" forms a subtextual parallel to the owner-worker relationship in capitalist factories in addition to the consumer-oriented culture of capitalism. Similarly, Christopher Sharrett thinks the film is about the diminishment of capitalist hegemony in "a world dissolving into primordial chaos set in an archetypal wasteland where the sustaining forces of civilization are not operative" (262).

Such is the plight of the slaughter family; in being denied work, they are stripped of their masculinity. This void is manifested in several ways. Conditioned by a capitalist, patriarchal society to value the act of labor, when legitimate means for satisfying this need are denied to them, the family seeks work in the only way it can: by murdering human victims and selling the flesh, as they had formerly done with cattle. Ironically, the slaughter family is trying to do what is expected of them, but because the system no longer has any need for their obsolete skills, their adapted labor is a brutal perversion.

Apart from these various interpretations, what is clear is that the film is deliberately designed to create a sense of panic and hysterical anxiety, as if the relentless Texas heat has finally driven everyone insane. Its atmosphere creates a sense of disruption and dislocation that occurs on a variety of levels simultaneously: *Chainsaw Massacre* poses a microcosm where dialogue is impossible (Sally screams more than she talks); societal values are completely abandoned (humans dining on other humans that they have murdered and barbecued); whatever is normal is aborted and distorted (time is "killed" with a nail through the face of a watch on the cannibal property); and the entire cosmos is in disarray (explosive sun storms erupt like geysers of blood). *Chainsaw* managed to capture the general mood of America after the crippling double blow of Vietnam and Watergate: A place that had lost touch with its core values and optimistic spirit. For so many reasons this picture should be regarded as *the* archetypal horror film—a two-hour nightmare as relentless as the scream of a chainsaw. Unfortunately, the remake of *Chainsaw* is not nearly as effective as the original; what the remake gains in improved production sophistication and increased budget, only serves to detract from the raw assault of the original.

Lots of Tricks, No Treats: *Halloween*

Less frenetic and obsessively violent than *Chainsaw Massacre*, *Halloween*, released in 1978, four years after *Chainsaw*, relies more on the conventional tropes typically aligned with the horror genre: moments of silence designed to heighten suspense and startle the viewer when they end abruptly, a musical score featuring a jarring and repetitive combination of piano and strings that is as unsettling as the one found in *Psycho*, dark and claustrophobic domestic spaces—kitchens, closets, and stairwells—where it is impossible to see clearly, startling silhouettes of Michael standing alone in the shadows of a front yard across the street. Conversely, the film also follows the formula established in *Chainsaw* in its reliance on the importance of imperiled females endangered by a relentless sociopath. In *Halloween*, however, we find a less emotional version of the slasher paradigm: Both Laurie and Michael have moments where they actually have time to consider their options and plot a strategy against one another. Leatherface literally imposes himself on the screen in full attack mode from the moment we make his introduction; Michael is much more subtle, even to the point of being self-disciplined and patient. He spends most of the film simply watching and waiting for the appropriate moment to strike. As Adam Rockoff notes, "The murders punctuate the suspense, they do not overshadow it" (57). While Leatherface appears as out of control as his raging chainsaw, Michael is a study in steady determination and careful selection of victims. Indeed, their choice of murder weaponry highlights the difference in the two serial killers respective styles of violence: Leatherface slashes indiscriminately with a machine—becoming merely an extension of its terrible technology—while Myers, emulating the kind of skill that produces a carved pumpkin face, wields a knife to probe and cuts deliberately. Perhaps the element that distinguishes these two films most sharply, however, is that Laurie is a far more proactive heroine than Sally is in *Chainsaw*; *Halloween* features the first—and one of the best—examples of Clover's Final Girl archetype.

Laurie is clearly distinguished from her two friends, Lynda and Annie. While they are obsessed with boyfriends, alcohol, and cigarettes, Laurie is a thoughtful student, capable of responding to a complex question raised by her teacher in class while she keeps an eye on the looming figure of Michael out the window. While her friends show little compunction for manipulating one another either to avoid baby-sitting responsibilities or to make use of an empty house for a romantic assignation, Laurie demonstrates her level-headedness and unselfish concern for others all through the film. When Michael attacks her directly, she makes sure that the two children she is baby-sitting are safely locked within a bedroom. Her two girlfriends are focused exclusively on "having a good time tonight," which translates into promiscuous sexual activity, while Laurie—although the most attractive of the three women—conforms to Clover's observation that the Final Girl is "with few exceptions sexually inactive" (46). Annie and Lynda are easy prey for Myers, in large part because boys and sex distract them. Both girls are murdered because of their deep involvement in these concerns; out of frantic rush to meet her boyfriend, Annie is slain when she doesn't realize the killer is in the parked car with her, and Lynda dies because, like Goldilocks, she trespasses into a stranger's house in order to make use of an available bedroom. Laurie's marginal interest in boys and sex, in contrast, allows her the ability to concentrate on other matters; we note on several occasions early in the film that her friends mock her nervous response to the looming presence of Myers, especially when she sees him lurking behind a set of bushes. Unlike her clueless girlfriends, Laurie senses intuitively that there is trouble brewing, and it is more serious than the harmless tricks typically associated with Halloween.

Laurie's true pluck is reserved for her personal battle against Myers. Although she begins the contest in passive mode, screaming while she runs from Michael's assault and cowering in fear when she notes that he is in the house with her, she turns more aggressively proactive the closer he comes to her. Again, following Clover's paradigm, Laurie "stops screaming, faces the killer, and reaches for the knife [to] address the monster on his own terms" (48). That Myers will not stay dead has less to do with Laurie's success at self-defense—she stabs him with both a knitting needle in the neck and his own butcher knife—than with the film's adherence to the premise that "you can't kill the bogeyman."

The bogeymen killers in slasher movies are seldom very articulate. Similar to the sniper/assassin films that were also popular in the 1970s, the serial murderers in the slasher genre never stop to explain their motivations or to engage in dialogue on any subject with either their victims or the audience. Leatherface emits only grunts and squeals, Michael Myers has not spoken a word in fifteen years, while Jason must find it hard enough to breathe underneath his hockey mask, much less to talk. The notable exception, which we will soon explore, is Freddy Krueger, the comic custodian in A Nightmare on Elm Street. His ghoulish banter notwithstanding, the typical silence of the serial killer is indicative of his antisocial nature. He does not wish to communicate; in fact, it is possible to argue that his propensity toward violence is, at least in part, a response to the failure in his ability to communicate his feelings—about sex, violence, women, or, for that matter, anything else. After he strangles Lynda in Halloween, Myers places her corpse on a bed directly beneath the gravestone that once marked his sister's cemetery plot. However rudimentary, this gesture is Michael's sole attempt at self-expression. Because he associates all women with his sister—especially sexually active women—Michael's deadly pursuit of them is an effort to duplicate again and again his crime against Judith, and thus his urge to juxtapose the dead Lynda with bed and gravestone. Myers telegraphs a staple convention in the slasher genre: The bed forms a direct conduit to the grave. Furthermore, the personal is synonymous with the political, as male ambivalence toward mothers and sisters is translated into action against all women.

In addition to the level of personal alienation that their violence reflects, the males who occupy center focus in slasher films also embody the reductive simplicity of a fascist credo: bludgeon whatever you do not understand. The serial murderer in these films shares something in common with the worst aspects of modern and postmodern man. Tortured by some horrific event that has reduced the present into a cyclic re-enactment of the past, unable to view women as individual beings whose lives exist beyond their sexual transgressions, and inhabiting a microcosm where traditional values of love, family, and morality have been rendered meaningless, the male slasher leads a deliberately circumscribed existence. Although he has simplified his life's philosophy drastically, he has done so in order to function; funneling his prodigious energies into pure violence allows the serial murderer to elude the personal chaos that always threatens to engulf him.

Thus, the killer feels a need to hide himself behind an omnipresent mask. This mask provides the serial monster with a high degree of anonymity, and thus increases our dread. More than just disguising the killer's identity, however, the male mask in the slasher film is about providing a connection among the various sociopaths: the blank face of random fury. The leather skins of Leatherface, the hockey mask of Jason, and the pasty white latex face that covers the front of Michael's head are all suggestive of the degree of their common alienation and anomie, of characters that have lost or abandoned their basic humanity. Just as they interpret their random female victims as personalized mother or sister substitutes, their masks allow us to view these serial murderers as random males—as men who are defined not by their individuality or uniqueness, but instead by their identical acts of unexplained violence and an emptiness of spirit reflected in their expressionless faces. The actor who played Leatherface, Gunnar Hansen, understood that his inability to use language or facial expressions forced him to emphasize the character as a physical presence exclusively: "The whole idea [of Leatherface] was that the mask reflected who he was now—my feeling was that under the mask there was nothing—if you take the mask away there's no face there—that's how I tried to play him, and I think that's why he's such a horrifying character. The mask defines who he was" (Jaworzyn 43).

Myers's white mask or Jason's blank hockey mask supplies a kind of tabula rasa upon which the audience is invited to project its most primal terrors. All through the film, Laurie attempts to calm both herself and the children she is baby-sitting by claiming, "There's no such thing as a bogeyman. It's all just make-believe." Myers turns out to be the refutation of Laurie's belief system: a very real bogeyman whose identity is made all the more terrifying because of its inability to be categorized. His masked persona forces a direct confrontation with all the blank voids we try to deny—the *nothingness* that interposes itself into discussions of the various mysteries we will never totally understand about human existence: death and what may exist beyond it, of course, but also the mysteries of abnormal human psychology, and the impossibility of controlling our fate or destiny. As a student, Laurie listens to her high school English teacher attempt to provide a definition of fate as an element at work in a narrative the class is studying. All the while the young girl is vaguely distracted by the presence of Michael, who is standing just outside the schoolroom window. Laurie will soon learn that Myers is a manifest figure of fate that will come to shape her own life, as well as the lives of her imperiled girlfriends.

The white mask covering Myers's face poses a link to several other icons of American whiteness, the "pasteboard mask" that disguises whatever truth is hidden beneath the symbolism of the white whale in Melville's *Moby-Dick*, a conundrum that the frustrated Captain Ahab is unable to penetrate. As a figure of whiteness, Michael's haunting presence is also reminiscent of the conclusion to Poe's *Narrative of Arthur Gordon Pym*, when the narrator is confronted with a foreboding and mysterious albino form that is impossible for Pym to comprehend, much less to control. Like these other famous images of blank whiteness on the American cultural landscape, Myers is a figure finally beyond our ability to explain rationally. Just as white signifies the absence of color as well as the merging of the entire color spectrum, Michael's expressionless white mask symbolizes both the void created by God's absence in the slasher universe and the collapse of rational order. The decision to permit Myers to exit *Halloween* exhibiting supernatural survival abilities is more than a cheap horror trick; the inability to vanquish Michael suggests that his existence is beyond the ultimate purview of whatever is human. Director John Carpenter has justified his reluctance to kill this cinematic monster in arguing, "evil never dies. It can't be killed. In the movie [Myers] really is just a force of evil, he's like nature" (Rockoff 57).

Into the Woods: *Friday the 13th*

Like *Halloween*, the *Friday* movies show the burden of history. The serial killer is motivated by a specific date on the calendar; that is why the full moon is featured in the mise-en-scène to start the film: It serves as a reminder that Jason's wrath is cyclical, linked not only to the cycles of the moon and the fact that this date happens to mark the killer's birthday, but also to the attempt to restore Camp Crystal Lake back into a working facility.

The film certainly opens with a degree of excessive cuteness: Camp counselors sing "Tom Dooley" around a rustic fireplace that makes their rosy teenage cheeks positively glow. If the diegetical music in the background both before and after the songfest—piercing strings and horns that pose a variation on *Psycho*'s score—fails to provide enough of a threat to this hokey pastoral moment, then the frequent cuts to the full moon that hangs low amid clouds carry sufficient foreboding. The cutest couple ventures away from the safety of the group to find privacy for a romantic interlude. The boyfriend, who appears somewhat to sense why the adult

Jason is after him, tries to buy immunity by claiming, "we haven't done anything" of a sexual nature, but he is nonetheless quickly dispatched by a knife in the stomach. His girlfriend, however, is given ample time to scream and try to find an escape before the opening sequence concludes in a close-up still of her open mouth. Her face, frozen in fear, will be repeated endlessly in the course of the film—from the third-tier face pictured on the totem pole at the camp entrance, to the false moments of terror that the teenage girls experience when one of the boys plays a trick on them, to the individual murders that take place in full frontal view of the camera.

The movie is very deliberate in balancing the beauty of the natural landscape of lake, woods, and open sky with a sinister presence lurking behind a tree, the driver of the Jeep that offers the naïve Annie a ride, or on the occasions in which the teenagers vaguely suspect that someone in the woods is watching them. Even more than *Chainsaw* or *Halloween*, *Friday* features teenagers reveling in so much illicit play—smoking pot, drinking beer, pretending to drown for a lark, wearing as few clothes as possible, participating in sexual intercourse, and an attractive young woman hitchhiking alone on strange roads—that Jason's rampage cannot be separated from their transgressive behavior. His violent retribution, in other words, is stimulated by their stupid and self-indulgent actions. In this way, then, it is impossible not to view Freddy's directed violence and victim selection, at least in part, as a backlash against the excesses of the 1960s.

According to the logic of the juxtapositions that *Friday* makes between the teenagers' conduct and Jason's compulsive urge to punish—particularly their acts of sexual expression—the film implies that the killer is meting out a punishment that is somehow "deserved." Indeed, as Cynthia A. Freeland points out in her essay "The Slasher's Blood Lust," Jason is similar to the vampire insofar as he is likewise driven by the actions of his victims. Just as Dracula is mutually stimulated by Mina's purity and Lucy's promiscuity, Jason is "revivified" by the camp's reopening; but more to the point, he is compelled into murderous action again as a direct consequence of watching the teenage camp counselors violate an ultraconservative agenda prohibiting taboo behavior. Because Jason reserves his wrath only for young adults associated with the camp (the townspeople, for example, are afraid of his reputation, but they themselves are left untouched until Ralph is killed early in the second sequel), it is difficult to concur completely with Crane's assessment that *Friday* is devoid of any kind of moral basis, and that "The counselors bear no responsibility for their gruesome passing. They have not been tempted by secret knowledge. They have not acted rashly and gone where no man or woman should tread and they have not really committed any cardinal sins" (147). During the opening sequence, Jason is shown wandering amidst beds filled with sleeping children as he stalks his first victims. He could easily have butchered the entire room

but chooses instead to ignore the young campers and go after their teenage counselors. It is as if Jason is a composite force of all the backwater adult males in town
that the teenagers ridicule as fools and "American originals"—the truck driver, the
cop, and the village idiot savant/alcoholic Ralph—who try to warn the counselors
about the "curse" of the camp, the danger of doing drugs and engaging in promiscuous sex, or the inherent troubles they will bring on themselves as highly vulnerable "babes in the woods."

Although Crane's thesis argues that the murders which occur in *Friday* are all
completely random and devoid of any kind of meaning, the film's conclusion
would suggest that Jason is seeking retribution for his drowning, which occurred
because he was a weak swimmer unsupervised by the Crystal Lake counselors. While
the various teenagers who become his future victims have had, of course, nothing
to do with Jason's childhood demise, this is hardly the point. The fact that they are
young, easily distracted (especially by one another), prone to selfish behavior,
and occupying the roles of camp counselors poses enough of a parallel to reactivate
the film's psychologically disturbed mother and son.

Each slasher film has a perverse logic of its own that always hinges on a single pivotal event from the past: The sexual violation/murder of Michael's sister finds
a similar locus in Jason's drowning. So obsessive does this event become that the
filmmakers who created the epic battle *Jason vs. Freddy* returned to Jason's drowning and the negligence of the camp counselors in a flashback meant to signify once
again the past's crucial influence on Jason's present. Every subsequent action that
takes place in a slasher film revolves around one of these primal events, like the
"eye" of a hurricane that manages to bring destruction for miles outside its core.
As a consequence, the genre creates its own circular vortex in which patterns of
past behavior are repeated in the present, not only in the identical deaths that populate the individual films, but also in the myriad sequels that resemble one another so indistinctly. This repetitive structure necessarily restricts and limits the
narrative range available to the genre because the characters as well as the audience find themselves essentially trapped within the monster's subjective reality. A
certain logic to these movies does exist, however self-reflexive and truncated; it is
the solipsism of a psyche that has witnessed—and cannot forget—a traumatic
event. The abject terror of the slasher universe emerges not only from the visceral violence to which the audience is relentlessly subjected, but also in the fact that
we must share the unwholesome inner space of a man doomed to wander (literally forever) through such a limited psychic terrain. More than any other horror subgenre, the slasher and its parade of sequels take the audience inside the "eye" of the
monster, forcing us to re-experience again and again the violent explanation for
why a man remains locked in childhood. The slasher film verifies the psychological likelihood that an abused child will grow up to become an abusive adult. It sim-

ulates the effect of being in a recurring nightmare where we are forced to relive and duplicate the same frightening experience where nothing much changes each night; it is the dream's predictability that contributes most to our unease.

Horror's Psychic Landscape: *A Nightmare on Elm Street*

Leatherface contains the unbridled energy of the mid-day Texas summer sun; he pursues his victims with the same relentless intensity. Michael and Jason spend the majority of their time quietly stalking; Ian Conrich views them as "deadly but mechanical and silent, with the films structured upon a series of repetitive and predictable killings" (226). In contrast to these other serial killers at the center of the genre, Freddy Krueger, the former child molester and killer who was murdered by vengeful parents, prefers to torment and humiliate his victims over a period of time, as much an interloper into their dreams as he is a projection of their worst personal fears. As David Edelstein remarks in *The Village Voice*: "The dreams are big production numbers and Freddy presides over them like a nightclub master-of-ceremonies" (58). In keeping with his desire to transform the dreamscapes of his victims into a spectacle of terror, his murdering is usually extravagant and bizarre: geysers of blood that literally paint the entire bedroom. As with Jason, Krueger preys on both sexes, but it is clear that his preference is for women. The two male deaths in the original *Nightmare* are dispatched without fanfare and without any effort for the boys to become acquainted with their killer. Tina and Nancy, in contrast, are visited in their sleep on multiple occasions, teased and chased before Freddy begins his grisly work. The women are aware of Freddy as a personality—the "Cagney swagger and cool-clown style" (Conrich 224) that Robert Englund's acting has brought to his character—and when Krueger does lash out at them with his razor finger-glove, the assault is personal, protracted, and visceral.

Krueger shares many traits in common with Dracula. Both horror icons inhabit the nether-realm of the undead, and they prey on the living. Like Stoker's vampire, which tends to visit his victims when they sleep, Freddy is similarly brought to life at moments when the barrier that protects the rational mind rests and the unconscious mind takes over. That he can only manifest his physical presence while his victims dream is the most distinguishing aspect of the *Nightmare* series. It permits Freddy to revel in the absurdity of a surreal existence. He makes use of typically claustrophobic places—back alleyways, bathtubs that transform into deep underwater pools, basement corridors, and beds that collapse into black holes—that suggest womb-like confinement and thus can be linked to the abject as Barbara Creed defines it. He enjoys contorting his face into wild horror masks, lengthening his arms in front of a disbelieving dreamer until they stretch out absurdly into space, and disappearing mysteriously only to reappear directly in front of a fleeing victim. Like the vampire, Freddy is a shape changer—capable of taking on the form of something abject, erotic, or even switching genders in a constant effort to confuse, trick, and seduce his hapless victims. Midway through the first *Nightmare* film, Shakespeare's *Hamlet* is the subject of discussion in Nancy's high school English class. The worlds of the "melancholic Dane" and suburban Elm Street resemble one another insofar as they feature locales where it is increasingly difficult to separate objective reality from the inner workings of a disturbed psyche. Ghosts they cannot control burden these young adults, Nancy and Hamlet, and their personal torments extend to the point at which both the characters themselves and others around them come to question their very sanity.

What *Nightmare* brings to the slasher genre is the logical culmination of an illogical experience—that is, the domestic surrealism of the inside of Leatherface's house, Michael's suburban obsession with innocent baby-sitters, and the total absence of mothers and fathers in supervisory or support roles are pushed to their furthest extreme. In *Nightmare*, the mind is as much under assault as the body; the distinctions between the real world and the dream world are deliberately blurred and conjoined. Walls and bedsheets appear as membranes that push out and pulsate, symbolizing the transformation of once fixed borders into permeable ones. In these films, Freddy breaks through the porous barrier that separates dream from reality whenever his victims enter the area of the personal subconscious; the imaginary is always on the verge of rupturing into the real. *Nightmare 1* and its sequels create a deliberate back and forth sense of dislocation as the audience—along with the teenage protagonists—are pulled between the two planes of consciousness/unconsciousness so frequently and abruptly that it is often difficult to distinguish one from the other. If *Chainsaw Massacre* creates a cinematic texture that is intrusively aggressive, the *Nightmare* series presents a cinema of increasingly incoherent spaces. At the end of the first *Nightmare* film, for example, it is not at all clear whether Nancy is still dreaming or not; she has willed her dead friends and mother back to life, and her own life appears to be returning back to normal as she prepares for school. Then, the windows of Glen's car rise magically, and Nancy watches helplessly as her mother's body is elongated and pulled like a piece of warm taffy through the small window above the front door of their house. In *Nightmare*, the slasher genre's reliance on the supernatural in a monster that cannot be killed extends to include Freddy's every action and very existence—he is a manufactured entity inside the mind of his victim, less real than surreal. Conversely, the series also insists that Freddy is directly linked to objective reality as well, as he leaves evidence that his victims do not merely die in their sleep but that they are brutally slaughtered.

As in *The Exorcist, Panic Room*, and many other horror films, the main female characters in *Nightmare 1* live with their mothers in homes that underscore the pervasiveness of divorce and the gender warfare that exists between men and women where fathers are notably absent. As one of the few adult male figures in the *Nightmare* series, Freddy enters the domestic vacuum when the teenage girls are sleeping and left most susceptible to personal fears in the wake of broken families. In his *loco parentis* role, Krueger continues to serve as an example of the "bad" father who exploits his unions with highly vulnerable daughters. Nancy, the heroine of the first *Nightmare* film and one of the great Final Girls in the slasher genre, recognizes that she must take control over her own life if she wishes to avoid her friend Tina's fate and survive Krueger's nocturnal assault. When Freddy is chasing Nancy near the end of the picture, the daughter tries in vain to summon her father, who, as a police officer, is investigating the murder of Glen at the house just across the street. Although her cries for help pierce the night, the father never does rescue his child, arriving well after Nancy is forced to employ her own resources and ingenuity to outwit the monster. At the end of the film, she asserts herself against Freddy, challenging him to "Come out and show yourself. Where are you, Krueger?" This independence of spirit serves her well, as it becomes the basis for her survival against all the threatening nightmares in her life: her father's anger and continued absence, her mother's alcoholism, and Freddy's will to destruction—the last merely a symbolic embodiment of Nancy's domestic situation.

During and since its reign of terror—generally considered to be from 1974 to 1986—the slasher film has received the most bifurcated criticism of any of the horror film subgenres. Either the films are staunchly defended, as is often the case with the genre's teenage fan base and a select group of feminist film scholars; or they are reviled, as is typically the reaction from mainstream film critics and most people beyond the age of serious acne. There seems to be very little middle ground available on the topic. Perhaps indicative of the visceral nature of the stories they tell, slashers inspire passionate reactions from everyone who views them. For many years I have subscribed to the belief that a pejorative attitude toward horror art—and especially the slasher film—is often an accurate barometer for measuring an individual's political and cultural values. For whatever reasons, if a person, who is completely immune to the importance of horror, can explain the genre only in terms of its contribution to the lamentable dissolution of culture and civilization, my experience is that person will more often than not possess a certain narrow-mindedness bordering on condescension regarding many other cultural topics as well. I find myself concurring with Carol Clover when she argues "that the standard critiques of horror . . . need not only a critical but a political interrogation" (19).

Regardless of one's opinion on the genre, here are several points with which everyone might agree:

- The spectacle of endless death brought—and continues to bring—to Hollywood producers an enormous financial profit on films that generally cost very little to make. The concept of the sequel was born and reached a level of grotesque absurdity as a direct response to the popularity and financial success of the slasher film.

- Special effect advances paralleled the rise of the slasher movie, providing an evermore sophisticated and convincing technology for visually portraying the body's graphic assault. The special effects are so critical to the *A Nightmare on Elm Street* series that the people who create them are grouped into teams of "operators" that have an average of six members and are provided elaborate credits at the end of each sequel.

- Following the shocking displays of violence presented in films such as *Straw Dogs* and *Clockwork Orange*, the slasher genre continued to push the boundaries of public censure defining acceptable levels of cinematic aggression. The level of escalating carnage that came to demarcate the genre is a major reason why critics such as Robin Wood and filmmaker Wes Craven have interpreted slasher movies as a reaction to and reflection of American involvement in Vietnam. As we have seen throughout this chapter, splatter films also suggest a specific misogyny that needs to be coupled with the progress of women's liberation.

- The fifteen-year reign of the classic slasher genre proved to be enormously influential on horror films that followed.

It is this last point that I now wish to address. The original slashers covered in this chapter gave birth to the next generation of horror cinema (the second half of the 1980s to the present) where the monster is a serial killer. Close to exhausting the concept, films such as *Silent Night, Deadly Night, Child's Play, April Fool's Day, Killer Party, Terror Train, Slaughter High,* and *Prom Night,* as well as many of the sequels based on these films and the original slashers themselves, tried desperately to rekindle interest in the genre by focusing on a greater gore content and increasingly more bizarre sociopathic personalities (e.g., a serial killer dressed as Santa Claus, a plastic doll animated with murderous life). The slasher film clearly required a transfusion of new blood at this juncture—and new ideas—in order to reinvent itself and become again a viable art form. As we will consider in the next chapter, *Scream* and *Scary Movie* provided a fresh imaginative infusion to a genre that two decades earlier had taken the horror film to unprecedented places. Witty and irreverent, these films parodied the very subject matter and conventions that had been treated with deadly seriousness in the original slasher pictures and their sequels.

By the end of the 1980s and all through the following decade, the slasher genre likewise morphed into mainstream cinema, attracting a broader audience that was neither primarily composed of teenagers nor was it necessarily attracted to classic slasher cinema. It is nevertheless crucial to recognize the slasher's bloodline in movies such as *Dressed to Kill*, *Henry: Portrait of a Serial Killer*, *The Dark Half*, *Candyman*, *Copycat*, *Silence of the Lambs*, *American Psycho*, *Kiss the Girls*, *Red Dragon*, and *Taking Lives*, to name just a few of the genre's most direct descendants. In these films—all of which were, incidentally, reviewed and marketed outside the slasher genre as "legitimate mainstream" cinema (*Silence of the Lambs*, for instance, winning several Academy Awards)—the serial killer is frequently a more articulate and complex monster (e.g., Hannibal Lecter) than the reticent Michael or inarticulate Leatherface. It would be a mistake, however, not to see the importance of the *Chainsaw Massacre* or *Halloween* series as establishing the archetypes for the narrative tropes and conventions, character types, and cinematography that were provided with a more cerebral slant in the generation of films that followed.

Conversely, the killers in *Dressed to Kill* and *Silence of the Lambs*, for example, are even more obsessed with gender transformation than the slasher monsters considered in this chapter. The transsexual quests of Dr. Robert Elliott and Buffalo Bill are really throwbacks to the cross-dressing, maternally identified Norman Bates in *Psycho*. The simple formula of kill all the pretty girls in the typical slasher film assumes a more perverse, psychosexual complexity in *Dressed to Kill* and *Silence*. While there is not much doubt that Leatherface and his slasher brethren suffer serious Oedipal challenges, by the time we get to *Dressed to Kill* and *Silence of the Lambs* it is no longer possible to distinguish the rampage of the serial killer from his effort to affirm himself as a woman, so fully has the male killer come, albeit unconsciously, to identify himself with the female object of his wrath. In the evolution of the slasher film the basic representations of victim/victimizer become muddied and less coherent. Jame Gumb and Dr. Elliott's complex psychosexual transference to and association with the feminine is clearly linked to an identification with lost maternal images, but their own sexual identities and preferences are not so easily fixed. Are these serial murderers transvestites? Transsexuals? Homosexuals? Neither or both? How is their compulsion to kill women connected to their desire to become women? Neither *Dressed to Kill* nor *Silence* addresses adequately any of these questions. Indeed, their compulsion to associate serial killing as a direct expression of gender distress complicates further the full range of what represents final "girl" status in the contemporary generation of slasher films.

Clover's observations about the anatomically female Final Girl as an integral development during the slasher history are also operative elsewhere in contemporary horror cinema. *Dressed to Kill, Silence of the Lambs, Kiss the Girls,* and *Taking Lives* all feature biological female protagonists whose courage and wits are severely tested. The women survivors in horror films that follow Sally, Laurie, and Nancy are even more adept at reconfiguring the hero as "an anatomical female" who recognizes "that at least one of the traditional marks of heroism, triumphant self-rescue, is no longer strictly gendered masculine" (Clover 60). Their independence, moreover, cannot be divorced from the crisis in white male masculinity that we have traced historically throughout this chapter and serves as an unspoken motivation for men in horror films to pursue the violent deaths of the women they wish either to dominate or appropriate (the latter suggests the degree of gender jealousy that femininity inspires in men). Many postmodern male horror monsters are symbolic representations of a patriarchal urge to regain the power—political, sexual, and psychological—that women have steadily usurped from men. As in the slasher paradigm, female survival skills remain the primary weapons horror's most recent generation of Final Girls employ against his intrusive force. What makes these later films also interesting, though, is that the Final Girls who star in them are now not only involved with self-survival, but have become empowered enough to take on the job of rescuing other imperiled women as well.

9.

Terror Parodies

The Wicker Man, The Rocky Horror Picture Show, Young Frankenstein, The Lost Boys, Scream, Scary Movie

The major conventions, characters, and tropes the creators of horror films have employed to disquiet our sleep have, over the years, also been featured in quite a different vein—in horror parodies and comedies. This tradition, resembling parasite fish that swim alongside sharks to feast on their discarded carrion, is nearly as old as the earliest horror films treated in chapter 2. The inimitable line that commences with Abbott and Costello and their mock-horror encounters with classic horror monsters extends to include Roger Corman's 1960s adaptations of Edgar Allan Poe's terror tales as well as to other horror exploitation films under Corman's direction (e.g., *Swamp Women, A Bucket of Blood, The Undead*). The comedic-horror connection includes the made-for-drive-in fare of the Hammer films and B-girl sexploitation horror such as *Vampire Hookers, Frankenhooker, Hollywood Chainsaw Hookers* as well as more adept and polished spoofs such as *Young Frankenstein, Love at First Bite,* and *The Rocky Horror Picture Show*. Finally, the parodistic nature of productions such as *Dracula: Dead and Loving It, Scream,* and *Scary Movie* represent the most recent efforts in the genre.

Although largely ignored by those who chronicle histories of the horror film, this comedic line represents an important component in the genre's oeuvre. The penchant for distorted bodies and situations that merge satire, horror, and comedy in varying ratios is an essential ingredient of the horror film tradition. Terror parodies reflect the resonate impact of horror film—in terms of a director's inspiration to make the parody as well as the audience's desire to see it—because it is first necessary to appreciate a genre in order to possess skill enough to satirize it. The genre of the film parody also frequently performs in the role of a film critic—selecting representative scenes and "interpreting" them by way of the type of commentary implicit in the parody itself. As work that often crosses over into the category of cult/exploitation, however, terror parodies should probably be distinguished from higher end horror—the *art* of the genre—that would include much of the work examined in the preceding chapters of this book. Moreover, it is probably fair to speculate that the audience interested in *Don't Look Now* or *Eyes Wide Shut* would not likely be the same as the one viewing *Hollywood Chainsaw Hookers*, although it is also very probable that viewers watching *Hollywood Chainsaw Hookers* would appreciate exactly what is being parodied. For a parody to invoke humor, the audience must be able to recognize the tradition, tropes, and conventions that are being parodied, whether it is classic horror cinema in *Young Frankenstein*, or the slasher genre in *Hollywood Chainsaw Hookers*.

The parody adaptations constituting the subject matter of this chapter are seldom treated seriously either by their large fan base or by film scholars, but there are some notable exceptions, such as *The Wicker Man*, which has spawned both a Web site and a journal, *Nuada*, devoted to the explication of the many arcane elements related to the picture and the strange mysteries it provokes. Furthermore, *The Rocky Horror Picture Show* continues to attract and delight successive generations of new fans while also receiving its share of scholarly attention from Twitchell in *Dreadful Pleasures*, Picart in *Remaking the Frankenstein Myth*, and others dedicated to tracing *Frankenstein's* lineage through the popular arts. The critical reception these two films garnered over the years is perhaps best explained in light of their audiences, as both pictures blur the thin border that distinguishes horror parody from cult status. Moreover, these two films are not neatly categorized. *The Wicker Man* is a comedy insofar as it holds Sergeant Howie up for ridicule as a symbol of authority, sexual repression, and fundamental Christianity; other aspects of the film, however, create a sobering debate between conflicting ideologies that demand careful study and are not easily resolved. *Rocky Horror*, on the other hand, is a highly irreverent romp on the *Frankenstein* myth, and it spares no one's dignity; Dr. Frank N. Furter's gender confusion—a blurring that in a serious horror film would signal monstrosity instead of laughter—and self-reflexive consciousness echo aspects of the *Frankenstein* legend, providing, in Twitchell's words, "for this generation what print and celluloid *Frankensteins* have been doing for the last five generations" (197).

William Paul's *Laughing/Screaming: Modern Hollywood's Horror and Comedy* perhaps comes closest to approximating the purpose of this final chapter. While Paul appreciates that "both laughing and screaming possess an echoing effect" (65), however, he seldom recognizes this effect when it occurs simultaneously in a single filmic text. His effort is mainly to explore various groupings of films that fit into the comedic *or* horrific categories, not both concurrently. The movies treated in this chapter represent a sometimes deliberately awkward blend of horror and comedy, and their comic elements can be appreciated only in the context of the established tradition of horror art that preceded the making of the parody. Thus, unlike Paul, I am most interested in the relationship between horror and comedy in these films, not their separation—the manner in which parody, as I am applying the term, also implies parity, or the admixture of terror and laughter, and typically at the expense of the former. Horror, not surprisingly, loses a great deal of its dark potency when it is diluted by the laughter of mockery or satire.

In many ways, the parody formulations in the films discussed here illustrate the theory of the carnivalesque as Mikhail Bakhtin has articulated in his book *Rabelais and His World*. Bakhtin's analysis of the medieval carnival draws comedy and horror together because, in their most excessive forms, they both emphasize grotesque exaggerations of the body, particularly its degradation. Many of the characters in horror parody films are trapped in narratives that blur the line separating horror and hilarity, the grotesque and the sublime, to the point where some of these film narratives are quite impossible to take seriously as terror-inducing productions, as their purpose, after all, is to mock the very conventions and tropes of the horror legacy and tradition they emulate. The films in this chapter dramatize what Bakhtin observed about the purpose of the pre-Lenten carnival: that mocking and misrule reign in the subversion of routine and established order.

Many movies manage to employ comedy as a means for highlighting terror, rather than as a means for subverting it. *Texas Chainsaw*, *Misery*, and *Nightmare on Elm Street* are good examples of films where comic elements are so absurdly juxtaposed with moments of terror that the two in fact cross-fertilize and interdefine one another. In all of these filmic texts, viewers often get their emotional wires crossed, become confused as to what reaction is appropriate, and how best to respond to a scene in the larger context of the narrative. Comedy is revealed in privileging life's banal absurdities: "Look what your brother did to the door," the gas station attendant notes in *Chainsaw*—choosing to focus his and the audience's attention on the rips in the front door while overlooking the carnage that Leatherface's chainsaw has performed to living human beings elsewhere in the house. The absurdity of his comment in the midst of such horror creates a momentary dislocation and reprieve for the viewer, eliciting a nervous kind of laughter usually reserved for comments from drunks on the street. In a film such as *Carrie*, which also seems to create and sustain this particular blend, the comic is always subservient to the horrific. Chris' and Billy's sexual titillations in the front seat of Billy's car, while memorable for their physical slapstick, really belie a cruelty and degree of manipulation that lead to events that are decidedly unfunny. Similarly, in *Misery*, Annie Wilkes's genuine respect for Liberace's music stimulates derisive laughter from the audience, and she keeps Paul Sheldon in situations that constantly provoke humor. So, when she hobbles his ankle with a sledgehammer the viewer does not know what to do: Is this still funny or not? Just when the audience gets comfortable laughing along with or at Annie, she does something that completely dispels the film's comic atmosphere, chilling it with a sobering act of cruelty. Through the course of the movie, Paul and the audience both learn there is a fatal danger in relaxing even for a moment while in Annie's psychotic company, and in order to be most effective, comedy requires a certain level of relaxation. In the end, comic elements in *Misery* and *Carrie* serve to distract the viewer just long enough so that when terror is reintroduced we are caught off guard, more vulnerable to its effects. It is like the effect of a winter snowstorm in late April. When comedy is used to underscore horror, we never really relax long enough to savor the comedy; the horror quotient is there to keep us on the edge of the seat in spite of the brief respite supplied by a comic moment.

When this formula is inverted, however, that is, when the horrific is undercut by the comic, the result is parody. The degree to which this is encouraged regulates the level of seriousness that the audience invests in the picture. Nothing in *Ghostbusters* is ever truly scary because Bill Murray's character is constantly undermining our response to the paranormal by inviting us to laugh at it. The same can be said about the film version of *The Addams Family* and the television situation comedy *The Munsters*. In *The Lost Boys*, however, our reactions are not so easily categorized. While committed to a level of comedy that threatens to take over the film, there are also moments of genuine terror, such as when Michael watches himself transform into a vampire or when the intoxicated vampires lose their grip underneath a train trestle and free fall into the mist below. Thus, deciding whether or not a cinematic work should be called terror or parody probably comes down to which of the two exerts the greater influence over the atmosphere of the film. There is, however, one clear measurement that usually works: When horror conventions descend into physical pratfalls or are treated with extreme silliness, the picture is no longer a conventional (i.e., terror-producing) horror film. As Freud observed in his essay, "The Uncanny," "Even a 'real' ghost, as in Oscar Wilde's *Canterville Ghost*, loses all power of arousing *gruesome* feelings in us as soon as the author begins to amuse himself by being ironical about it and allows liberties to be taken with it" (252). Once the monster is degraded into an object of derision, the monster loses all power to terrify; where he once inspired fear, he now inspires ridicule. For many historical observers of the genre, this is the reason the Abbott and Costello horror films marked the end of the era of classical monster movies, or why *Scream* may signal the death knell for the slasher film. Once a serious tradition is under-

mined by over-the-top comedy, it is a sign that the tradition itself has lost its via-
bility and, in the case of the horror genre, its critical capacity to arouse and sustain fear.

The Edge of Terror and Parody: *The Wicker Man*

In the final scene of this very strange picture, Sergeant Howie, the film's ambas-
sador of law, upholder of Western values, and Christian acolyte, finds that the entire
town of Summerisle has tricked him into becoming its pagan sacrifice: a human virgin offered to the gods to ameliorate the island's blighted harvest. Locked inside
the "heart" of the enormous wicker man as it is steadily consumed by fire, Howie
prays for the last time, offering himself in literal martyrdom to Jesus. Meanwhile,
the citizens of the island join hands and encircle the burning pyre singing their own
prayers to a pagan godhead; while Howie's face is wrought with distress, the
islanders appear rapturous, swaying back and forth in delirious harmony. As the
camera moves away to face a fierce red sun descending into the ocean, the audience is left to consider a series of contradictory questions: Are we to sympathize
with Howie's awful fate? Should we view his personal sacrifice as symbolizing the
triumph of pagan virtues over a repressive civilization or join with the islanders in
mocking the ultraserious policeman for failing to recognize that he has been played
as a fool? Should we view the song of the islanders as the single voice of a cruel bar-
barian society desperate for any scapegoat to alleviate the recent failure of their
crops?

The true brilliance of this unsettling cinematic parable is that, unlike a typical parable, it offers no comforting maxims, no clear position to any of the disturbing questions it accumulates. *The Wicker Man* opens with Howie piloting an
airplane high over the ocean while consulting a map. When he lands the airplane
on a remote island, alien (palm trees grow alongside apple orchards!) and private,
the first words offered by a weathered native are: "Have you lost your bearings?"
Howie has arrived at a place that is "off the map" of his—and our—understanding, a place where he will forever feel lost, spiritually as well as geographically. He
flies from an urbane world of machines and technology and goes back in time to
a pagan culture of horse-drawn carriages, sailboats, and agrarian fertility rituals.
Searching for evidence about the murder of a young girl, Howie is himself murdered,
and the young girl he purports to investigate helps to kill him. As a police officer,
he is a detective, and a representative of authority and civilized values. However,
he also always is *the fool*, even to the extent of wearing the official costume of this
character during the island's spring parade. During the course of the narrative, his
role as fool is confirmed as Howie is steadily tricked and teased by the entire

town. At the end, just when he appears to have figured out the mystery of the missing girl, Howie is made to play the fool one more time in a horrible act of deception that wholly undermines the police sergeant's patronizing certitude.

Midway into the film, Howie's search for the missing girl brings him into her classroom where inside one of the school desks he discovers a beetle with a string tied around its waist circling around and around a fixed pin. It is significant that this bug is pursuing its circular motion at the exact same moment that young island boys perform a similar circle dance around a maypole to a ribald song about sexual potency. Although the rituals and the information the island children receive outrage Howie, they are really not so different from children in any society, including Howie's. The children here and elsewhere on Summerisle are taught at an instructional level that emphasizes the importance of following established behavioral patterns. Never are they allowed to examine why they, like the bug or the boys around the maypole, are locked in this designated pattern. Following the rituals of the adults in this culture, they are taught to be mindless believers—the string, after all, keeps them circling around the same monotonous pole dance. The core values of the island, in contrast to Howie's rational Christianity, center on a pagan hedonism that proves in the end, however, to be no less rigid than Howie's "I don't believe in [sex] before marriage" mantra of bodily purity, or his own commitment to the Resurrection. The female schoolteacher and the police officer pride themselves on the righteousness of their philosophies, defending their respective belief systems, but neither realizes that they are each attached to their own set of strings, both circling deathlessly around different maypoles and pins.

The film interestingly endorses neither a pagan nor a Christian ideology. Both are portrayed as rigid and uncompromising. The sergeant so fiercely resists the culture of Summerisle that he comes across as an arrogant prig, while the pagan villagers mock and manipulate him for their own amusement and devious purpose. The horror of *The Wicker Man* comes from the audience's realization that neither of these religious ideologies—both of which are parodied throughout the film—offer a fully acceptable code of conduct. Howie's repressive Christianity and the island's cruel paganism prove too extreme in their respective sacrificial demands. The citizens of Summerisle criticize Howie and the culture he represents as a system of illusions that submit to the will of an uptight Christianity. However, these free-spirited pagans are really no better as they blindly follow their own Lord Summerisle, overlooking the sharp class differences and pseudoscience he promulgates. While the people of the village live in modest cottages, their Lord inhabits a magnificent castle with elaborate gardens in the back and plenty of opportunity for him to seduce comely local maidens. His citizens may not adhere to an organized church, but they certainly maintain a passionate faith in the specious science of Lord Summerisle, trusting in his primitive superstition that the earth gods will accept the violent sacrifice of the virginal policeman and bring abundant fruit back to their apple orchards.

The Wicker Man taps into the historical reality of the 1960s from the vantage point of its release date in 1973. Howie is appalled by the quasimystical fervor of nude flower children with long flowing hair, who, when they are not strumming guitars and singing syrupy folk ballads, appear in a state of perpetual sexual arousal, and this despite the fact that the climate is cold enough to require gloves. In this atmosphere of fecundity, however, the island suffers from apple blight, and its people are desperate. Underneath the visionary love fest and the relaxed decadence that makes Howie so uncomfortable, there lurks a violent will. The hippielike children of Summerisle design to sacrifice the outsider, the other, in the hope that his death will serve their selfish purposes. In constructing the premeditated murder of the police officer, not one person in the entire village protests the murderous action of the collective, even when Howie begs for his life. It is as if every individual on the island conforms to a unified way of thinking directed by Lord Summerisle. Moreover, the policeman's destruction is not only about the seasonal harvest; it is also about preserving the microcosm of the island from the intrusively "corrupt" modern values that Howie represents and insuring, at the same time, that Lord Summerisle's vision of the world goes unchallenged.

As serious as these issues become, the film continually frames them in a grotesquely comic context. The sergeant is not much of a detective, and his aggressive demeanor in dealing with people from whom he is trying to obtain information is also subject to parody. Howie's stubborn prudishness culminates in a bedroom scene where the naked innkeeper's daughter, played by a voluptuous Britt Ekland, tries in vain to seduce him out of his bedroom. Howie's inner torment—as he listens to her siren's song and sweats against the heat he seems to feel radiating from the wall separating their two bodies—is finally more humorous than it is in any way psychological. Additionally, the number of naked bodies that appear on the island engaged in acts of copulation and various fertility rituals only repulse the conservative man; their behavior never fires his curiosity to any degree even as a tourist in the midst of cultural pluralism. For most of the movie, Howie confronts the wayward behavior of Summerisle wearing an iron mask of sullen scorn, his lipless mouth clenched in a line so tight that he comes to resemble the world's most constipated cop. Because the sergeant adheres to such a narrow and uptight perspective, we accept readily his identification with the role of the fool, and watching him bullying the natives of the island in his aggressive and officious capacity as a police officer makes us initially sympathize with the island natives. It is only when we discover that Howie is to pay such a terrible price for doing his job that our response becomes more complicated: What begins as a narrative that parodies clashing cultures in the end pivots against the people with whom we have steadily identified. This sequence of events does not necessarily mean that we gain new respect for Howie when he is forced into the role of human sacrifice, but the audience certainly loses respect for the "free spirited" natives of Summerisle when their duplicitous design unfolds.

Do the Time Warp: *The Rocky Horror Picture Show*

Rocky Horror pushes terror parody beyond the mildly amusing or satiric into the realm of the debauched and the outrageous. The most raucous song performed in *Rocky Horror* is "The Time Warp," a performance piece that always manages to pull the enthusiastic theater audience into the aisles to dance along with the actors whenever the film is shown during one of its traditional midnight weekend time slots. The song, appearing early in the film, is a wonderful dance participation number, but it also speaks directly to the picture's narrative purposes. *Rocky Horror* draws its mythic energy from a metatextual suturing to the tradition of early horror cinema. While the earnest seriousness of the classic novels and film adaptations of *Frankenstein*, *Dracula*, and *The Wolf Man* is radically undermined in this musical parody, *Rocky Horror* is nonetheless a homage to them, and it ends up following their didactic warnings against the dangers of extreme behavior which are the consequences of monstrous transgressions.

When the bland and naïve Brad and Janet are stranded on a dark rainy road, all the traditional iconography and paraphernalia of the horror film are summoned: The two lost protagonists surrounded by dark woods during a lightning storm find refuge in Dr. Frank N. Furter's isolated Gothic castle. Indeed, a taller version of Igor himself answers the door appearing in the role of a butler while his sister finishes the film wearing a hairstyle inspired by *The Bride of Frankenstein*. In case anyone in the audience has missed the allusions to the filmic tradition *Rocky Horror* seeks to parody, the black and white RKO Picture logo long associated with productions of early Hollywood horror cinema serves as the backdrop for the film's final dance floor routine. Inside this castle, where one would expect to find Dracula or the mad scientist of the classic horror film narrative, Janet and Brad stumble upon a collection of party revelers who have as much in common with a college frat party as they do with Halloween. Dr. Furter, a "sweet transvestite from Transvestite, Transylvania," who is a composite parody of all the libidinous energies unleashed by the horror monster, serves as master of ceremonies for this obscene celebration.

Furter follows Frankenstein in pursuing "the secret to life," but whereas the creature in Shelley's novel and Whale's film adaptation is an unsavory amalgamation of parts from local graveyards that ends up repulsing his creator, Furter births a muscular gold-lamé trophy boy that absolutely fulfills his master's homoerotic desire for "exceptional beauty." The scene where Rocky is born to the utter delight of his maker is a composite of Las Vegas cabaret show meets Fire Island gender bending. Like Dracula, Dr. Furter's gender alignment is ambiguous, and he is similarly possessed of a deviant sexuality. His guiding philosophy of the bedroom is "Give yourself over to absolute pleasure/ . . . Don't dream it, be it." He welcomes readily the addition of Janet and Brad to his pleasure palace and is not at all distracted by their simple desire to locate a telephone and get their flat tire fixed. Instead, he takes advantage of his naïve visitors, seducing them both, and they, in turn, come to revel in a personal sexual liberation that is reminiscent of what Dracula himself practices and bestows upon his various victims. After her sexual violation, Janet sings out an anthem of libidinous excess: "Oh I—I feel released/ Bad times deceased/ My confidence has increased/ . . . My mind has been expanded/ It's a gas that Frankie's landed/ His lust is so sincere."

Furter embodies so much sexual energy, he is "so gleefully transsexual, so raucously alive, so husky beneath the sequins" that, as Twitchell correctly assesses, "it's hard not to be swept along" (198). His energies, however, again similar to the self-indulgent excesses of both Frankenstein and Dracula, are extreme and transgressive, and the film demands that they be placed back under control so that Janet and Brad can return to bourgeois normalcy. As Dr. Furter is told at the end of the film, "Your mission is a failure; your lifestyle's too extreme." Thus, even as *Rocky Horror* is an outrageous parody of monster movies that precede it (and also the cult Hammer films from the 1960s), it subscribes to the paradigm that serves as a common foundation for all classic horror cinema in its insistence that the monster's power to cause societal and personal upheavals must be negated and the status quo reaffirmed. Furter, like Dracula and Frankenstein, is really a representative of the unconscious, particularly embodying Brad and Janet's urge to experiment with a full range of sexual self-expression. They arrive at his castle at the moment where they have declared their love for one another but have not yet consummated it through marriage; "I was saving myself," Janet acknowledges, but neither she nor her fiancé require much convincing before submitting to a range of premarital debauchery with Furter as their mutual sex therapist and bedmate. As the film's stodgy narrator comments: "Just a few hours after announcing their engagement, Brad and Janet had both tasted forbidden fruit." Like Lucy after her violation by Dracula, Brad's and Janet's desire for such fruit, though consciously repressed until their arrival at Furter's castle, is nearly as voracious as Furter's own. The normal merely requires enough direct physical contact with the monstrous for the repressed Hyde to be unleashed. Their initiation into Frank's world of depravity culminates in an underwater orgy of floating high heels, clinging bodies, and smeared makeup that is as sexually decadent as it is an exercise in over-the-top musical camp.

At the end of *Rocky Horror*, however, it is important that Brad relinquishes his garter belt, stockings, corset, and heels—fetish objects to which he has become so erotically attached—and that Janet recognizes who is her proper reproductive partner despite her growing attraction to promiscuous sex. For this reorientation to occur, Furter must be vanquished and his mixed up bisexual mystification straightened out into a clear confirmation of heterosexual monogamy. Dr. Scott, the film's voice of rational moderation, applauds Furter's demise by reminding the characters in the film—as well as the picture's late-night adolescent audience, many of whom are dressed in full costume and makeup to replay and mime events on the screen—that "Society must be protected." His sentiment echoes the same righteous indignation that animated the angry multitudes carrying pitchforks and torches to seek out transgressive monsters from an earlier cinematic epoch. Frank's banishment back to the planet of Transsexual is the equivalent of a wooden stake through Dracula's heart, a silver bullet into the WolfMan, or the incineration of the Frankenstein creature inside the windmill: Only after the monster is dead and discredited as a symbol of alternative sexuality and behavior is it possible for the other characters to regain personal equilibrium and reaffirm the values of the status quo.

Raising the Monster: *Young Frankenstein*

Like *Rocky Horror*, the comic parody of *Young Frankenstein* relies on an understanding of Hollywood's *Frankenstein* movies and achieves much of its humor by continually placing Frankenstein's quest to reanimate his monster in a contemporary context. For example, jokes about the relative size of the monster's penis—Igor speculates that because of it, the creature is "going to be very popular"—would not have been likely before the 1974 release of this film. Although certainly offering no less serious a treatment of the *Frankenstein* myth than *Rocky Horror*, *Young Frankenstein* works hard to recreate the atmospheric effects of classical horror cinema: The deserted nocturnal streets of Transylvania, the castle laboratory replete with electronic machinery that closely approximates the original film sets from the 1930s and 1940s, misty forests of barren trees, all rendered in a black and white cinematography that is presented in stark detail. Even more than *Rocky Horror*, *Young Frankenstein* appreciates the mise-en-scène visual effects that still make the earliest *Frankenstein* adaptations inspiring cinema. Further, although Mel Brooks exploits every opportunity to wrest laughter from his audience, his screenplay is a wonderful composite parody of Shelley's novel and the Whale films. Brooks's monster, for example, is a tormented soul, more interested in finding acceptance (and great sex with Elizabeth) than in causing destruction. *Young Frankenstein* is probably best described as a hybrid homage to Whale's films and Shelley's novel as interpreted by a vaudeville comedian. In addition to the creature battling the requisite angry villagers carrying torches, for example, an audience of Budapest surgeons also humiliates Brooks's monster after he falters in a soft-shoe dance routine while dressed in a tuxedo.

Brooks's film clearly owes something to the early Abbott and Costello parodies, as the director never misses an opportunity to capitalize on physical sight gags: Igor's hump is always shuffling around to different spots on his back; young Frankenstein and his curvaceous assistant, Inga, share an entire scene where they keep getting stuck in the castle's secret revolving bookshelf; while the monster is strangling Frederick, the doctor has to resort to pantomime in order to get his assistants to deliver a sedative to his assailant; and the inspiration for young Frankenstein to pursue his grandfather's research is a book in the laboratory library entitled *How I Did It*. The humor is of a kinder and gentler variety than the wickedness found in *Rocky Horror*; there is, finally, no monster present in *Young Frankenstein* that even approximates the wildly threatening excesses of Frank N. Furter. Brooks's Frankenstein is a lovable if madcap mad scientist who is not really very mad; his decision to pursue his grandfather's research, ironically, instead of leading to isolation and tragedy, becomes a personally liberating exercise.

Perhaps the major element that *Rocky Horror* shares in common with *Young Frankenstein*, and they, in turn, with the energies of the creation myth itself is that the quest to "reanimate dead tissue" produces in all those who pursue it a corresponding revivification. In fact, both of these parodies continue to link the monstrous with a liberated libido. When Dr. Frankenstein and the creature exchange bodily fluids at the conclusion of *Young Frankenstein*, the doctor is transformed into a more physical being to complement the monster's newly elevated level of sophistication. Frederick gains a penis enlargement, which is what the monster provides him in return for improved language and culture skills, and the doctor comes to recognize his love for the affectionate Inga and wisely follows his passions in marrying her instead of the fastidious Elizabeth. Sexuality also transforms Elizabeth, however, as she ends up marrying the creature. In *Young Frankenstein*, sexual expression is an exclusively positive force because it has none of the transgressive— i.e., homoerotic—properties that are associated with it in *Rocky Horror*. Dr. Furter's sexual appetite is so inclusive that in spite of the humor it provokes, it simultaneously represents the threat of the abject. *Young Frankenstein* appears tame in comparison because the film avoids the gender complications that *Rocky Horror* flagrantly imposes. *Young Frankenstein* confirms the hegemony of heterosexuality; the "abnormally large" monster penis—because it is "gender appropriate" and aligned with a "normal" and therefore unthreatening heterosexuality—is treated as a positive attribute that contributes to the film's orgasmic happy ending.

The Vampire Wears Shades: *The Lost Boys*

The Lost Boys is no more a typical vampire film than *Rocky Horror* and *Young Frankenstein* are typical monster movies. The lost boy vampires are as much in need of some good mothering as they are in need of a good staking. The heroes of the film are a motley collection of comic book enthusiasts, the Frog brothers, Edgar and Allan; two other brothers who feel as abandoned as the vampire lost boys themselves, Michael and Sam; and an eccentric senior citizen taxidermist. The vampire fighters are about as far removed from *Dracula*'s Crew of Light as California is from Transylvania. The film even pokes fun at the sacred traditions of the revenant legend by having them comically misapplied by the Frog brothers, whose knowledge is gleaned exclusively from reading vampire comic books. A couple of the teenage vampires in *The Lost Boys* are vanquished by holy water shot from high-powered squirt guns and mixed with garlic in a bathtub. These humorous elements notwithstanding, the film is a parody at the same time as it is a terrifying vampire narrative. It manages to balance its dark excursions into the lair of the vampire with light comic touches.

The opening credits roll to accompany a series of jump cuts featuring the boardwalk of Santa Clara. Among the happy faces of young people riding amusement park rides and playing video games, there are several cuts to posters featuring the faces of missing children. The sequence concludes with a shot of a sign on the edge of the ocean indicating that there is no lifeguard on duty. This opening sequence is a stunning visual pastiche of Santa Clara's double-sidedness. On the one hand, there is the brilliance of a California coastal town, its sexy bodies and eternal youthfulness. On the other, the town also reveals some of its dark underside, especially in the "Welcome to Santa Clara" billboard that hides "Murder Capital of the World" spray painted on its flip side, and the selected jump cuts to boardwalk kids— more evidence of "lost boys"—eating food out of dumpsters.

While the opening sequence/credits roll, in the background on the car radio Michael, Sam, and their mother listen to a rendition of the Doors' well-known song "People Are Strange." The Doors, and particularly their hedonist lead singer, Jim Morrison, are quietly referenced throughout the film. A huge black and white headshot of Morrison, his long hair and youthful beauty strikingly similar to the vampire boys themselves, resides on the wall of the cave where the rock star presides over their lives like a shaman. Morrison haunts the fringes of this film, its love of dark spectacle, transformation, rebellion, drug use, alienation, and crowd incitement to riot. The various allusions to Morrison and the Doors is important as a way of perceiving the pessimistic side of Santa Clara itself—for the Doors, a group that was originally formed in southern California in the late 1960s, posed a disturbing alternative to the idealistic "flower children" of the Woodstock generation. The

Doors were a reminder to the Age of Aquarius that violence and death were still omnipresent elements stalking America. It is worth noting that one of the songs the family hears on their drive into town only to bypass on the car radio is "Groovin'" by The Young Rascals, an appropriate anthem for the syrupy sweet side of the 1960s and the antithesis to the theme of stark alienation epitomized in the lyrics of "People Are Strange." As such, Morrison and the Doors speak for and to the lost children of Santa Clara; they all come to embody the nightmare of California dreaming. Just as the "Summer of Love" in the 1960s gave way to the sobering realities of Viet Nam and urban violence at the end of the decade, Santa Clara's amusement part atmosphere barely disguises a town under the grip of punk vampires and alienated "lost boys." Morrison, who was also a "lost boy" estranged from both his family and era, is the mythical god of the film's abandoned and way-ward youth. The radical iconoclast, who wrote haunting songs and poetry about abandonment and "blood in the streets," was himself a kind of boy vampire—the Lizard King—whose youthful immortality remains a big part of his continuing lega-cy in both his songs and deathless physical beauty.

The concept of boys either lost or in danger of becoming lost is of core impor-tance to this film, and in each case a missing parent is what precipitates the crisis. Fragmented families extend to include the Frog brothers, who are completely without parental supervision, as well as Star and Laddy, the adolescent vampires-in-training whose faces are among posters of Santa Clara's missing children. David and his motorcycle vamps are like the "lost boys" of Peter Pan's gang: Not only capa-ble of flight, these are children who operate outside the purview of a traditional fam-ily and who find themselves, as vampires, in a position where they will never grow old or die. Appropriate to the Peter Pan myth, Max, the vampire father-surrogate of the lost boys, is searching for a mother to help him raise his misguided revenant children. He clearly recognizes that his clan is fragmented, somehow vulnerable in the absence of a perceived wholeness available in a traditional two-parent nuclear family: "Boys need a mother. One big happy family. Your boys and my boys." For Michael and Sam, divorce has put the two brothers in a position where they are similarly lost; their current familial disaffection is continually manifested both in the aggressive way in which they treat each other and in their mutual desire to pro-tect one another. Michael is himself old enough to take on the role of father, and the film suggests that after straying unintentionally into the vampire realm—flirt-ing dangerously with David's taunt "How far you willing to go?"—Sam's subsequent endangerment and Star's affections guide Michael back home where he assumes the mantle of the father-protector. He proves his bravery by helping to rescue the film's endangered females, his mother and Star, and their lost sons, Sam and Laddy. Even before Michael chooses to reject his emerging vampire persona and accept his role as a hero, Max correctly recognizes him as "the head of the household," and asks his permission to be invited inside.

It is Grandpa, however, who turns out to be the viable paternal figure in the film, and the vampire slayer that Michael eventually comes to emulate. At first, the old man appears as a curmudgeon who is not very pleased that his recently divorced daughter and teenage sons have moved into his home. Like the town of Santa Clara, however, the grandfather is not what he appears. Underneath his gruff and eccentric exterior, the old man is wise to the "bad elements around here," and he is the one who takes it on himself to rid the town of its vampires while helping to rescue his besieged family. Grandpa insists on the preservation of "rules" that need to be respected in his home (a home, by the way, that contains a great deal of wood—even the wind chimes in front—as if foreshadowing his role as a staker of vampires). Initially, the "rules" refer merely to the second drawer of the refrigerator, where Grandpa stores his soda and cookies, or the demand that his car be filled with gas whenever someone takes it out. His comical set of "rules" become more serious, however, when the vampire family violates his home, and Grandpa returns to quell the chaos of the vampire invasion by slaying the vampire king. All through the film, while he pretends to be oblivious to what is happening to his grandsons and community, he is conscious of what is going on, as he acknowledges in the last line of the movie: "One thing I never could stomach about Santa Clara: all the damn vampires." In reality, his is the voice of wisdom and authority as well as courage in the face of forces that endanger his family and town. Crashing through the wall of his house at the end of the film with giant phallic fence poles that are used to stake his patriarchal rival, Grandpa's reemergence signals the triumphant return of a legitimate order to the upheaval unleashed by the vampire. While his grandsons begin the film sharing little in common with their grandfather (both mock his interest in taxidermy, and Sam complains about the absence of a television in his house), by its conclusion they are warriors fighting on the same side. The line of descent is revealed, as Grandpa has presided over a kind of initiation ritual for Michael and Sam, watching both establish their independence from their mother even as they risk their lives to protect her. Under his indirect tutelage, the lost boys are no longer lost.

Reinventing Genre: *Scream*

What distinguishes *Scream* from the generation of slasher films that preceded it is its script's clever ability to tread carefully along the line separating homage from parody. *Scream* really is both: A truly terrifying movie that emulates the tradition of the most effective slasher films while at the same time managing to deconstruct and reinvent the genre that had nearly exhausted itself a decade earlier. Although following the plotline of the typical slasher with its multiple brutal murders of teenagers at the hands of a relentless serial killer, its witticism and self-conscious parody of the conventions it draws upon gives *Scream* a completely different tone from the films it parodies. Indeed, instead of being afraid of the serial killer stalking them, most of the high school students of Woodsboro are excited to be at the center of such drama and national media attention. They mock the murderer in their midst even to the point of dressing up in his disguise; when the school cancels classes after the deaths of two students, the other carefree teens throw a massive party. Its sense of cynical parody amidst the carnage ends up connecting *Scream* more to Freddy's bizarre sense of humor in the *A Nightmare on Elm Street* movies (a brief shot of a janitor mopping the high school hallway outside the principal's office is a deliberate allusion to Freddy himself) than to the lethally grim *Halloween* or *Friday the 13th* sagas.

Scream supplied the slasher tradition with an overdue face-lift. In the conventional slasher film, the Final Girl is the only teenager aware of the monster and his intentions; her friends are either killed by random surprise or ignore naïvely whatever danger signs are associated with his presence. All the teenagers in *Scream* have grown up watching multiple films from slasher cinema and thus possess an intimate knowledge of the various conventions associated with the genre. *Halloween*, *Friday the 13th*, and *A Nightmare on Elm Street* are all referenced in the first fifteen minutes of the movie. At one point in *Scream*, several teenagers, who will themselves soon be attacked, watch a video of the film, *Halloween*. One of the students tells his peers that "There are certain rules that one must abide by to successfully survive a horror movie," and then proceeds to list them. The killer also possesses his own understanding of these rules and uses this expertise as a means for tormenting his victims by making them aware of the fact that their lives have become "meta-connected" with a slasher movie. As the film develops, it is clear that the murderers possess a deep appreciation of horror film, and they employ their personal knowledge of the genre to help design their own serial spree: The murderers understand their place—and purpose—and are guided by the celluloid stalkers who have influenced and inspired them. While stalking his women victims on the telephone, the killer asks them, "What's your favorite scary movie," and then quizzes them on details relevant to their choice. It is a bizarre version of the game "Trivia"; the women stay alive as long as their film knowledge keeps supplying the killer with correct answers. *Scream* does not just imply that life mirrors art, it also goes so far to suggest that life also parodies art. This point is brought home by one of the killers—there are two—when he informs his girlfriend after making love with her that the distinction between movies and real life is always an artificial one and that the two realms continually influence and intersect with one another.

Like the various serial killers in the slasher genre from whom they are descendants, the murderers in *Scream* wear a mask to disguise their identity. It is a white plastic reproduction of Edvard Munch's famous Ghostface figure from his painting "The Scream." Munch's painting is an apt representation of the degree of alienation from other people that inspires the killers' murderous agenda. Rockoff sees in the face "an exaggerated, almost mocking grin, as if reflecting the look of terror and surprise on his victims' faces" (181). However, Munch's Ghostface is also an ironic choice, because the killers featured in *Scream* are by far the most loquacious psychopaths found in the slasher genre. They enjoy conversing with their victims prior to their killing, and part of what stimulates them is how well women in particular understand and verbalize their role as active participants in the horror tradition. While all the monsters in the conventional slasher film are outsiders—that is, they are usually older males and thus do not belong to the social group upon whom they prey—Ghostface is himself a teenager and intimately connected to all of his victims.

As Ghostface occupies a different position in relationship to his victims from that of the celluloid serial killers who precede him, *Scream* raises several unsettling parallels to the bloodbath at Columbine High School in 1999, less than two and a half years after the release of *Scream* in December 1996. First, there is the fact that two male killers plan and execute the bloodletting in both the film and inside the Colorado high school. More significantly, the teenage murderers at Columbine were similarly imbued and obsessed with the same culture of the Gothic, particularly the violent tradition of the horror film that we find continually cross-referenced in *Scream*. By the end of *Scream*, there are so many bodies strewn and so much blood around Stu's party house and yard that the murder scene is strongly reminiscent of the powerful images of murder pictured on surveillance tapes and news videos from Columbine. At points, Ghostface is killing teenagers randomly, just as the Columbine murderers shot classmates under desks and in hallways. More relevant to our purposes, however, in both instances, there is an overwhelming sense of the killers' self-consciousness: They understand themselves as pursuing a script, or, as it is called in *Scream*, a "formula" that is not entirely of their own design. Both sets of serial killers conduct their grisly business with a profound awareness of their potential roles as media stars, as mass murderers who understand too well that their legacy will prove so tantalizing to a popular culture with an insatiable appetite for violence that it will be analyzed even to the point of eventually inspiring parody.

The Parody of Excess: *Scary Movie*

Scary Movie draws from so many different film sources that it frequently and gleefully enters into the realm of self-parody. In addition to being a specific satire of films from the slasher genre, such as *Halloween* and *A Nightmare on Elm Street* (where a fountain of sperm replaces *Nightmare*'s geyser of blood in the bedroom), *Scary Movie* makes overt references to *I Know What You Did Last Summer*, *The Shining*, *When a Stranger Calls*, *The Blair Witch Project*, *The Sixth Sense*, and *All Cheerleaders Die*. Of course, its most important sourcework remains *Scream*, as it provided *Scary Movie* with the prototype for a slasher satire. *Scary Movie* not only purloins the original title of the script that eventually was renamed *Scream*, it also satirically parallels the latter's narrative plotline, including its Ghostface killer, an intrepid girl reporter, and a small town high school under siege. What we get in *Scary Movie* is essentially a parody of a parody. Unlike *Scream*, however, *Scary Movie* pushes the slasher genre all the way over into the comedic realm. In the first three days of its release, the film made $42.5 million; its worldwide gross is currently in excess of $250 million. Its status as a satiric homage notwithstanding, *Scary Movie* has ironically made more money than any of the films it parodied (Rockoff 192–93).

Scary Movie is a virtual encyclopedia of allusions to the most popular films in the postmodern horror canon. Because this film tries to take full advantage of every possible opportunity to parody other scary movies, there are many moments in *Scary Movie* when the film sacrifices its own narrative cohesion in order to digress into a comic homage of a specific scene or situation from an earlier horror movie. As a result, *Scary Movie* has less integrity as an independent work of art than *Rocky Horror*, *Young Frankenstein*, or even *Scream*, but this is because it is so shamelessly and self-consciously opportunistic and aware of its comic intentions. The parody simply must be accepted on its own terms: as a loosely plotted series of satiric sketches.

Scary Movie never gets any better than its opening, as this inventive sequence is destined to endure as a classic example of cinematic parody. Carmen Electra's Drew embodies all the essential assets of the female victim in the slasher genre. Alone in her parents' house, dressed as a cheerleader, and willing to explore and share cheerfully her sexual knowledge with a complete stranger on the telephone, Drew places herself in immediate danger. Even though she is appalled while listening to the killer detail his plan to cause her bodily harm, she unlocks all the doors in her house. She is the ultimate parody of Clover's Final Girl and, specifically, the character Casey Becker in *Scream* played by Drew Barrymore (thus, the choice to name the character in *Scary Movie*, Drew): a beautiful female who does everything in her power to enable her victimization and participate in her own slaughter. When offered two huge arrows pointing in different directions—"safety" and "danger"—as the killer pursues her, Drew chooses the latter path, and when provided a choice of weapons to counter the crazed killer, she eschews both gun and knife in favor of a banana. It is a wildly comic sequence that is deeply enriched when considered in the context of the slasher genre, and most particularly the opening scene in *Scream*. Although she is the first murder victim of the film's serial murderer, her death establishes the film's tone of comic absurdity: When the killer stabs at her chest with his hunting knife, he cleanly extracts a silicone implant from Drew's breast.

Much of *Scary Movie*'s comic sensibility is focused on bathroom humor, perverse sex jokes, and stoned drug scenes; in fact, so much of its plot is situated in the realm of what William Paul calls the adolescent gross-out comedy that the film vies as much for genre inclusion with pictures such as *Fast Times at Ridgemont High* and *American Pie* as it does a horror parody. There are, nevertheless, continual and specific references to the slasher tradition. The killer pursuing the students at B. A. Corpse High School, like Michael Myers and Leatherface before him, is masked throughout the film. While the unemotional masks that Jason and Michael wear remain fixed points in their fetishistic universes, the Ghostface mask of the serial murderer in *Scary Movie*—identical to the one in *Scream*—is constantly changing to reflect the varying moods of the killer: from a look of stoned ecstasy when he is smoking pot with his next murder victims to pained bewilderment when a girl fails to react with appropriate fear in his presence. While the slasher genre provides a parade of serial psychopaths who are devastating killing machines, the anonymous murderer in *Scary Movie* is a bungling idiot. He is a perfect foil to his female victims who parody the helpless women of the slasher genre. Like them, the killer plays his role more for laughs than for blood. When the film's Final Girl/heroine, Cindy Campbell, discovers the masked killer in her home, he makes her turn her back long enough so that he can find another hiding place behind the curtains. Like many of the other horror film satires considered in this chapter, *Scary Movie* and its sequel do not seek to evoke real terror, choosing instead to undercut the audience's fear factor by deliberately modeling scenes from a specific horror narrative, and then converting the audience's recollected terror at that moment into derisive laughter.

An important aspect of the slasher parody that continues to distinguish it from the seriousness of the slasher genre it emulates concerns the handling of violence and graphic gore. As discussed in the preceding chapter, the amount of violence and bloodshed in slasher pictures increased as the genre evolved, essentially upping the ante in technical effects and incidents of violence with the release of each new sequel. *Scary Movie*, while relying on acts of murdering and mayhem that mimic the slasher narratives, is careful not to follow its sourcework by wallowing in realistic and graphic portrayals of violence. Instead, we often do not see the killer's knife actually penetrate his victim's flesh, as the camera discretely pulls away at these critical moments; even when blood is revealed, it never simulates the elaborate and fetishistic gorefest found in conventional slasher cinema. This measure of self-restraint is the result of *Scary Movie* playing its scenes of violent intrusion for laughs—the comedy, in other words, takes precedence over what would normally evoke a horrific response. Further, too much graphic violence would likely distract from and diminish the audience's attention to the satiric aspects of a given scene. Thus, the film's director is attentive to moving the emphasis away from the actual bloodletting in the murder sequences.

There are many scenes in *Scary Movie* that illustrate such tendencies, but the most memorable one may occur when Ghostface attacks Buffy, one of Cindy's buxom friends. Isolated and trapped in the girl's high school locker room—the scene of so many horrible occurrences throughout the horror genre—her response is to parody the terror heroines who precede her. She asks if the killer would like her to scream, how much clothing she should remove, and the appropriately submissive position her body ought to assume in preparation for his violence. Even after her head is decapitated, Buffy will not stop talking and mocking both her killer and the other female victims of slasher cinema. Finally, out of confusion that bleeds into disgust, Ghostface simply disposes of her still-talking head in a dirty laundry basket. The scene perfectly illustrates the self-consciousness of parody as it is distinguished from the conventional slasher film: The audience is so amused by Buffy's deconstructive critical accuracy and good-natured willingness to facilitate her own self-destruction that the acts of violence that are perpetrated against her are diminished accordingly. Indeed, by the end of the scene she has brought nearly as much self-inflicted brutality to her own body as has the killer himself.

While terror parodies frequently take great liberties with the traditions they love to mock, it is also necessary that they adhere to many of the horror genre's conventions. Contradiction, after all, is a frequent and typical element in parody. The mad scientist creator in *Rocky Horror* may be an ostentatious transvestite who prefers wearing lipstick and high heels, but the film in which he appears still manages to underscore a somber tenet of the *Frankenstein* myth: the danger inherent in a liberated imagination that acts out of selfish interest rather than from a responsibility to others. Similarly, while *The Lost Boys* may poke fun at the bravado of adolescent vampire hunters who are, in reality, terrified of the revenants they hunt, it also views the vampire as a transgressive agent preying on the community in which he dwells. As in *Dracula*, *The Lost Boys* portrays the vampire as a challenger to traditional patriarchal authority, and he must be vanquished by the collective efforts of those males who would seek to reestablish a more conventional patriarchal dominance. Moreover, again borrowing from the vampiric tradition, the film features a maternal woman as the ultimate prize contested by both the vampire and his enemies.

Thus, while relying heavily on comic strategies, terror parodies never completely lose sight of those elements in the horror tradition that have likewise inspired fright and serious representation. In fact, often the closer a parody adheres to the essential gravity of the genre film(s) it spoofs, the more effective the parody. Consequently, a picture such as *Young Frankenstein* reveals its debt to the horror genre far more readily than do movies such as *Ghostbusters*, *Gremlins*, or *Scooby-Do*. While all of these films are comedies, only *Young Frankenstein* rises to the level of parody because the humor it evokes is dependent on the audience's knowledge of work that has preceded it. If the viewer has not seen Whale's *Frankenstein* movies or at least read Mary Shelley's novel, *Young Frankenstein* loses much of its satiric potency. The same can be said about *Scream* and *Scary Movie*: Without at least a basic understanding of the conventions featured in the slasher genre, the humor and referential dialogue in these parodies fail to resonate. No similar context, however, is necessary prior to viewing and appreciating *Ghostbusters*, *Gremlins*, or *Scooby-Doo*.

Illustrations

Figure I. The dinner party in *The Texas Chainsaw Massacre* that features Sally as guest of honor. The camera, moving continually around the table and the dining room, provides us here with a shot of the Hitchhiker, the man referred to as "just a cook," Grandpa, and Leatherface from Sally's point of view.

Figure 2. Norman Bates runs between the two most important buildings in *Psycho*, the Victorian mansion, associated with his mother and childhood, and the Bates Motel, located to the right of this shot.

Figure 3. Laura Baxter reaches through a locked iron gate in Venice that separates her from her husband and dead daughter during the climactic scene in *Don't Look Now*. Laura's last word in the film, "Darlings," is uttered

Figure 4. Miriam, the Queen Vampire, relies on dominatrix clothing and Catherine Deneuve's real-life persona as haute couture fashion model to complicate our response to vampirism in *The Hunger*.

Figure 5. An interior shot of the Korova milk bar in *A Clockwork Orange*. Note how the patrons, in various stages of dissolution, are surrounded by naked female ceramic figures that serve as tables, milk dispensers, and misogynist bondage art.

Figure 6. Ripley under siege in *Alien 3*. The Alien's dual mouths, both filled with sharp incisors, are clearly in evidence.

Films Cited

The Addams Family. Dir. Barry Sonnenfeld. Orion Pictures, Paramount Pictures, 1991.

Alien. Dir. Ridley Scott. Twentieth Century Fox, Brandywine Productions, 1979.

Alien 3. Dir. David Fincher. Twentieth Century Fox, 1992.

Alien Resurrection. Dir. Jean-Pierre Jeunet. Twentieth Century Fox, Brandywine Productions, 1997.

Aliens. Dir. James Cameron. Twentieth Century Fox, Brandywine Productions, 1986.

All Cheerleaders Die. Dir. Lucky McKee, Chris Sivertson. Milman Productions, 2001.

American Pie. Dir. Paul Weitz. Summit Entertainment, Universal Pictures, 1999.

American Psycho. Dir. Mary Harron. Edward Pressman Film Corporation, Muse Productions, Quadra Entertainment, 2000.

The Andalusian Dog. Dir. Luis Bunuel. Art House Video, Large Door Video, Video Yesteryear, 1929.

April Fool's Day. Dir. Fred Walton. Homefront Films, Paramount Pictures, 1986.

Apt Pupil. Dir. Brian Singer. Phoenix Pictures, TriStar Pictures, 1997.

Artificial Intelligence [A. I.]. Dir. Steven Spielberg. Amblin Entertainment, Dream Works, Stanley Kubrick Productions, Warner Brothers, 2001.

Barry Lyndon. Dir. Stanley Kubrick. Hawk Films, Peregrine, 1975.

Basic Instinct. Dir. Paul Berhoeven. Carolco, Le Studio Canal, TriStar Pictures, 1992.

Batman Returns. Dir. Tim Burton. Polygram Pictures, Warner Brothers, 1992.

Beverly Hills, 90210. [Television series]. Created by Darren Star. Spelling Television, 1990–2000.

The Bird with the Crystal Plumage. Dir. Dario Argento. CCC Filmkunst GmbH, Glazier, Seda Spettacoli, 1970.

The Birds. Dir. Alfred Hitchcock. Universal Pictures, 1963.

Blacula. Dir. William Crain. Power Productions, American International Pictures, 1972.

Blade. Dir. Stephen Norrington. Amen Ra Films, Imaginary Forces, New Line Cinema, 1998.

Blade Runner. Dir. Ridley Scott. Blade Runner Partnership, Ladd Company, 1982.

The Blair Witch Project. Dir. Daniel Myrick and Eduardo Sanchez. Haxan Films, 1999.

The Blob. Dir. Irwin S. Yeaworth, Jr. TonyLyn Productions, 1958.

Body Heat. Dir. Lawrence Kasdan. Ladd Company, 1981.

The Bone Collector. Dir. Phillip Noyce. Columbia Pictures, Universal Pictures, 1999.

Bound. Dir. Andy Wachowski and Larry Wachowski. De Laurentiis Group, Spelling Films, Republic Pictures, 1996.

Bram Stoker's Dracula. Dir. Francis Ford Coppola. Columbia Pictures, 1992.

The Bride of Frankenstein. Dir. James Whale. Universal Pictures, 1935.

The Brood. Dir. David Cronenberg. Les Productions Mutuelles, Elgin International Productions, 1979.

A Bucket of Blood. Dir. Roger Corman. Alta Vista Productions, 1955.

Buffy the Vampire Slayer [television series]. Created by Joss Whedon. Twentieth Century Fox Television, 1997—2003.

The Cabinet of Dr. Caligari. Dir. Robert Wiene. Decla-Bioscop, 1920.

Candyman. Dir. Bernard Rose. TriStar Pictures, 1992.

Carrie. Dir. Brian De Palma. United Artists, 1976.

Cat People. Dir. Jacques Tourneur. RKO Radio Pictures, 1942.

Children of the Corn. Dir. Fritz Kiersch. Angeles Entertainment Group, Cinema Group, Gatlin, Inverness Productions, 1984.

Child's Play. Dir. Tom Holland. United Artists, 1988.

Chinatown. Dir. Roman Polanski. Paramount Pictures, 1974.

Christine. Dir. John Carpenter. Columbia Pictures, 1983.

A Clockwork Orange. Dir. Stanley Kubrick. Hawk Films, Polaris Productions, Warner Brothers, 1971.

Copycat. Jon Amiel. New Regency Pictures, Warner Brothers, 1995.

Countess Dracula. Dir. Peter Sasdy. Hammer Films, 1971.

Cowboy Beebop: The Movie. Dir. Toshihiro Kawamoto. Sony Pictures, 2001.

Crash. Dir. David Cronenberg. The Movie Network, Telefilm Canada, 1996.

Cujo. Dir. Lewis Teague. Taft Entertainment, Warner Brothers, Republic Pictures, 1983.

Cursed. Dir. Wes Craven. Dimension Films, Outerbanks Entertainment, Craven-Maddalena Films, 2004.

The Dark Half. Dir. George Romero. Orion Pictures, 1992.

Dawn of the Dead. Dir. George A. Romero. Laurel, 1978.

Dawson's Creek. [Televison series]. Created by Kevin Williamson. Outerbank Entertainment, Columbia TriStar Televison, Sony Pictures Television, 1998–2003.

The Day After Tomorrow. Dir. Roland Emmerich. Twentieth Century Fox, Centropolis, Mark Gordon Productions, 2004.

Day of the Dead. Dir. George A. Romero. Dead Films, Laurel Entertainment, 1985.

The Day the Earth Stood Still. Dir. Robert Wise. Twentieth Century Fox, 1951.

The Deadly Mantis. Dir. Nathan Juran. Universal Pictures, 1957.

Dead Ringers. Dir. David Cronenberg. Morgan Creek Productions, Telefilm Canada, 1988.

The Dead Zone. Dir. David Cronenberg. De Laurentiis Group, Lorimar, 1983.

Dial "M" for Murder. Dir. Alfred Hitchcock. Warner Brothers, 1954.

The Deer Hunter. Dir. Michael Cimino. EMI Films, Universal Pictures, 1978.

Demon Seed. Dir. Donald Cammell. Metro-Goldwyn-Mayer, 1977.

The Devil's Manor. Dir. Georges Méliés. Star, 1896.

Dolores Claiborne. Dir. Taylor Hackford. Castle Rock Entertainment, 1995.

Don't Look Now. Dir. Nicholas Roeg. Paramount Pictures, 1973.

Dr. Jekyll and Mr. Hyde. Dir. Robert Mamoulian. Paramount Pictures, 1931.

Dr. Strangelove, or How I Learned to Stop Worrying and Love the Bomb. Dir. Stanley Kubrick. Hawk Films, 1964.

Dracula. Dir. Tod Browning. Universal Pictures, 1931.

Dracula: Dead and Loving It. Dir. Mel Brooks. Brooksfilms, Castle Rock Entertainment, 1995.

Dracula: The Musical. Dir. Richard Ouzounian. Ontario Educational Communications Authority, 2000.

Dracula's Daughter. Dir. Lambert Hillyer. Universal Pictures, 1936.

Dreamcatcher. Dir. Lawrence Kasden. Castle Rock Entertainment, Village Roadshow Productions, 2003.

Dressed to Kill. Dir. Brian De Palma. Cinema 77 Films, Filmway Pictures, Warwick Associates, 1980.

E. T.: The Extraterrestrial. Dir. Steven Spielberg. Amblin Entertainment, Universal Pictures, 1982.

Edward Scissorhands. Dir. Tim Burton. Twentieth Century Fox, 1990.

The Evil Dead. Dir. Sam Raimi. Renaissance Pictures, 1981.

eXistenZ. Dir. David Cronenberg. Telefilm Canada, Alliance Atlantis, Harold Greenberg Fund, The Movie Network, 1999.

The Exorcist. Dir. William Freidkin. Hoya Productions, Warner Brothers, 1973.

Eyes Wide Shut. Dir. Stanley Kubrick. Warner Brothers, 1999.

The Fall of the House of Usher. Dir. Jean Epstein, Films J. Epstein, 1928.

Fast Times at Ridgemont High. Dir. Amy Heckerling. Universal Pictures, 1982.

Fatal Attraction. Dir. Adrian Lyne. Paramount Pictures, 1987.

The Fly. Dir. David Cronenberg. Twentieth Century Fox, 1986.

Forbidden Planet. Dir. Fred M. Wilcox. Metro-Goldwyn-Mayer, 1956.

Frankenhooker. Dir. Frank Henenlotter. Levins-Henenlotter, 1990.

Frankenstein. Dir. James Whale. Universal Pictures, 1931.

Frankenstein Meets the Wolf Man. Dir. Roy William Neill. Universal Pictures, 1943.

Freddy vs. Jason. Dir. Ronny Yu. New Line Cinema, 2003.

Friday the 13th. Dir. Sean S. Cunningham. Georgetown Productions, Paramount Pictures, 1980.

From Dusk till Dawn. Dir. Robert Rodriguez. A Band Apart, Dimension Films, Los Hooligans Productions, Miramax Films, 1996.

Full Metal Jacket. Dir. Stanley Kubrick. Warner Brothers, 1987.

Ghost in the Shell. Dir. Mamoru Oshii. Bandai Visual, Kodansha, Manga Entertainment, Production I.G., 1995.

Ghostbusters. Dir. Ivan Reitman. Black Rhino Productions, Columbia Pictures, 1984.

The Giant Spider Invasion. Dir. Bill Rebane. Cinema Group 75, 1975.

Gremlins. Dir. Joe Dante. Amblin Entertainment, Warner Brothers, 1984.

The Grudge. Dir. Takashi Shimizu. Senator International, Ghost House Pictures, Vertigo Entertainment, Renaissance Pictures, 2004.

Halloween. Dir. John Carpenter. Falcon Films, 1978.

Halloween H2o: Twenty Years Later. Dir. Steve Miner. Dimension Films, Nightfall Productions, 1998.

Halloween Resurrection. Dir. Rick Rosenthal. Dimension Films, Nightfall Productions, Transcas International, 2002.

Harry Potter and the Sorcerer's Stone. Dir. Chris Columbus. 1942 Pictures, Warner Brothers, 2001

Henry: Portrait of a Serial Killer. Dir. John McNaughton. Filmcat, Fourth World Cinema, MPI, 1986.

The Hills Have Eyes. Dir. Wes Craven. Blood Relations Company, 1977.

Hollywood Chainsaw Hookers. Dir. Fred Olen Ray. American Independent Productions, Camp Motion Pictures, Savage Cinema, 1988.

The Howling. Dir. Joe Dante. AVCO Embassy Pictures, International Film Investors, Westcom
     Productions, 1981.
The Hunchback of Notre Dame. Dir. William Dieterle. RKO Radio Pictures, 1939.
The Hunger. Dir. Tony Scott. Metro-Goldwyn-Mayer, 1983.
I Know What You Did Last Summer. Dir. Jim Gillespie. Columbia Pictures, Mandalay Enterprises, 1997.
Interview with the Vampire. Dir. Neil Jordon. Geffin Pictures, 1994.
Invasion of the Body Snatchers. Dir. Don Siegel. Republic Pictures, 1955.
It Came from Outer Space. Dir. Jack Arnold. Universal Pictures, 1953.
It! The Terror from Beyond Space. Dir. Edward L. Cahn. Vogue Pictures, 1958.
It's Alive. Dir. Larry Cohen. Larco Productions, Warner Brothers, 1974.
Jaws. Dir. Steven Spielberg. Universal Pictures, Zanuck/ Brown Productions, 1975.
Killer Party. Dir. William Fruet. Marquis, Polar Entertainment, Telecom Entertainment, 1986.
King Kong. Dir. Merian C. Cooper, Ernest B. Schoedsack, RKO Radio Pictures, 1933.
Kiss the Girls. Dir. Gary Fleder. Rysher Entertainment, Paramount Pictures, 1997.
The Last House on the Left. Dir. Wes Craven. Metro-Goldwyn-Mayer, Orion, 1972.
The Last Seduction. Dir. John Dahl. Incorporated Television Company, 1994.
Legends of the Overfiend. Dir. Hideki Takayama. Anime 18, Island World, JAVN, West Cape, 1989.
Lolita. Dir. Stanley Kubrick. Anya, Harris-Kubrick Productions, Seven Arts Productions, Transwood,
     1962.
The Lord of the Rings. Dir. Peter Jackson. New Line Cinema, WingNut Films, Saul Zaentz Company,
     2001–2003.
The Lost Boys. Dir. Joel Schumacher. Warner Brothers, 1987.
Love at First Bite. Dir. Stan Dragoti. Melvin Simon Productions, 1979.
Macbeth. Dir. Roman Polanski. Caliban Films, Playboy Productions, 1971.
The Mangler. Dir. Tobe Hooper. New Line Cinema, 1994.
Marnie. Dir. Alfred Hitchcock. Geoffrey-Stanley Productions, Universal Pictures, 1964.
Maximum Overdrive. Dir. Stephen King. De Laurentiis Group, 1986.
M. Butterfly. Dir. David Cronenberg. Geffen Pictures, Miranda Productions, 1983.
Metropolis. Dir. Fritz Lang. Universum Film, 1927.
Minority Report. Dir. Steven Spielberg. Cruise/ Wagner Productions, Blue Tulip, DreamWorks, Amblin
     Entertainment, 2002.
Misery. Dir. Rob Reiner. Castle Rock Entertainment, 1990.
The Mummy. Dir. Karl Freund. Universal Pictures, 1932.
The Munsters [television series]. Dir. Norman Abbott, David Alexander. Kayro-Vue Productions,
     1964-1966.
Night of the Living Dead. Dir. George A. Romero. Image Ten and Laurel, 1968.
The Nightmare before Christmas. Dir. Henry Selick. Skellington Productions, Touchstone Pictures, 1993.
A Nightmare on Elm Street. Dir. Wes Craven. New Line Cinema, 1984.
Nosferatu: A Symphony of Terror. Dir. F.W. Murnau. Prana-Film, 1922.
Panic Room. Dir. David Fincher. Columbia Pictures, Hofflund/Polone, Indelible Pictures, 2002.
Paths of Glory. Dir. Stanley Kubrick. Harris-Kubrick Productions, Bryna Productions, 1957.
Peeping Tom. Dir. Michael Powell. Anglo-Amalgamated Productions, Michael Powell, 1960.
Pet Sematary. Dir. Mary Lambert. Paramount, 1990.
The Phantom Carriage. Dir. Victor Sjostrom. Svensk Filmindustri, 1921.
The Phantom of the Opera. Dir. Rupert Julian. Universal Pictures, 1925.
Poltergeist. Dir. Tobe Hooper. Metro-Goldwyn-Mayer, 1982.
Prom Night. Dir. Paul Lynch. Quadrant Trust Company, Simcom Limited, 1980.

Psycho. Dir. Alfred Hitchcock. Shamley Productions, 1960.

The Quick and the Dead. Dir. Sam Raimi. IndieProd, TriStar Pictures, 1995.

The Raven. Dir. Charles Brabin. The Essanay Film Manufacturing Company, 1915.

Rear Window. Dir. Alfred Hitchcock. Paramount Pictures, 1954.

Red Dragon. Dir. Brett Ratner. Universal Pictures, De Laurentiis Group, 2002.

Repulsion. Dir. Roman Polanski. Campton Films, Tekli, 1965.

The Ring. Dir. Gore Verbinski. DreamWorks, MacDonald/Parkes, Bender-Spink, Inc., 2002.

The Rocky Horror Picture Show. Dir. Jim Sharman. Twentieth Century Fox, 1975.

Rosemary's Baby. Dir. Roman Polanski. Paramount Pictures, 1968.

'Salem's Lot: The Movie. Dir. Tobe Hooper. Warner Brothers, CBS-TV, 1979.

Saturday Night Fever. Dir. John Badham. Paramount Pictures, Robert Stigwood Organization, 1977.

Scary Movie. Dir. Keenen Ivory Wayans. Dimension Films, Wayan Brothers Entertainment, 2000.

Schindler's List. Dir. Steven Spielberg. Amblin Entertainment, Universal Pictures, 1993.

Scooby-Do. Dir. Raja Gosnell. Atlas Entertainment, Hanna-Barbera Productions, Mosaic Media, 2002.

Scream. Dir. Wes Craven. Dimension Films, Woods Entertainment, 1996.

Secret Window, Secret Garden. Dir. David Koepp. Grand Slam Productions, Columbia Pictures, Pariah Entertainment, 2004.

Se7en. Dir. David Fincher. New Line Cinema, 1995.

The Shining. Dir. Stanley Kubrick. Warner Brothers, Peregrine Hawks Films, 1980.

The Silence of the Lambs. Dir. Jonathan Demme. Orion Pictures, 1991.

Silent Night, Deadly Night. Dir. Charles E. Sellier Jr. Slayride, TriStar Pictures, 1984.

Single White Female. Dir. Barbet Schroeder. Columbia Pictures, 1992.

The Sixth Sense. Dir. M. Night Shyamalan. Hollywood Pictures, Spyglass Entertainment, Kennedy/Marshall Group, 1999.

Slaughter High. Dir. George Dugdale. Spectacular Trading International, 1986.

Sleeping with the Enemy. Dir. Joseph Ruben. Twentieth Century Fox, 1991.

The Sopranos. [Television series]. Created by David Chase. Brad Grey Television, Home Box Office, Chase Films, 1999–2006.

Star Wars. Dir. George Lucas. Lucasfilm, 1977.

Stephen King's IT. Dir. Tommy Lee Wallace. Warner Brothers, ABC-TV, 1990.

Stephen King's Rose Red. Dir. Craig Baxley. ABC-TV, 2002.

Stephen King's The Stand. Dir. Mick Garris. Laurel, ABC-TV, 1994.

Stephen King's The Tommyknockers. Dir. John Power. K&S Partnership, Vidmark, ABC-TV, 1993.

Straw Dogs. Dir. Sam Peckinpah. ABC Pictures, Amerbroco, 1971.

Susperia. Dir. Dario Argento. Seda Spettacoli, 1977.

Swamp Women. Dir. Roger Corman. Bernard Woolner Productions, 1955.

Taking Lives. Dir. D. J. Caruso. Warner Brothers, Village Roadside Productions, Atmosphere Pictures, Taking Lives Films, 2004.

The Tenant. Dir. Roman Polanski. Paramount Pictures, 1976.

The Terminator. Dir. James Cameron. Cinema 84, Euro Film Fund, Hemdale Corporation, Pacific Western, 1984.

The Terminator 2: Judgment Day. Dir. James Cameron. Carolco Pictures, Canal, Lightstorm Entertainment, Pacific Western, 1991.

Terror Train. Dir. Roger Spottiswoode. Astral Films, Daniel Grodnik Productions, Sandy Howard Productions, 1980.

Tess. Dir. Roman Polanski. Renn Productions, Burrill Productions, 1979.

The Texas Chainsaw Massacre. Dir. Tobe Hooper. Vortex, 1974.

The Texas Chainsaw Massacre. Dir. Marcus Nispel. Chainsaw Productions, New Line Cinema, 2003.

The Texas Chainsaw Massacre 2. Dir. Tobe Hooper. Cannon Films, 1986.

Them! Dir. Gordon Douglas. Warner Brothers, 1954.

The Thing. Dir. Christian Nyby. RKO Pictures, Winchester Pictures, 1951.

Twelve Monkeys. Dir. Terry Gilliam. Atlas Entertainment, Classico, Universal Pictures, 1995.

28 Days Later. Dir. Danny Boyle. Twentieth Century Fox, 2002.

Twins of Evil. Dir. John Hough. Hammer Films, 1971.

2001: A Space Odyssey. Dir. Stanley Kubrick. Metro-Goldwyn-Mayer, 1968.

The Undead. Dir. Michael and Peter Spierig. Spierigfilm, 2003.

The Unforgiven. Dir. Clint Eastwood. Mapaso, Warner Brothers, 1992.

Vampire Hookers. Dir. Circo H. Santiago. Ariel Video, Continental Video, HQV Video, 1979.

Vampires. Dir. John Carpenter. Film Office, JVC Entertainment, Largo Entertainment, Spooky Tooth Productions, 1998.

Vampyres: Daughters of Darkness. Dir. Jose Ramon Larraz. Lurco Films, 1974.

Van Helsing. Dir. Stephen Sommers. Carpathian Pictures, Universal Pictures, Sommers Company, 2004.

The Velvet Vampire. Dir. Stephanie Rothman. New World Pictures, 1971.

Vertigo. Dir. Alfred Hitchcock. Paramount Pictures, 1958.

Videodrome. Dir. David Cronenberg. Universal Pictures, 1983.

The Village. Dir. M. Night Shyamalan. Touchstone, 2004.

The Werewolf of London. Dir. Stuart Walker. Universal Pictures, 1935.

When a Stranger Calls. Dir. Fred Walton. Columbia Pictures, 1979.

The Wicker Man. Dir. Robin Hardy. Anchor Bay Entertainment, Canal, Image, 1973.

The Wizard of Oz. Dir. Victor Fleming. Metro-Goldwyn-Mayer, 1939.

The Wolf Man. Dir. George Waggner. Universal Pictures, 1932.

Young Frankenstein. Dir. Mel Brooks. Twentieth Century Fox, 1974.

Works Cited

Auerbach, Nina. *Our Vampires, Ourselves*. Chicago: U of Chicago P, 1995.

Bakhtin, Mikhail. *Rabelais and His World*. 1965. Trans. Helene Iswolsky. Bloomington: Indiana UP, 1984.

Baudelaire, Charles. *The Painter of Modern Life and Other Essays*. Trans. and ed. Jonathan Mayne. New York: Phaidon Press, 1964.

Beard, William. *The Artist as Monster: The Cinema of David Cronenberg*. Toronto: U of Toronto P, 2001.

Bettelheim, Bruno. *The Uses of Enchantment: The Meaning and Importance of Fairy Tales*. 1975. New York: Vintage, 1977.

Blackmore, Tim. "'Is This Going to Be Another Bug Hunt?' S-F Tradition Versus Biology-as-Destiny in James Cameron's *Aliens*." *Journal of Popular Culture* 29 (1996): 211–26.

Bosky, Bernadette Lynn. "Making the Implicit, Explicit: Vampire Erotica and Pornography." *The Blood Is the Life: Vampires in Literature*. Ed. Leonard G. Heldreth and Mary Pharr. Bowling Green, OH: The Popular Press, 1999. 217–34.

Brand, Dana. "Rear-View Mirror: Hitchcock, Poe, and the Flaneur in America." *Hitchcock's America*. Ed. Jonathan Freedman and Richard Millington. New York: Oxford UP, 1999. 123–34.

Burke, Edmund. *A Philosophical Enquiry into the Origins of Our Ideas of the Sublime and Beautiful*. 1757. Ed. James T. Boulton. Oxford: Basil Blackwell, 1987.

Canby, Vincent. "Has Movie Violence Gone Too Far?" *New York Times*. January 16, 1972, sec. 2, p. 1.

Caputi, Jane. *The Age of Sex Crimes*. Bowling Green, OH: The Popular Press, 1987.

Carroll, Noël. *The Philosophy of Horror or Paradoxes of the Human Heart*. New York: Routledge, 1990.

Clover, Carol. *Men, Women, and Chainsaws: Gender in the Modern Horror Film*. Princeton, NJ: Princeton UP, 1992.

Cohen, Paula Marantz. *Alfred Hitchcock: The Legacy of Victorianism*. Lexington: Kentucky UP, 1995.

Coleridge, Samuel Taylor. *Christabel*. 1800. *The Portable Coleridge*. New York: Viking Press, 1950. 105–27.

Conrich, Ian. "Before Sound: Universal, Silent Cinema, and the Last of the Horror-Spectaculars." *The Horror Film*. Ed. Stephen Prince. New Brunswick, NJ: Rutgers UP, 2004. 40–57.

———. "Seducing the Subject: Freddy Krueger, Popular Culture and the *Nightmare on Elm Street* Films." *Horror Film Reader*. Ed. Alain Silver and James Ursini. New York: Limelight Editions, 2000. 223—35.

Cook, Pam, and Mieke Bernink, eds. *The Cinema Book*. 1985. London: British Film Institute, 1999.

Coppola, Francis Ford, and James V. Hart. *Bram Stoker's Dracula: The Film and the Legend*. New York: New Market Press, 1992.

Craft, Christopher. "'Kiss Me with Those Red Lips': Gender and Inversion in Bram Stoker's *Dracula*. *Dracula*. Ed. Nina Auerback and David J. Skal. New York: Norton, 1997. 444–59.

Crane, Jonathan Lake. *Terror and Everyday Life: Singular Moments in the History of the Horror Film*. Thousand Oaks, CA: Sage, 1994.

Creed, Barbara. "Freud's Worst Nightmare: Dining with Hannibal Lecter." *Horror Film and Psychoanalysis*. Ed. Steven Jay Schneider. Cambridge: Cambridge UP, 2004. 188–202.

———. *The Monstrous-Feminine: Film, Feminism, Psychoanalysis*. New York: Routledge, 1993.

Cronenberg, David. "Interview." *Gadfly Magazine* 3 (June 1999): 14–17.

Dickinson, Emily. *The Complete Poems of Emily Dickinson*. Ed. Thomas H. Johnson. Boston: Little, Brown, 1960.

Dika, Vera. "The Stalker Film, 1978–81." *American Horrors: Essays on the Modern American Horror Film*. Ed. Gregory A. Waller. Urbana: U of Illinois P, 1987. 86–101.

Doherty, Thomas. "Genre, Gender, and the *Aliens* Trilogy." *The Dread of Difference: Gender and the Horror Film*. Ed. Barry Keith Grant. Austin: U of Texas P, 1996. 181–99.

Dostoevski, Fyodor. *Notes from the Underground*. 1864. Ed. and trans. Michael R. Katz. New York: W. W. Norton, 1989.

Durgnat, Raymond. *A Long Hard Look at "Psycho"*. London: British Film Institute, 2002.

Edelstein, David. "Drilling for Fresh Nerves." *The Village Voice*. November 20, 1984, p. 58.

Edmundson, Mark. *Nightmare on Main Street: Angels, Sadomasochism and the Culture of the Gothic*. Cambridge, MA: Harvard UP, 1997.

Faulkner, William. *Absalom, Absalom!* 1936. New York: Vintage, 1987.

Fawell, John. "Torturing Women and Mocking Men: Hitchcock's *Rear Window*." *The Midwest Quarterly* 44 (2002): 88–104.

Ferraro, Susan. "Novels You Can Sink Your Teeth Into." *New York Times Book Review*. October 14, 1990, pp. 27, 67.

Fiedler, Leslie A. *Love and Death in the American Novel*. New York: Stein and Day, 1966.

Fisher, Benjamin Franklin. "The Residual Gothic Impulse: 1824–1873." *Horror Literature*. Ed. Marshall B. Tymn. New York: Bowker Company, 1981. 176–89.

Frank, Frederick S. "The Gothic Romance: 1762–1820." *Horror Literature*. Ed. Marshall B. Tymn. New York: Bowker Company, 1981. 3–33.

Freeland, Cynthia A. *The Naked and the Undead: Evil and the Appeal of Horror*. Boulder, CO: Westview Press, 2000.

———. "The Slasher's Blood Lust." *Dark Thoughts: Philosophic Reflections on Cinematic Horror*. Ed. Steven Jay Schneider and Daniel Shaw. Lanham, MD: Scarecrow Press, 2003. 198–211.

Freud, Sigmund. "The Uncanny." *The Complete Works of Sigmund Freud*. Vol. 17. Edited by James Strachey. London: The Hogarth Press, 1995. 219–52.

Fuss, Diana. "Fashion and the Homospectatorial Look." *On Fashion*. Ed. Shari Benstock and Suzanne Ferriss. New Brunswick, NJ: Rutgers UP, 1994. 211–32.

———. *Identification Papers*. New York: Routledge, 1995.

Gallardo C., Ximena, and C. Jason Smith. *Alien Woman: The Making of Lt. Ellen Ripley*. New York: Continuum, 2004.

Gelder, Ken. *Reading the Vampire*. New York: Routledge, 1994.

Golden, Christopher, Stephen R. Bissette, and Thomas E. Sniegoski. *Buffy the Vampire Slayer: The Monster Book*. New York: Pocket Books, 2000.

Grunenberg, Christoph. "Unsolved Mysteries: Gothic Tales from *Frankenstein* to the Hair Eating Doll." *Gothic: Transmutations of Horror in Late Twentieth Century Art*. Ed. Christoph Grunenberg. Cambridge, MA: MIT Press, 1997. 213–160.

Halberstam, Judith. *Skin Shows: Gothic Horror and the Technology of Monsters*. Durham, NC: Duke UP, 1995.

Horwitz, Margaret M. "*The Birds*: A Mother's Love." *A Hitchcock Reader*. Ed. Marshall Deutelbaum and Leland Poague. Ames: Iowa State UP, 1986. 279–87.

Iaccino, James F. *Psychological Reflections on Cinematic Terror: Jungian Archetypes in Horror Films*. Westport, CT: Praeger, 1994.

Jaworzyn, Stefan. *The Texas Chainsaw Massacre Companion*. London: Titan Publishing Group, 2003.

Jensen, Jeff. "Fright Night." *Entertainment Weekly*. October 8, 2004, pp. 31–41.

Jones, Ernest. *On the Nightmare*. 1951. New York: Liveright, 1971.

Kavka, Misha. "The Gothic on Screen." *The Cambridge Companion to Gothic Fiction*. Ed. Jerrold E. Hogle. Cambridge: Cambridge UP, 2002. 209–28.

King, Stephen. *Danse Macabre*. New York: Berkley Books, 1982.

Kristeva, Julia. *The Powers of Horror: An Essay on Abjection*. Trans. Leon S. Roudiez. New York: Columbia UP, 1982.

Lane, Anthony. "Village People." [Review of *The Village*]. *The New Yorker*. August 23, 2004, 90–91.

Lasch, Christopher. *Haven in a Heartless World: The Family Besieged*. New York: Basic Books, 1979.

LeFanu, J. Sheridan. *Carmilla*. 1872. *The Penguin Book of Vampire Stories*. Ed. Alan Ryan. New York: Penguin Books, 1987. 71–137.

Lovecraft, Howard Phillips. *Supernatural Horror in Literature*. 1927. New York: Dover Publications, 1973.

Magistrale, Tony. *Stephen King: The Second Decade*. New York: Twayne/ Macmillan, 1992.

Manchel, Frank. "What About Jack? Another Perspective on Family Relationships in Stanley Kubrick's *The Shining*." *Discovering Stephen King's The Shining*. Ed. Tony Magistrale. San Bernardino, CA: The Borgo Press, 1998. 82–94.

Melville, Herman. *Moby-Dick; or, The White Whale*. 1852. New York: Penguin, 1972.

Modleski, Tania. *The Women Who Knew Too Much: Hitchcock and Feminist Theory*. 1988. New York: Routledge, 1989.

Morgan, Robin. *The Demon Lover: On the Sexuality of Terrorism*. New York: Norton, 1989.

Mulvey, Laura. "Visual Pleasure and Narrative Cinema." 1975. *Visual and Other Pleasures*. Indianapolis: Indiana UP, 1990. 14–26.

Nelson, Thomas Allen. *Kubrick: Inside a Film Artist's Maze*. Bloomington: Indiana UP, 1982.

Norden, Eric. "Interview with Stanley Kubrick." *Playboy Magazine* (September 1968): 83–86.

Oates, Joyce Carol. "Afterword: Reflections on the Grotesque." *Haunted: Tales of the Grotesque*. New York: Dutton, 1994. 303–07.

Otto, Rudolf. *The Idea of the Holy*. Trans. John W. Harvey. London: Oxford UP, 1938.

Paglia, Camille. *The Birds*. London: British Film Institute, 1998.

Paul, William. *Laughing Screaming: Modern Hollywood Horror and Comedy*. New York: Columbia UP, 1994.

Perry, Dennis R. *Hitchcock and Poe: The Legacy of Delight and Terror*. Lanham, MD: Scarecrow Press, 2003.

Picart, Caroline Joan S. *Remaking the Frankenstein Myth on Film: Between Laughter and Horror*. Albany: State U of New York, 2003.

Pinedo, Isabel Cristina. *Recreational Terror: Women and the Pleasures of Horror Film Viewing*. Albany: State U of New York, 1997.

Poe, Edgar Allan. "The Cask of Amontillado." 1846. *Edgar Allan Poe: Poetry, Tales, and Selected Essays*. Ed. Patrick F. Quinn, 1984. New York: Library of America, 1996. 848–54.

———. "The Fall of the House of Usher." 1839. *Edgar Allan Poe: Poetry, Tales, and Selected Essays*. Ed. Patrick F. Quinn, 1984. New York: Library of America, 1996. 317–36.

———. "Ligeia." 1838. *Edgar Allan Poe: Poetry, Tales, and Selected Essays*. Ed. Patrick F. Quinn, 1984. New York: Library of America, 1996. 262–277.

———. "The Murders in the Rue Morgue." 1841. *Edgar Allan Poe: Poetry, Tales, and Selected Essays*. Ed. Patrick F. Quinn, 1984. New York: Library of America, 1996. 397–431.

———. *The Narrative of Arthur Gordon Pym*. 1838. Ed. Richard Kopley. New York: Penguin, 1999.

———. "The Philosophy of Composition." 1846. *Edgar Allan Poe: Poetry, Tales, and Selected Essays*. Ed. Patrick F. Quinn, 1984. New York: Library of America, 1996. 1373–85.

———. "The Purloined Letter." 1844. *Edgar Allan Poe: Poetry, Tales, and Selected Essays*. Ed. Patrick F. Quinn, 1984. New York: Library of America, 1996. 680–98.

———. "The Tell-Tale Heart." 1843. *Edgar Allan Poe: Poetry, Tales, and Selected Essays*. Ed. Patrick F. Quinn, 1984. New York: Library of America, 1996. 555–59.

Reep, Diana C., Joseph F. Ceccio, and William A. Francis. "Anne Rice's *Interview with the Vampire*: Novel Versus Film." *The Gothic World of Anne Rice*. Ed. Gary Hoppenstand and Ray B. Browne. Bowling Green, OH: The Popular Press, 1996. 123–48.

Rockoff, Adam. *Going to Pieces: The Rise and Fall of the Slasher Film, 1978–1986*. Jefferson, NC: McFarland and Company, 2002.

Rushing, Janice Hocker, and Thomas S. Frentz. *Projecting the Shadow: The Cyborg Hero in American Film*. Chicago: U of Chicago P, 1995.

Sanderson, Mark. *Don't Look Now*. London: British Film Institute, 1996.

Sardar, Ziauddin, and Sean Cubbitt, eds. *Aliens R Us: The Other in Science Fiction Cinema*. London: Pluto Press, 2002.

Sartre, Jean-Paul. *No Exit*. 1944. *No Exit and Three Other Plays*. New York: Vintage International, 1989.

Schelde, Per. *Androids, Humanoids, and Other Science Fiction Monsters*. New York: New York UP, 1993.

Seltzler, Mark. *Serial Killers: Death and Life in America's Wound Culture*. New York: Routledge, 1998.

Shakespeare, William. *Hamlet*. 1603. Ed. Susanne L. Wofford. New York: Bedford Books, 1994.

Sharrett, Christopher. "The Idea of Apocalypse in *The Texas Chainsaw Massacre*." *Planks of Reason: Essays on the Horror Film*. Ed. Barry Keith Grant. Lanham, MD: The Scarecrow Press, 1996. 255–76.

Shelley, Mary. *Frankenstein*. 1818. Ed. Johanna M. Smith. Boston: Bedford/St. Martin's, 2000.

Skal, David. *Hollywood Gothic: The Tangled Web of Dracula from Novel to Stage to Screen*. New York: W. W. Norton, 1990.

———. *The Monster Show: A Cultural History of Horror*. New York: Penguin, 1993.

Spoto, Donald. *The Art of Alfred Hitchcock*. New York: Hopkinson and Blake, 1976.

Stevenson, Robert Louis. *The Strange Case of Dr. Jekyll and Mr. Hyde*. 1886. Ed. Martin A. Danahay. Ontario, Canada: Broadview, 1985.

Stoker, Bram. *Dracula*. 1897. Ed. Nina Auerbach and David Skal. New York: Norton, 1997.

Truffaut, François, and Helen G. Scott. *Hitchcock*. New York: Simon and Schuster, 1967.

Tutor, Andrew. *Monsters and Mad Scientists: A Cultural History of the Horror Movie*. Oxford: Basil Blackwell, 1989.

Twitchell, James. *Dreadful Pleasures: An Anatomy of Modern Horror*. New York: Oxford UP, 1985.

Verniere, James. "Screen Previews: *The Dead Zone*." *Twilight Zone Magazine* (November/ December 1983): 52–55.

Walker, Alexander, Sybil Taylor, and Ulrich Ruchti. *Stanley Kubrick, Director: A Visual Analysis*. 1971. New York: W. W. Norton, 1999.

Waltje, Jörg . *Blood Obsession: Vampires, Serial Murder, and the Popular Imagination*. New York: Peter Lang , 2005.

Wells, Paul. *The Horror Genre: From Beelzebub to Blair Witch*. 2000. London: Wallflower Press, 2002.

Wicke, Jennifer. "Vampiric Typewriting: *Dracula* and Its Media." *The Horror Reader*. Ed. Ken Gelder. New York: Routledge, 2000. 172–83.

Wilde, Oscar. *The Canterville Ghost*. 1887. New York: North-South Books, 1996.

Williams, Linda. "Film Bodies: Gender, Genre, and Excess." *Film Genre Reader II*. Ed. Barry Keith Grant. Austin: U of Texas P, 1995. 140–58.

———. "When the Woman Looks." 1983. *The Dread of Difference: Gender and the Horror Film*. Ed. Barry Keith Grant. Austin: U of Texas P, 1986.

Williams, Tony. *Hearths of Darkness: The Family in American Horror Film*. Madison, NJ: Fairleigh Dickinson UP, 1966.

Wood, Robin. *Hitchcock's Films*. New York: Castle, 1965.

———. *Hollywood from Vietnam to Reagan*. New York: Columbia UP, 1986.

———. "An Introduction to the American Horror Film." *The American Nightmare*. Ed. Robin Wood and Richard Lippe. Toronto: Festival of Festivals, 1979. 7–28.

Young, Iris Marion. "Women Recovering Our Clothes." *On Fashion*. Ed. Shari Benstock and Suzanne Ferriss. New Brunswick, NJ: Rutgers UP, 1994. 197–210.

Zimmerman, Bonnie. "Daughters of Darkness: The Lesbian Vampire on Film." *The Dread of Difference: Gender and the Horror Film*. Ed. Barry Keith Grant. Austin: U of Texas P, 1996. 379–87.

Index

T

U

V

W